JOURNEYS INTO DANGER

JOURNEYS INTO DANGER

THE LURE OF THE UNKNOWN

Chosen by *ALAN C. JENKINS*

Blackie: London and Glasgow

Contents

Acknowledgements

For permission to reprint copyright material in this anthology I have to thank the following:

Messrs. Charles Scribner's Sons for the extract from the MS. of Captain Robert Stuart's *Narrative of his Overland trip eastward from Astoria.*

Brian Fawcett and the Hutchinson Publishing Group Ltd. for the extract from *Exploration Fawcett* by Lt.-Colonel P. H. Fawcett DSO.

The Author and Messrs. J. M. Dent & Sons Ltd. for the extract from *Men Under the Sea* by Egon Larsen.

Messrs. John Johnson for the extract from *Tschiffeley's Ride* by A. F. Tschiffeley (originally published by Messrs. William Heinemann).

Penguin Books Ltd. for the extract from *The Conquest of New Spain* translated by J. F. Cohen.

Robert de la Croix for the extract from his book *Mysteries of the North Pole.*

The Author and Messrs. J. M. Dent & Sons Ltd. for the extract from *The Darkness under the Earth* by Norbert Casteret.

The Author and Messrs. George Allen & Unwin Ltd. for the extract from *The Kon-Tiki Expedition* by Thor Heyerdahl.

The Estate of Peter Fleming and Messrs. Jonathan Cape Ltd. for the extract from *News from Tartary* by Peter Fleming.

Messrs. Victor Gollancz Ltd. and Anthony Sheil & Co. Ltd. for the extract from *The Kanchenjunga Adventure* by F. S. Smythe.

The Author and Messrs. André Deutsch Ltd. for the extract from *The Bombard Story* by Dr. Alain Bombard.

Messrs. Cassell & Co. Ltd. for the extract from *The Seven Lost Trails of Africa* by Hedley A. Chilvers.

The Champlain Society of Canada for the extract from *Documents relating to the Early History of Hudson's Bay*, ed. J. B. Tyrell, trans. David Keys.

Every effort has been made to trace the owners of copyright material and if any omissions have inadvertently occurred, it is hoped that our apologies will be accepted and that contact will be made with Messrs Blackie so that corrections can be made in subsequent editions of this anthology.

Introduction

Exploration Earth and *Journeys into Danger* are not only companion anthologies, but really their titles are interchangeable, for all exploration involves dangers of some kind or another – from Nansen in his epic two-year 'drift' across the Arctic, to Livingstone racked by fever in tropical swamps.

It is impossible to exaggerate the courage of the early explorers – the perils they encountered – the hardships they endured. Nowadays expeditions set off with every conceivable advantage and comfort – wireless, helicopters, power-boats, land-rovers, sno-cats, lightweight tents and so on. At the drop of a hat help can be sent to them, whereas in the days of a Cabot or a Burton, a Freuchen or a Franklin, men disappeared for months, years, on end – and often forever, in their particular quest. Often, like Mungo Park, for instance, in his nankeen breeches, they had no idea of appropriate clothing; even the early Everest expeditions had scant equipment available.

Why were men prepared to face the dangers entailed in exploration? Mainly, as we said in *Exploration Earth*, because of their insatiable curiosity, their eagerness to reach into the uttermost corners of the earth, their refusal to admit defeat at the hands of nature, the innate spirit of adventure which has always spurred men on.

There were of course many other reasons: some exploration was undertaken because of the rivalry that always exists in human affairs – national rivalry, for instance, which set Britain in urgent quest of the Australian continent lest Napoleon should turn his eyes thither; or individual rivalry which caused such bitterness between Burton and Speke in the search for the headwaters of the Nile; or which added tension to the 'race' for the South Pole between Scott and Amundsen.

Religion as well as the search for knowledge of Africa inspired David Livingstone; but he also bore in mind the existence of coalfields, the prospects for growing cotton, and of commerce between the native kings and Britain. The interests of science were the prime concern of men such as Sir Joseph Banks, who accompanied Captain Cook, or Darwin when he went on his voyage in the *Beagle*. Some adventurers went in search of gold and conquest, notably the Spaniards in the Americas; others sought profit in human merchandise – notably a Hawkins and his lucrative slave-trade. Some 'discoveries' were made by accident – the classic instance being Columbus who chanced upon the New World when in search of the Far East.

Few of the explorers could have foreseen the consequences of their quests. A Hudson or a Parry would have been amazed at the way the Arctic has been ransacked for minerals. Livingstone could have no idea of the grab for Africa that largely resulted from his explorations. The Sieur de la Salle, explorer of the Mississippi Valley, striving to form an alliance with the Iroquois, would have been appalled at the eventual fate of the Red Indians in general.

But always the chief considerations that inspired and drove on the explorers in the face of all the dangers can be pointed by two quotations. In the seventeenth century Sir Thomas Browne wrote 'Man is the whole world' – and man certainly thought he should know the whole world. Swin-

burne in the last century wrote 'Man is the master of things'
– and man has certainly wanted to be that.

Once again, as in *Exploration Earth*, it is possible in
Journeys into Danger to give only a representative idea of
man's readiness to risk everything in his thirst for knowledge of his world. But once again also, there is here a vast
range of examples.

A. C. J.

1 Blazing the Oregon Trail

CAPTAIN ROBERT STUART

The American explorers Lewis and Clark had proved in 1804–06 that the Pacific domains of the United States could be reached overland, instead of by the long sea-voyage round Cape Horn. But historic though their journey was, it left much of the way still to be adequately traced if the Oregon Trail (as it became known) was to be blazed sufficiently for the settlers of the future. Stuart, born in Scotland, first emigrated to Canada, but became interested in the Far West through association with John Jacob Astor of fur-trade fame. In 1810, in order to augment the discoveries of Lewis and Clark, he made the journey in the opposite direction, from west to east, and his journal, from which this extract is taken, gives a vivid picture of the dangers and privations the 'mountainy men' and the frontiersmen had to face.

We were all up soon after dawn and I had just reached the river bank, when I heard the Indian yell raised in the vicinity of our camp and the cry 'To Arms' – 'There's Indians!' echoed by all our party. We had just time to snatch our arms when two Indians at full gallop passed 300 yards to one side of our station driving off, by their yells, every horse we had, notwithstanding their being tethered and hobbled. We rushed towards them and got almost within shot of the nearest, when repeated yells in the direction from which they had come made us desist from the pursuit in order to defend ourselves and baggage; for there being only two Indians after the horses, we very readily imagined that the main body were in reserve to attack our rear if we had pursued the first Indians, or to plunder the camp if opportunity offered.

At the rate the horses were going all attempts to catch up with them were unavailing, and if we had continued the pursuit everything else would have been lost for a certainty – which would undoubtedly have made our situation far worse than ever. The savages whose yells had made us return to the baggage passed soon after at full speed in the others' tracks and we saw that the whole party did not amount to more than twenty – which had we known only three minutes sooner, a few horses might have been saved and a scalp or two fallen into our hands. From a few words we heard, they were beyond all doubt members of the Crows.

This method of stealing horses is deserving of being more minutely described; one of the party rode past our camp and placed himself on a conspicuous knob in the direction they wanted to run them off; when the others (who were hidden behind our camp) seeing him prepared, rose the war-whoop, or yell – which is the most horribly discordant howling imaginable, being in imitation of the different beasts of prey. At this diabolical noise the horses naturally rose their heads to see what the matter was – and at that instant he who had placed himself in advance put spurs to his steed, and our horses seeing him gallop off in apparent fright, started all in the same direction, as if a legion of infernals were in pursuit of them. In this manner a dozen or two of those fellows have sometimes succeeded in running off every horse belonging to war parties, of perhaps five or six hundred men; for once those creatures take fright, nothing short of broken necks can stop their progress.

On the whole it was one of the most daring and intrepid actions I ever heard of among Indians, and convinced me how determined they were on having our horses, for which they would unquestionably have followed us any distance, and nothing but seeing us prepared and ready to defend ourselves prevented their attacking us where we first saw them. . . . We have been busy all day making preparations to set out in the morning on foot down the river, along the plains of which below Henry's Fort, we have hopes of meeting some of the Snakes, from which if we can procure a couple of horses we shall continue our former determination and if possible reach the Cheyenne River before the winter sets in.

At the portage of the long narrows the Cathlaskas Indians not only behaved impudently, but they carried off two bales of goods with some other articles which were intrusted to their care to be by them transported on horses to the upper end of the carrying place, and our canoes being too heavy for the number of men, we were constantly compelled to employ these villains to carry them – this they executed well, but while five men were watching them, they maliciously threw large stones on one, which damaged it considerably, at the same time pillaging what knives, handkerchiefs etc. they could lay their hands on.

Being dusk before we succeeded in getting all together, it was impossible to better our forlorn situation before morning, so we passed the night under arms without one of us closing an eye, and when day was yet scarcely visible in the East, every thing was embarked, and we gladly bid adieu to this abominable den of robbers –

Elated I suppose with the success of yesterday, we were this day escorted by the whole tribe who by the time we reached the Celilo Falls had augmented their numbers to upwards of 400 armed principally with bows and arrows, and where these were deficient war clubs, battle-axes, etc. were substituted. Surrounded by this host they requested permission to make the portage for us, which I declined by saying that it was now too late, but that if they behaved well, I would accept their offer in the morning, and in the meantime engaged them to take up the canoes, a service they executed with fidelity. But no sooner were they recompensed for their trouble than they manifested an intention to destroy them, notwithstanding the presence of ten well armed men whom I had despatched as a guard – and were only at last prevented by the interference of an old man, who seemed to be a considerable personage among them.

With the exception of thirty the whole of this hostile band crossed to the north side soon after the termination of the hoary gentleman's lecture, which I suppose only tended to dissuade them for the present and to watch an opportunity to strike a more decisive blow. Well aware that their proffered assistance was not for the best of purposes, I determined to defeat if possible their infernal machinations, and, at 1 a.m. by the aid of moonlight, began the transportation of the goods with the hopes of getting all over before dawn. Two loads were only remaining at daybreak, when those spies who had remained to watch our motions perceived what had been going on and thinking themselves too weak for an attack gave the alarm to those on the opposite side, who, to the number of about 130, embarked without loss of time in several large canoes.

I immediately sent the people to the lower end for another load, with orders to Mr. Reed to keep what men he thought necessary with him as I supposed the gentry from the other side were not crossing with any good intention.

But he, very imprudently, refused to retain any of them, saying he would with Mr. Robert McClellan take care of what little remained. No sooner did the canoes touch the shore than the Indians leaped on the rocks and, making direct for the goods, began an indiscriminate pillage, which the two gentlemen vainly attempted to oppose.

Mr. McClellan soon perceived how unavailing any exertions of human strength would be and retired with his arms, calling to Mr. Reed to do the same and that 'they would give it to them while plundering'. Reed, however, was wrestling with a savage who had hold of his gun. At the same time another Indian threw a buffalo robe over McClellan's head, but McClellan jumped back and disengaged himself from the skin and just had time to draw up his piece when the villain made a lunge at him with his knife and received the contents of his rifle in the breast, which laid him lifeless on the spot.

Mr. Reed was still scuffling for his gun, and Mr. McC. attempted in vain to get off the cap and shoot the scoundrel who held it, just as another rascal made a blow at him with an axe handle, which by springing over a canoe he avoided, but the blow fell on Mr. Reed's head a little below the ear and deprived him of his senses. A small pocket pistol was all the reserve Mr. McC. had and this he instantly discharged at the fellow who finished Mr. R. and saw him fall apparently as dead as the first.

Among Indians unaccustomed to fire-arms one would have supposed that seeing two of their comrades fall, the rest would have sought safety in flight. But far different was their conduct: they continued to press forward and inflicted tomahawk wounds on Mr. R. Mr. McC.'s only hope depended on the effect of his empty gun. This he presented and rushed at them, on which they gave ground, and he loaded his piece at once. He was still unharmed and, running directly at the main body of them, raised the Indian Yell, which put them partially to flight.

He followed them some distance and gave up the pursuit on account of seeing a party of savages coming from above. On his return to the field of action he found the Indian he had shot with his pistol to be missing, but Mr. Reed and the other Indian lay weltering in their blood. He examined the former – who yet gave some faint sign of existence which he supposed to be his last struggles – and found in his pocket a well-loaded pistol. Taking this, he set out to encounter those whom he saw coming from above; there were but three and they went off a considerable way to avoid him.

Having heard the report of a gun a short time before the people with their loads came to the upper end, I was suspicious of the cause, and as soon as enough arrived to take care of the goods, I sent Mr. Farnham to see what was the matter. He met Mr. McC. on the road and they returned together. Our canoes were leaky and the oars were still at the lower end – some hands began caulking and Mr. McC. with four others returned for what was left. During his absence the dead Indian was carried off, while Mr. Reed had recovered from his wounds but was weak from the loss of blood and was wandering about on the rocks, not knowing whither he went. He was accordingly assisted in getting to the upper end where soon after he fainted and in this situation was embarked and we continued our voyage up the south shore.

News of this affair no sooner reached the Cathlasko village than two horses were killed and the blood in its crude state was drunk by the warriors in order to give them additional courage. This ceremony, with their dead-dance and war-song finished, they to the number of 120 men clothed with their garments and furnished with every other accoutrement for war, mounted their horses and followed us, panting for revenge. We however fortunately discovered them some distance above the Shoshone River crossing to the side by which we were ascending, and when near the place found them posted among some steep eroded rocks along which we must unavoidly pass.

Finding they had the advantage of the ground, we stopped about 400 yards below, discharged and reloaded our arms, made a fire and Mr. McC. dressed Mr. Reed's head, on which were five tomahawk gashes, about 2 inches in length each. This done we lashed the canoes together went to a rock a small distance from the shore, from which we could retreat with facility in the event of being too hard pushed, and there awaited the onset.

Not long after, the war chief with three others came to us in a canoe, and after a long preamble said we had killed two of his nation and that their relatives, incensed at this, had compelled him to take command of the party against his will – but that they were come purposely to fight, determined on having satisfaction in some shape or other. He proposed as the only means of appeasing their fury that we should deliver up Mr. Reed (who, he observed, was already dead) to the friends of the savages who had died, to be by them cut in pieces – this would, he said, completely obliterate their present animosity, and that the greatest harmony would prevail for the future.

Our answer was No. The man you wounded is our brother and you must destroy all of us before you get him. We are prepared and ready for your warriors – bring them on and we will teach you a more serious lesson than you learned this morning. This they considered for some time and after mature deliberation the business was soon after compromised for three blankets to cover the dead and some tobacco to fill the Calumet (Pipe) of Peace – on condition that they should immediately cross the river and leave our passage free, which was soon complied with, and we saw no more of them.

But hostile Indians were by no means the only miseries we faced. Often we were on the brink of death from starvation. During one period of three weeks twelve of us subsisted on no more than two ibexes and five beaver; even the skins of these we preserved and consumed. The best and indeed the only method of dressing those skins is first to singe them well, after which they must be boiled for several hours, then cut into small pieces so as to be fit for bolting or gulping.

Frequently we found nothing but choke-berries to eat, though these were excellent, because the frost had taken away their tartness. On one occasion we shot a poor wolf from which we made an immediate meal. The skins and bones were pounded, mixed with roots and made into broth. The remaining flesh we sliced and dried for future use.

Our plight for the time-being improved when we met some friendly Shoshone Indians. From them we purchased a fat dog, a little dried salmon and an excellent sort of cake made of pulverized roots and service-berries. We made a hearty supper on the dog's carcase and between the evening and the morning caught a sufficiency of trout for breakfast which we found delicious, they being fried with dog's fat and a little flour we had preserved.

Indeed, the flesh of dogs seemed to us well flavoured,

healthful and strengthening; whereas horsemeat (which we were forced to use, killing one of our horses), however well cooked, did not nourish, no matter how much one ate of it.

But worse was to come. We had overtaken Mr. McClellan, from whom we had parted. We found him emaciated and worn to a perfect skeleton and hardly able to raise his head or speak from extreme debility.

Soon after camping we made an unsuccessful attempt to procure some meat, and after dark returned to camp with heavy hearts – but I must confess we could not in justice enter the same complaint against our stomachs!

Before going once again supperless to bed, we set our old trap in hopes of procuring us something for breakfast. We were up at dawn and visited the trap in anxious expectation, but nothing in it except the forepaw of a large beaver, which has greatly dampened our spirits, as we do not feel in very good trim to resume our journey.

When we did, greater disappointment ensued. We were now in country where we expected to find buffalo in abundance, but a few old bull tracks was all we had for hope, with the exception of a few antelopes on the brow of a mountain which were so wild as to preclude all hope of getting near them.

As we were preparing for bed one night, after yet another near-starvation day, one of our men advanced towards me with his rifle in hand, saying that as there was no appearance of our being able to procure any provisions at least until we got to the extreme of this plain, which would take us three or four days, he was determined to go no farther, but that lots should be cast and one die to preserve the rest, adding as a farther inducement for me to agree to his proposal that I should be exempted in consequence of being their leader.

I shuddered at the idea and used every endeavour to create an abhorrence in his mind against such an act, urging also the probability of our falling in with some animal on the morrow. But, finding that every argument failed and that he was on the point of converting some others to his cannibalistic purpose, I snatched up my rifle, cocked and levelled it at him with the firm resolution to fire if he persisted. This affair so terrified him that he fell instantly upon his knees and asked the whole party's pardon, solemnly swearing he should never again suggest such a thought.

After this matter was settled I felt so agitated and weak that I could scarcely crawl to bed.

We resumed our line of march a little before daylight and had scarcely proceeded two miles when, to our great joy, we discovered an old run-down buffalo bull, which after considerable trouble we succeeded in killing. So ravenous were our appetites that we ate part of the animal raw. Then we cut up the most of what was eatable and carried it to a brook. Here we sat up the greater part of the night eating and barbecueing meat.

I was much alarmed at the ravenous way in which all ate, but happily none felt any serious effects therefrom, probably in consequence of my not allowing them to eat freely before they had supped a quantity of broth.

2 The Lost Mines in the Green Hell

LT.-COLONEL P. H. FAWCETT

For long, Africa was regarded as the 'Dark Continent', but such a title could equally have been given to South America, with its fever-haunted jungles, thirty-foot anacondas, and savage tribes that hunted with poisoned arrows. Fawcett was drawn by those perilous, mysterious lands partly because of legends of ancient, abandoned cities, rich in the treasure of strange civilizations. He became a legend himself, for on his last expedition in 1925 he disappeared without trace in the wilds of Brazil. His fate remains a mystery to this day, in spite of various expeditions that searched for him. One legend current for a time was that he had been captured by an unknown Indian tribe who appointed him as their god. The story he tells here, based on old Portuguese documents, is an indication of the fascination he always felt for the dangerous haunts where eventually he, too, met his fate.

When Diego Alvarez struggled landwards through the Atlantic swell in a welter of wreckage from the disintegrating caravel, it was to land, exhausted, on a shore absolutely unknown to this sixteenth-century Portuguese. Only twenty-four years previously Columbus had discovered the New World and fired the imaginations of Iberian adventurers. The dawn of knowledge was only just breaking after the dark night of the Middle Ages; the world in its entirety was yet a mystery, and each venture to probe it disclosed new wonders. The border between myth and reality was not fixed, and the adventurer saw strange sights with an eye distorted by superstition.

Here, on the coast of Brazil where Bahia now stands, anything might exist. Behind the forest's edge on top of those cliffs were surely to be found wonderful things, and he – Diego Alvarez – would be the first of his race to set eyes on them. There might be dangers from the natives of the country – perhaps even those weird people, half human, half monster, who, tradition had it, lived in this land – but they had to be faced if he was to find food and water. The spirit of the pioneer had driven him to join the ill-fated voyage; it spurred him on, and nothing short of death could stop him.

The place where he came ashore, sole survivor from the wreck, was in the territory of the cannibal Tupinambas. Perhaps he escaped being eaten by reason of his strangeness; perhaps his captors considered it a triumph over neighbouring tribes to display their captive alive. For his salvation the Portuguese had principally to thank an Indian girl named Paraguassu, the Pocahontas of South America, who took a fancy to him and became his wife – ultimately the favourite among several.

For many years the Portuguese mariner lived with the Indians. A number of his countrymen came to Brazil, and he was able to establish friendly relations between them and the savages. Finally he managed to bring Paraguassu into the fold of the Church, and a sister of hers married another Portuguese adventurer. The child of her sister's marriage, Melchoir Dias Moreyra, spent most of his life with the Indians, and was known by them as Muribeca. He discovered many mines, and accumulated vast quantities of silver, gold and precious stones, which were worked by the skilful Tapuya tribes into so wonderful a treasure that the early European colonists were filled with envy.

Muribeca had a son called Roberio Dias, who as a lad

was familiar with the mines where his father's vast wealth originated. About 1610 Roberio Dias approached the Portuguese King, Dom Pedro II, with an offer to hand over the mines in exchange for the title of Marquis das Minas. He showed a rich specimen of silver-bearing ore and temptingly promised more silver than there was iron at Bilbao. He was only partly believed, but the royal greed for treasure was strong enough to cause a patent to be drawn up for the marquisate.

If Roberio Dias thought he would leave the court a marquis he was mistaken. Old Dom Pedro II was too cunning for that. The patent was sealed and delivered to a Commission entrusted to hand it over only after the mines had been disclosed. But Dias in his turn had suspicions. He was not one to trust blindly to the King's faith. While the expedition was some distance from Bahia he managed to persuade the officer in command of the Commission to open the envelope and allow him to see the patent. He found that he was down for a military commission as captain, and no more – not a word about the marquisate! That settled it. Dias refused to hand over the mines, so the enraged officer took him back by force to Bahia, where he was flung into prison. Here he remained for two years, and then he was allowed to buy his freedom for 9,000 crowns. In 1622 he died, and the secret of the mines was never disclosed. Diego Alvarez had been dead for a long time; Muribeca himself had gone, no Indian would talk even under the most frightful tortures, so Dom Pedro was left to curse his ill-judged deceit and read over again and again the official reports of the assays made of Roberio Dias's specimens.

The secret of the mines was lost, but for years expeditions scoured the country in an effort to locate them. As failure succeeded failure, belief in their existence died away to survive only as myth, yet there were always some hardy souls ready to brave hostile savages and slow starvation for the chance of discovering a New Potosi.

The region beyond the São Francisco River was as unknown to the Portuguese colonists of those times as the forests of the Gongugy are to the Brazilians of today. Exploration was too difficult. Not only was it too much to contend with hordes of wild Indians shooting poisoned arrows from impenetrable cover, but food was not available to provide for an expedition large enough to protect itself from attack. Yet one after another ventured it, and more often than not was never heard of again. They called these expeditions *Bandeiras*, or Flags, for they were officially sponsored, accompanied by Government troops, and usually by a contingent of missionaries. Occasionally civilians banded together for the purpose, armed a number of negro slaves, enlisted tame Indians as guides, and disappeared into the Sertao (bush) for years at a time, if not for ever.

If you are romantically minded – and most of us are, I think – you have in the foregoing the background for a story so fascinating that I know none to compare. I myself came upon it in an old document still preserved at Rio de Janeiro, and, in the light of evidence gleaned from many quarters, believe it implicitly. I am not going to offer a literal translation of the strange account given in the document – the crabbed Portuguese script is broken in several places – but the story begins in 1753, when a native of Minas Gerais, whose name has not been preserved, decided to make a search for the Lost Mines of Muribeca.

Franciso Raposo – I must identify him by some name – was not to be deterred by wild beasts, venomous snakes, savages and insects from attempting to enrich himself and his followers as the Spaniards in Peru and Mexico had done only two centuries before. They were a hardy lot, those old pioneers – superstitious, perhaps, but when gold called all obstacles were forgotten.

It was always difficult to take cargo animals through the trackless hinterland. There were numerous rivers and bogs everywhere; pasture was coarse, and the continuous attacks of vampire bats soon finished the animals off. Climate ranged from very cold to extreme heat, and total drought would be followed by days of sheer deluge, so that a fair amount of equipment had to be carried. Yet Raposo and his band gave little consideration to such drawbacks, and set out hopefully into the wilds.

Exactly where they went I have only lately discovered. It was roughly northwards. There were no maps of the country in those days, and no member of the party knew anything about land navigation, so the clues in the record they left are entirely unreliable. Indians accompanied them from point to point and suggested the routes taken, otherwise they merely wandered into the unknown and left it to fortune to bring them to the coveted objective. In the manner of all pioneers, they lived on what fish and game they could secure, and on fruit and vegetables pilfered from Indian plantations or begged from friendly tribes. It was thin living, for game is timid in the South American wilderness, but men lived more simply in those days and consequently their endurance was greater. Raposo, his compatriots, and their black slaves survived to continue their wanderings for ten years. Not counting the Indians who joined them from time to time and who would vanish when it suited them, the party was about eighteen strong. Perhaps that was the secret of their survival, for the usual *Bandeiras* numbered at least five hundred, and there is a record of one 1,400 strong, not a single member of which ever returned! Few might live where many would starve.

The time came when the party was travelling eastward again, towards the coast settlements, tired of this seemingly endless wandering, and disheartened by their failure to locate the lost mines. Raposo was almost ready to believe them a myth, and his companions had long ago decided that no such mines existed. They had come through swamp and bush country when jagged mountains showed up ahead, beyond a grassy plain broken by thin belts of green forest. Raposo in his narrative describes them poetically, 'They seemed to reach the ethereal regions and to serve as a throne for the wind and the stars themselves.' Anyone who has passed months on end in the monotonous flatness of the plains will appreciate his rhapsody.

These were no ordinary mountains. As the party came nearer, the sides lit up in flame, for it had been raining and the setting sun was reflected from wet rocks rich in crystals and that slightly opaque quartz which is so common in this part of Brazil. To the eager explorers they seemed to be studded with gems. Streams leaped from rock to rock, and over the crest of the ridge a rainbow formed, as though to hint that treasure was to be found at its feet.

'An omen!' cried Raposo. 'See! We have found the treasure house of the great Muribeca!'

Night came down and forced them to camp before reaching the foot of those wonderful mountains; and next morning, when the sun came up from behind them, the crags appeared black and menacing. Enthusiasm waned; but there is always something fascinating about mountains for the explorer. Who knows what may be seen from the topmost ridge?

To the eyes of Raposo and his comrades their height was

vast, and when they reached them it was to find sheer, unscalable precipices. All day they struggled over boulders and crevices, seeking a way up those glassy sides. Rattlesnakes abounded – and there is no remedy for the bite of the Brazilian species. Wearied by the hard going and constant vigilance to avoid these snakes, Raposo called a halt.

'Three leagues we have come and still no way up,' he said. 'It would be better to return to our old trail and find a way northwards. What do you say?'

'Camp!' was the reply. 'Let's camp. We've had enough for one day. Tomorrow we can return.'

'Very well,' answered the leader; and then to two of the men, 'You, José and Manoel – off you go to find wood for the fire!'

Camp was pitched and the party was resting when confused shouting and a crashing in the bush brought them to their feet, guns in hand. José and Manoel burst into view.

'*Patrão, Patrão!*' they cried. 'We've found it – the way up!'

Searching for firewood in the low scrub they had seen a dead tree at the edge of a small wooded creek. This was the best fuel to be had, and they were making their way towards it when a deer sprang up on the other side of the creek and disappeared beyond a corner of the cliff. Unslinging their guns the two men followed as quickly as they could, for here was meat enough to last them several days.

The animal had vanished, but beyond the outcropping of rock they came on a deep cleft in the face of the precipice, and saw that it was possible to climb up through it to the summit. Deer and firewood were forgotten in the excitement.

They broke camp at once, shouldered their packs, and set off with Manoel leading. With ejaculations of wonder they entered the crevice in single file, to find that it widened somewhat inside. It was rough going, but here and there were traces of what looked like old paving, and in places the sheer walls of the cleft seemed to bear the almost obliterated marks of tools. Clusters of rock crystals and frothy masses of quartz gave them the feeling of having entered a fairyland, and in the dim light filtering down through the tangled mass of creepers overhead all the magic of their first impressions returned.

The climb was so difficult that three hours passed before they emerged torn and breathless on a ledge high above the surrounding plain. From here to the ridge was clear ground, and soon they were standing shoulder to shoulder at the top, gazing, dumb with amazement, at the view spread out below them.

There at their feet, about four miles away, was a huge city.

Immediately they flung themselves down and edged back behind the cover of rocks, hoping that the inhabitants had not seen their distant figures against the sky, for this might be a colony of the hated Spaniards. Then again, it might be such a city as Cuzco, the ancient capital of the Incas in Peru, inhabited by a race of highly civilized people still holding out against the encroachments of the European invaders. Was it perhaps a Portuguese colony? It might be a stronghold of the Orizes Procazes, remnant of the mysterious Tapuyas, who showed unmistakable signs of having once been a highly civilized people.

Raposo wriggled up to the crest once more and, still lying flat, looked around him. The ridge stretched as far as he could see from south-east to north-west, and away over to the north, hazy with distance, was unbroken forest. In the immediate foreground was an extensive plain patched with green and brown, broken in places by shining pools of water. He could see where a continuation of the rocky trail they had ascended dropped down the side of the mountain to vanish below the range of vision, appearing again and winding over the plain to lose itself in the vegetation surrounding the city walls. No sign of life could he see. No smoke arose in the still air; no sound broke the utter silence.

He gave a quick sign to his followers, and one by one they crawled over the ridge and dropped down beyond the skyline to the shelter of scrub and rock. Then they made their way cautiously down the mountainside to the valley floor, and left the trail for a camp site near a small stream of clear water.

No fires were lit that night, and the men talked in whispers. They were awed by the sight of civilization after those long years in the wilds, and by no means confident of their safety. Two hours before nightfall Raposo had sent off two Portuguese and four negroes to reconnoitre and find out what sort of people lived in this mysterious place. Nervously the rest of the party awaited their return, and every forest noise – every insect song and whisper of the foliage – was sinister. But the scouts had nothing to tell when they came back. Lack of cover had kept them from venturing too near the city, but no sign of occupation had they seen. The Indians of the party were as mystified as Raposo and his followers. By nature superstitious, certain parts of the country to them were 'taboo', and they were filled with alarm.

Raposo, however, was able to prevail on one of the Indians to scout forward singlehanded after sunrise next morning. No one had slept much during the night, and their curiosity about the Indian's fate kept them from resting in the more comfortable light of day. At midday he crept back into camp, obviously terrified, and insisting that the city was uninhabited. It was too late to push forward that day, so they spent another restless night listening to the strange forest sounds around them, ready to face some unknown danger at any moment.

Early next morning Raposo sent ahead an advance guard of four Indians and followed towards the city with the rest of the party. As they came near the overgrown walls the Indians met them with the same story – the place was deserted – and so with less caution they followed the trail to an entrance under three arches formed of huge stone slabs. So impressive was this cyclopean structure – similar, probably, to much that can yet be seen at Sacsahuaman in Peru – that no man dared speak, but slipped by the blackened stones as stealthily as a cat.

High above the central arch characters of some sort were graven deeply into the weatherworn stone. Raposo, uneducated though he was, could see that this was no modern writing. A feeling of vast age brooded over everything, and it took a distinct effort for him to issue in a hoarse, unnatural voice the orders to advance.

The arches were still in a fair state of preservation, but one or two of the colossal uprights had twisted slightly on their bases. The men passed through and entered what had once been a wide street, but littered now with broken pillars and blocks of masonry rank with the parasitic vegetation of the tropics. On either side were two-storeyed houses built of great blocks fitting together with mortarless joins of almost incredible accuracy, the porticos, narrow above and wide below, decorated with elaborate carvings of what they took to be demons.

The descriptions, coming from men who had never seen Cuzco and Sacsahuaman, or the other wonder cities of old

Peru – which were incredibly ancient when the Incas first came upon them – cannot be lightly dismissed. What they saw and related tallies closely with much that we can still see today. Uneducated adventurers could hardly invent an account so closely corroborated by the cyclopean remains now familiar to so many.

There was ruin everywhere, but many buildings were roofed with great slabs still in position. Those of the party who dared to enter the dark interiors and raise their voices ran out at the echoes flung back at them from walls and vaulted ceilings. It was impossible to say if any remnants of furnishings remained, for in most cases inner walls had collapsed, covering the floors with debris, and the bat droppings of centuries formed a thick carpet underfoot. So old was this place that perishables such as furniture and textiles must have disintegrated long ago.

Huddled together like a flock of frightened sheep, the men proceeded down the street and came to a vast square. Here in the centre was a huge column of black stone, and upon it the effigy, in perfect preservation, of a man with one hand on his hip and the other pointing towards the north. The majesty of this statue struck deep into the hearts of the Portuguese and they crossed themselves reverently. Carved obelisks of the same black stone, partially ruined, stood at each corner of the square, while running the length of one side was a building so magnificent in design and decoration that it must have been a palace. The walls and roof had collapsed in many places, but its great square columns were still intact. A broad flight of ruined stone steps led up and into a wide hall, where traces of colour still clung to the frescoes and carvings. Bats in countless thousands winged in circles through the dim chambers and the acrid reek of their droppings was suffocating.

The explorers were glad to get out into the clean air. The figure of a youth was carved over what seemed to be the principal doorway. It portrayed a beardless figure, naked from the waist up, with shield in hand and a band across one shoulder. The head was crowned with what looked to them like a wreath of laurel, judging by Grecian statuary they had seen in Portugal. Below were inscribed characters remarkably like those of ancient Greece. Raposo copied them on a tablet and reproduced them in his narrative.

Opposite the palace was the ruin of another huge building, evidently a temple. Eroded carvings of figures, animals and birds covered the walls that remained, and over the portal were more characters which again were copied as faithfully as Raposo or one of his followers was capable of doing.

Beyond the square and the main street the city lay in complete ruin, in some places actually buried under mounds of earth on which not a blade of grass or other vegetation grew. Here and there were gaping chasms, and when the explorers dropped rocks into these not a sound came up to indicate bottom. There was little doubt now what had devastated the place. The Portuguese knew what earth-quakes were and what destruction they could do. Here whole buildings had been swallowed, leaving perhaps only a few carved blocks to show where they had stood. It was not difficult to imagine something of the awful cataclysm that had laid waste this glorious place, tumbled columns and blocks weighing perhaps fifty tons and more, and that had destroyed in a matter of minutes the painstaking labour of a thousand years!

The far side of the square terminated in a river about thirty yards wide, flowing straight and easily from the north-west and vanishing in distant forest. At one time a fine promenade had bordered on the river, but the masonry was now broken up and much had subsided into the water. On the other side of the river were fields that were once cultivated, still covered with abundant coarse grass and a carpet of flowers. Rice had propagated and thrived in the shallow swamps all about, and here the waters were alive with duck.

Raposo and his party forded the river and crossed the swamps towards an isolated building about a quarter of a mile away, and the ducks scarcely troubled to move from their path. The building was approached by a flight of steps in stone of many colours, for it stood on a rise and its frontage extended for 250 paces. The imposing entrance, behind a square monolith with deeply engraved characters, opened into a vast hall where carvings and decorations had resisted the depredations of time in an amazing manner. They found fifteen chambers opening off the great hall, and in each was a carved serpent's head with a thin stream of water still flowing from it into the open mouth of another stone serpent beneath. The place could have been the college of a priesthood.

Deserted and ruined the city was, but its environs of rice fields provided far more food for the explorers than they could find in the virgin forest. It is therefore not surprising that in spite of their awe of the place none of the men was anxious to leave it. Their fear gave way to a lust for treasure, and this increased when João Antonio – the only member of the party to be mentioned by name in the document – found a small gold coin in the rubble. On one face it bore the effigy of a youth on his knees, and on the other a bow, a crown and a musical instrument of some sort. The place must be full of gold, they told themselves; when the inhabitants fled they would have taken only the things most necessary for their survival.

The document hints at the finding of treasure, but no details are given. It may well be that the heavy aura of calamity hanging over the place was in the long run too much for the nerves of these superstitious pioneers. Perhaps the millions of bats deterred them. At any rate, it is unlikely that they brought any quantity of it out with them, for they still had a formidable journey ahead if they were ever to see civilization again, and none of them would have been anxious to burden himself with more equipment than he already had.

Gathering rice from the swamps and hunting duck – if hunting it could be called – were perilous. Anacondas big enough to kill a man were common; and poisonous snakes, attracted by the game, swarmed everywhere, feeding not only on the birds but also on jerboas – 'rats jumping like fleas', as the narrator describes them. Wild dogs, large grey brutes as big as wolves, haunted the plains, yet not a man would sleep within the city. Camp was pitched just beyond the gate where they first entered, and from here they watched at sunset the legions of bats emerging from the great buildings to disperse in the gloaming with a dry rustling of wings like the first breath of an approaching storm. By day the sky was black with swallows, greedy for the prolific insect life.

Franciso Raposo had no idea where they were, but at last decided to follow the river through the forest, hoping that his Indians would remember the landmarks when he returned with a properly equipped expedition to comb the wealth out of these ruins. Fifty miles down they came to a mighty waterfall, and in an adjoining cliff face were found distinct signs of mine workings. Here they tarried longer.

Game was plentiful, several of the men were down with fever and the Indians were nervous about the possibility of hostile tribes in the vicinity. Below the fall the river broadened out into a series of swampy lagoons, as these South American rivers have a way of doing.

Investigation proved the suspected mineshafts to be holes they had no means of exploring, but at their mouths lay scattered about a quantity of rich silver ore. Here and there were caves hewn out of the cliff by hand, some of them sealed off by great stone slabs engraved with strange glyphs. The caves might have been tombs of the city's monarchs and high priests. The men tried in vain to move the stone slabs.

The adventurers pictured themselves as rich men and agreed to say nothing to anybody except the Viceroy, to whom Raposo owed a debt of gratitude. They would return here as soon as possible, take possession of the mines, and remove all treasure from the city.

In the meantime a scouting party had been sent out to explore farther down river. After traversing the lagoons and backwaters for nine days they caught a glimpse of a canoe paddled by two 'white people' with long black hair and dressed in some sort of clothing. They fired a shot to attract attention, but the canoe made off and vanished from view. Weary of the fatiguing business of making wide detours around the swamps, and afraid to continue farther down with so small a party, they returned to the fall.

Raposo felt the need of caution now that he and his followers had fortunes within their grasp. He had no wish to risk an encounter with hostile Indians and so he struck off eastwards. After some months of hard travel they reached the bank of the São Francisco River, crossed from there to the Paraguassu, and at length came to Bahia. From here he sent to the Viceroy, Don Luiz Peregrino de Carvalho Menezes de Athayde, the document from which this story is taken.

Nothing was done by the Viceroy, and one cannot say if Raposo returned to his discovery or not. At all events, he was never heard of again. For nearly a century the document was pigeonholed at Rio de Janeiro, till the then State Government turned it up and commissioned a young priest to investigate. This exploration was entirely unsuccessful, apparently carried out with little intelligence.

It was difficult for an administration steeped in the narrow bigotry of an all-powerful Church to give much credence to such a thing as an old civilization. Egypt in those days was still a mystery, and the ecclesiastical spirit which wilfully destroyed the priceless records of Peru and Mexico was rife as ever.

I know that Raposo's lost city is not the only one of its kind. The late British consul at Rio was taken to such a place in 1913 by a half-caste Indian; but it was a city far more easily reached, in non-mountainous country, and completely buried in forest. It too was distinguished by the remains of a statue on a great black pedestal in the middle of a square. Unfortunately a cloudburst carried away their cargo animal and they had to return immediately to avoid starvation.

There are other lost cities besides these two; and there exists another remnant of an old civilization, its people degenerate now, but still preserving records of a forgotten past in mummies, parchments and engraved metal plates. It is just such a place as described in the story, but far less ruined by earth-quakes – and very difficult to reach. The Jesuits knew of it, and so did a Frenchman who in the present century made several unsuccessful attempts to reach it. So too did a certain Englishman, much travelled in the interior, who had learned of it from an old document in Jesuit keeping. He was a victim of advanced cancer, and either died of it or was lost.

I am probably the only other who knows the secret.

3 The Fatal Month

LIEUTENANT-COMMANDER GEORGE W. DE LONG, U.S.N.

From Frobisher to Franklin, men had eagerly tried to fight their way through the North-West gateway of the Arctic. But ever since Chancellor in 1553 discovered the backdoor to Muscovy or Russia, explorers had also sought to open the North-East Passage. In 1879, de Long made the attempt from the Bering Straits end. But his ship, the Jeannette, *fell a victim to the ice and when she sank, de Long and his men had to endeavour to reach safety in the Lena delta as their only hope of survival. This extract from de Long's diaries speaks for itself and reminds us of Scott's last diaries at the South Pole thirty-three years later. As for the North-East Passage, it was the Swedish explorer Nordenskjiold who finally penetrated it in 1878–79 in the* Vega, *making his attempt from the opposite direction.*

October 1st, Saturday. – One hundred and eleventh day, and a new month. Called all hands as soon as the cook announced boiling water, and at 6.45 had our breakfast; one half pound of deer meat and tea. Sent Nindemann and Alexey to examine main river, other men to collect wood. The doctor resumed the cutting away of poor Ericksen's toes this morning. No doubt it will have to continue until half his feet are gone, unless death ensues, or we get to some settlement. Only one toe left now. Temperature 18°.

At 7.30 Nindemann and Alexey were seen to have crossed, and I immediately sent men to carry one load over.

Left the following record:

Saturday, October 1, 1881.

Fourteen of the officers and men of the U.S. Arctic Steamer *Jeannette* reached this hut on Wednesday, September 28th, and having been forced to wait for the river to freeze over, are proceeding to cross to the west side this a.m. on their journey to reach some settlement on the Lena River. We have two days' provisions, but having been fortunate enough thus far to get game in our pressing needs, we have no fear for the future.

Our party are all well, except one man, Ericksen, whose toes have been amputated in consequence of frostbite. Other records will be found in several huts on the east side of this river, along which we have come from the northward.

George W. de Long,
Lieutenant U.S. Navy, Commanding Expedition.

At 8.30 we made the final trip, and got our sick man over in safety. From there we proceeded until 11.20, dragging our man on the sled. Halted for dinner; one half pound meat and tea each. At one went ahead again until 5.05.

Actually under way: 8.30 to 9.15, 9.30 to 10.20, 10.30 to 11.20, 1.00 to 1.40, 1.50 to 2.10, 2.20 to 2.40, 3.00 to 3.25, 3.35 to 4.00, 4.15 to 4.35, 4.45 to 5.05. Total, 5 h. 15 m. At least two miles an hour. Distance made good ten to twelve miles.

And where are we? I think at the beginning of the Lena River at last. 'Sagastyr' has been to us a myth. We saw two old huts at a distance, and that was all, but they were out of our reach, and the day not half gone. Kept on ice all the way, and therefore I think we were over water, but the stream was so narrow and so crooked that it never could have been a navigable water. My chart is simply useless. I must go on plodding to the southward, trusting in God to guide me to a settlement, for I have long since realized that we are powerless to help ourselves.

A bright, calm, beautiful day. Bright sunshine to cheer us up, an icy road, and one day's rations yet. Boots frozen, of course, and balled up. No hut in sight, and we halt on a bluff to spend a cold and comfortless night. Supper one half pound of meat and tea. Made a rousing fire, built a log bed, set a watch (two hours each) to keep the fire going, and at eight p.m. crawled into our blankets

October 2nd, Sunday. – I think we all slept fairly well until midnight; but from that time it was so cold and uncomfortable that sleep was out of the question. At 4.30 we were all out and in front of the fire, daylight just appearing. Ericksen kept talking in his sleep all night, and effectually kept those awake who were not already awakened by the cold.

Breakfast five a.m. One half pound meat and tea. Bright, cloudless morning. Light N. airs. At seven went ahead, following frozen water wherever we could find it, and at 9.20 I feel quite sure we have gone some distance on the main river. I think our gait was at least two miles an hour, and our time under way two hours four minutes. I call our forenoon work at least six miles: 7.00 to 7.35, 7.45 to 8.05, 8.15 to 8.30, 8.40 to 8.50, 9.20 to 9.40, 9.50 to 10.12, 10.22 to 10.40, 10.55 to 11.15. Dinner camp. 1.00 to 1.30, 1.40 to 2.00, 2.15 to 2.35, 2.45 to 3.00, 3.20 to 3.40, 3.50 to 4.05, 4.15 to 4.20.

Divine service before dinner. Dinner one half pound meat and tea. Started ahead at one p.m., and by 4.15 had completed two marching hours and made four miles. I was much bewildered by the frequent narrowing of the river to a small vein of ice, and the irregular rambling way in which it ran. Frequently it led us into a sand bank or deep snow, and our floundering around was both exhaustive of energy and consumptive of time. There is no use denying it, we are pretty weak. Our food is not enough to keep up our strength, and when we lose a night's sleep we feel it keenly. I had several bad falls on the ice this afternoon which shook me up pretty badly. A freshening N.E. wind had blown the efflorescence off the ice, and left smooth, clear spots as clear as glass. Frozen boots are but poor foot gear, and besides cramping the feet, are like boots of iron in walking. Slip, slide, and down you are on your back.

At 4.05 p.m. I saw more wood than we had sighted since our dinner camp, and but little ahead. I therefore called a halt and 'camped', i.e., sat down, made a fire and got supper. Then we stood by for a second cold and wretched night. There was so much wind that we had to put our tent halves up for a screen, and sit shivering in our half blankets.

October 3rd, Monday. – One hundred and thirteenth day. At midnight it was so fearfully cold and wretched that I served out tea to all hands, and on that we managed to struggle along until five a.m., when we ate our last deer meat and had more tea. Our remaining food now consists of four fourteenths pounds pemmican each, and a half-starved dog. May God again incline unto our aid. How much farther we have to go before reaching a shelter or a settlement, He alone knows.

Brisk wind. Ericksen seems failing. He is weak and tremulous, and the moment he closes his eyes talks incessantly in Danish, German and English. No one could sleep even if our other surroundings permitted.

For some cause my watch stopped at 10.45 last night

while one of the men on watch had it. I set it as near as I could come to the time by guessing, and we must run by that until I can do better. Sun rose yesterday morning at 6.40 by the watch when running all right: 7.05 to 7.40 (35 m.), 7.50 to 8.20 (30 m.), 8.30 to 9.00 (30 m.), 9.15 to 9.35 (20 m.), 9.50 to 10.10 (20 m.), 10.25 to 10.40 (15 m.), 11.00 to 11.20, 11.30 to 11.50, 11.50 dinner – 1 h. 55 m. – 2 h. 35 m., say five miles.

Our forenoon's walk I put as above at five miles. Some time and distance was lost by crossing the river upon seeing numerous fox-traps. A man's track was also seen in the snow, bound south, and we followed it until it crossed the river to the west bank again. Here we were obliged to go back in our tracks, for the river was open in places, and we could not follow the man's track direct. Another of the dozen shoals which infest the river swung us off to the eastward, too, and I hastened to get on the west bank again, reaching there at 11.50 for dinner. Our last four fourteenths pound pemmican.

At 1.40 got under way again and made a long fleet until 2.20. While at the other side of the river Alexey said he saw a hut, and during our dinner camp he again saw it. Under our circumstances my desire was to get to it as speedily as possible. As Alexey pointed out it was on the left bank of the river of which we were now on the right side looking south. But a sand bank gave us excellent walking for a mile, until we took to the river ice and got across it diagonally. Here, at 2.20, I called a rest, and Alexey mounted the bluff to take a look again. He now announced that he saw a second but about one and a quarter miles back from the coast, the first hut being about the same distance south and on the edge of the bluff. The heavy dragging across country of a sick man on a sled made me incline to the hut on the shore, since, as the distance was about the same, we could get over the ice in one third of the time. Nindemann, who climbed the bluff, while he saw that the object inland was a hut, was not so confident about the one on the shore. Alexey, however, was quite positive, and not seeing very well myself I unfortunately took his eyes as best and ordered an advance along the river to the southward.

Away we went, Nindemann and Alexey leading, and had progressed about a mile when, splash! in I went through the ice up to my shoulders before my knapsack brought me up. While I was crawling out, in went Gortz to his neck about fifty yards behind me, and behind him in went Mr. Collins to his waist. Here was a time. The moment we came out of the water we were one sheet of ice, and danger of frost-bite was imminent. Along we hobbled, however, until we came, at 3.45, abreast the point on which the hut was seen. Here Nindemann climbed the bluff, followed by the doctor. At first the cry was, 'All right, come ahead,' but no sooner were we all up than Nindemann shouted, 'There is no hut here.'

To my dismay and alarm nothing but a large mound of earth was to be seen, which, from its regular shape and singular position would seem to have been built artificially for a beacon; so sure was Nindemann that it was a hut that he went all around it looking for a door, and then climbed on top to look for a hole in the roof. But of no avail. I ordered a camp to be made in a hole in the bluff face, and soon before a roaring fire we were drying (and burning) our clothes, while the cold wind ate into our backs.

And now for supper! Nothing remained but the dog. I therefore ordered him killed and dressed by Iversen, and soon after a kind of stew was made of such parts as could not be carried, of which everybody except the doctor and myself eagerly partook. To us it was a nauseating mess and – but why go on with such a disagreeable subject. I had the remainder weighed, and I am quite sure we had twenty-seven pounds. The animal was fat and – as he had been fed on pemmican – presumably clean, but –

Immediately upon halting I had sent off Alexey with his gun toward the hut island, to determine whether that was a myth like our present one. He returned about dark, certain that it was a large hut, for he had been inside of it, and had found some deer meat, scraps and bones. For a moment I was tempted to start everybody for it, but Alexey was by no means sure he could find it in the dark, and if we lost our way we should be worse off than before. We accordingly prepared to make the best of it where we were.

We three wet people were burning and steaming before the fire. Collins and Gortz had taken some alcohol, but I could not get it down. Cold, wet, with a raw N.W. wind impossible to avoid or screen, our future was a wretched, dreary night. Ericksen soon became delirious, and his talking was a horrible accompaniment to the wretchedness of our surroundings. Warm we could not get, and getting dry seemed out of the question. Nearly everybody seemed dazed and stupefied, and I feared that some of us would perish during the night. How cold it was I do not know, for my last thermometer was broken in my many falls on the ice, but I think it must have been below zero. A watch was set to keep the fire going and we huddled around it, and thus our third night without sleep was passed. If Alexey had not wrapped his sealskin around me and sat down alongside of me to keep me warm by the heat of his body, I think I should have frozen to death. As it was I steamed, and shivered, and shook. Ericksen's groans and rambling talk rang out on the night air, and such a dreary, wretched night I hope I shall never see again.

October 4th, Tuesday. – One hundred and fourteenth day. At the first approach of daylight we all began to move around, and the cook was set to work making tea. The doctor now made the unpleasant discovery that during the night Ericksen had got his gloves off and that now his hands were frozen. Men were at once set to work rubbing them, and by six a.m. we had so far restored circulation as to risk moving the man. Each one had hastily swallowed a cup of tea, and got his load in readiness. Ericksen was quite unconscious, and we lashed him on the sled. A S.W. gale was blowing, and the sensation of cold was intense; but at six a.m. we started, made a forced fleet of it, and at eight a.m. had got the man and ourselves, thank God, under the cover of a hut large enough to hold us. Here we at once made a fire, and for the first time since Saturday morning last got warm.

The doctor at once examined Ericksen and found him very low indeed. His pulse was very feeble, he was quite unconscious, and under the shock of the exposure of the past night he was sinking very fast. Fears were entertained that he might not last many hours, and I therefore called upon every one to join with me in reading the prayers for a sick person before we sought any rest for ourselves. This was done in a quiet and reverent manner, though I fear my broken utterances made but little of the service audible. Then setting a watch we all, except Alexey, laid down to sleep at ten a.m. Alexey went off to hunt, but returned at noon wet, having broken through the ice and fallen in the river.

At six p.m. all roused up, and I considered it necessary to think of some food for my party. Half a pound of dog was fried for each one and a cup of tea given, and that constituted our day's food. But we were so grateful that we were not exposed to the merciless S.W. gale that tore around us that we did not mind short rations.

October 5th, Wednesday. – One hundred and fifteenth day. The cook commenced at 7.30 to get tea, made from yesterday's tea leaves. Nothing can be served out to eat until evening. One half pound dog per day is our food until some relief is afforded us. Alexey went off hunting again at nine, and I set the men to work collecting light sticks enough to make a flooring for the house, for the frozen ground thawing under everybody has kept them damp and wet and robbed them of much sleep.

S.W. gale continues. Mortification has set in in Ericksen's leg and he is sinking. Amputation would be of no use, for he would probably die under the operation. He is partially conscious. At twelve Alexey came back, having seen nothing. He crossed the river this time, but unable longer to face the cold gale was obliged to return.

I am of the opinion that we are on Tit Ary Island, on its eastern side, and about twenty-five miles from Ku Mark Surka, which I take to be a settlement. This is a last hope, for our Sagastyr has long since faded away. The hut in which we are is quite new, and clearly not the astronomical station marked on my chart. In fact this hut is not finished, having no door and no porch. It may be intended for a summer hut, though the numerous set fox-traps would lead me to suppose that it would occasionally be visited at other times. Upon this last chance and one other seem to rest all our hopes of escape, for I can see nothing more to be done. As soon as this gale abates I shall send Nindemann and one other man to make a forced march to Ku Mark Sarka for relief. At six p.m. served out one half pound of dog meat and second-hand tea, and then went to sleep.

October 6th, Thursday. – One hundred and sixteenth day. Called all hands at 7.30. Had a cup of third-hand tea with one half ounce of alcohol in it. Everybody very weak. Gale moderating somewhat. Sent Alexey out to hunt. Shall start Nindemann and Noros at noon to make the forced march to Ku Mark Surka. At 8.45 a.m. our messmate Ericksen departed this life. Addressed a few words of cheer and comfort to the men. Alexey came back empty-handed. Too much drifting snow. What in God's name is going to become of us – fourteen pounds dog meat left, and twenty-five miles to a possible settlement? As to burying Ericksen, I cannot dig a grave, for the ground is frozen and we have nothing to dig with. There is nothing to do but to bury him in the river. Sewed him up in the flaps of the tent, and covered him with my flag. Got tea ready, and with one half ounce alcohol we will try to make out to bury him. But we are all so weak that I do not see how we are going to move.

At 12.40 p.m. read the burial service and carried our departed shipmate's body down to the river, where, a hole having been cut in the ice, he was buried; three volleys from our two Remingtons being fired over him as a funeral honor.

A board was prepared with this cut on it:

IN MEMORY
H. H. ERICKSEN,
Oct. 6, 1881.
U.S.S. Jeannette.

and this will be stuck in the river bank abreast his grave.

His clothing was divided up among his messmates. Iversen has his Bible and a lock of his hair. Kaack has a lock of his hair.

Supper at five p.m. – one half pound dog meat and tea.

October 7th, Friday. – One hundred and seventeenth day. Breakfast, consisting of our last one half pound dog meat and tea. Our last grain of tea was put in the kettle this morning, and we are now about to undertake our journey of twenty-five miles with some old tea-leaves and two quarts alcohol. However, I trust in God, and I believe that He who has fed us thus far will not suffer us to die of want now.

Commenced preparations for departure at 7.10. Our Winchester rifle being out of order is, with one hundred and sixty-one rounds ammunition, left behind. We have with us two Remingtons and two hundred and forty-three rounds ammunition. Left the following record in the hut:

Friday, October 7, 1881.

The undermentioned officers and men of the late U.S. Steamer *Jeannette* are leaving here this morning to make a forced march to Ku Mark Surka, or some other settlement on the Lena River. We reached here on Tuesday, October 4th, with a disabled comrade, H. H. Ericksen (seaman), who died yesterday morning, and was buried in the river at noon. His death resulted from frost-bite and exhaustion, due to consequent exposure. The rest of us are well, but have no provisions left – having eaten our last this morning.

Under way at 8.30 and proceeded until 11.20, by which time we had made about three miles. Here we were all pretty well done up, and, moreover, seemed to be wandering in a labyrinth. A large lump of wood swept in by an eddy seemed to be a likely place to get hot water, and I halted the party. For dinner we had one ounce alcohol in a pot of tea. Then went ahead, and soon struck what seemed like the river again. Here four of us broke through the ice in trying to cross, and fearing frost-bite I had a fire built on the west bank to dry us. Sent Alexey off meanwhile to look for food, directing him not to go far nor to stay long; but at 3.30 he had not returned, nor was he in sight. Light S.W. breeze, hazy; mountains in sight to southward.

At 5.30 Alexey returned with one ptarmigan, of which we made soup, and with one half ounce alcohol had our supper. Then crawled under our blankets for a sleep. Light W. breeze; full moon; starlight. Not very cold. Alexey saw river a mile wide with no ice in it.

October 8th, Saturday. – One hundred and eighteenth day. Called all hands at 5.30. Breakfast, one ounce alcohol in a pint of hot water. Doctor's note: Alcohol proves of great advantage; keeps off craving for food, preventing gnawing at stomach, and has kept up the strength of the men, as given, – three ounces per day as estimated, and in accordance with Dr. Anstie's experiments.

Went ahead until 10.30; one ounce alcohol 6.30 to 10.30; five miles; struck big river; 11.30 ahead again; sand bank. Meet small river. Have to turn back. Halt at five. Only made advance one mile more. Hard luck. Snow; S.S.E. wind. Cold camp; but little wood, one half ounce alcohol.

October 9th, Sunday. – One hundred and nineteenth day. All hands at 4.30 one ounce alcohol. Read divine service. Send Nindemann and Noros ahead for relief; they carry their blankets, one rifle, forty rounds ammunition, two ounces alcohol. Orders to keep west bank of river until they reach settlement. They started at seven; cheered them.

Under way at eight. Crossed creek. Broke through ice. All wet up to knees. Stopped and built fires. Dried clothes. Under way again at 10.30. Lee breaking down. At one strike river bank. Halt for dinner – one ounce alcohol. Alexey shot three ptarmigans. Made soup. We are following Nindemann's track, though he is long since out of sight. Under way at 3.30. High bluff. Ice running rapidly to northward in river. Halt at 4.40 upon coming to wood. Find canoe. Lay our heads on it and go to sleep; one half ounce alcohol for supper.

October 10th, Monday. – One hundred and twentieth day. Last half ounce alcohol at 5.30; at 6.30 send Alexey off to look for ptarmigan. Eat deerskin scraps. Yesterday morning ate my deerskin foot-nips. Light S.S.E. airs. Not very cold. Under way at eight. In crossing creek three of us got wet. Built fire and dried out. Ahead again until eleven. Used up. Built fire. Made a drink out of the tea-leaves from alcohol bottle. On again at noon. Fresh S.S.W. wind, drifting snow, very hard going. Lee begging to be left. Some little beach, and then long stretches of high bank. Ptarmigan tracks plentiful. Following Nindemann's tracks. At three halted, used up; crawled into a hole in the bank, collected wood and built fire. Alexey away in quest of game. Nothing for supper except a spoonful of glycerine. All hands weak and feeble, but cheerful. God help us.

October 11th, Tuesday. – One hundred and twenty-first day. S.W. gale with snow. Unable to move. No game. One spoonful glycerine and hot water for food. No more wood in our vicinity.

October 12th, Wednesday. – One hundred and twenty-second day. Breakfast; last spoonful glycerine and hot water. For dinner we tried a couple of handfuls of Arctic willow in a pot of water and drank the infusion. Everybody getting weaker and weaker. Hardly strength to get firewood. S.W. gale with snow.

October 13th, Thursday. – One hundred and twenty-third day. Willow tea. Strong S.W. wind. No news from Nindemann. We are in the hands of God, and unless He intervenes we are lost. We cannot move against the wind, and staying here means starvation. Afternoon went ahead for a mile, crossing either another river or a bend in the big one. After crossing, missed Lee. Went down in a hole in the bank and camped. Sent back for Lee. He had turned back, lain down, and was waiting to die. All united in saying Lord's Prayer and Creed after supper. Living gale of wind. Horrible night.

October 14th, Friday. – One hundred and twenty-fourth day. Breakfast, willow tea. Dinner, one half teaspoonful sweet oil and willow tea. Alexey shot one ptarmigan. Had soup. S.W. wind, moderating.

October 15th, Saturday. – One hundred and twenty-fifth day. Breakfast, willow tea and two old boots. Conclude to move on at sunrise. Alexey breaks down, also Lee. Come to empty grain raft. Halt and camp. Signs of smoke at twilight to southward.

October 16th, Sunday. – One hundred and twenty-sixth day. Alexey dying. Doctor baptized him. Read prayers for sick. Mr. Collins' birthday – forty years old. About sunset Alexey died. Exhaustion from starvation. Covered him with ensign and laid him in the crib.

October 18th, Tuesday. – One hundred and twenty-eighth day. Calm and mild, snow falling. Buried Alexey in the afternoon. Laid him on the ice of the river, and covered him over with slabs of ice.

October 19th, Wednesday. – One hundred and twenty-ninth day. Cutting up tent to make foot gear. Doctor went ahead to find new camp. Shifted by dark.

October 20th, Thursday. – One hundred and thirtieth day. Bright and sunny, but very cold. Lee and Kaack done up.

October 21st, Friday. – One hundred and thirty-first day. Kaack was found dead about midnight between the doctor and myself. Lee died about noon. Read prayers for sick when we found he was going.

October 22nd, Saturday. – One hundred and thirty-second day. Too weak to carry the bodies of Lee and Kaack out on the ice. The doctor, Collins and I carried them around the corner out of sight. Then my eye closed up.

October 23rd, Sunday. – One hundred and thirty-third day. Everybody pretty weak. Slept or rested all day, and then managed to get enough wood in before dark. Read part of divine service. Suffering in our feet. No foot gear.

October 24th, Monday. – One hundred and thirty-fourth day. A hard night.

October 25, Tuesday. – One hundred and thirty-fifth day.

October 26, Wednesday. – One hundred and thirty-sixth day.

October 27th, Thursday. – One hundred and thirty-seventh day. Iversen broken down.

October 28th, Friday. – One hundred and thirty-eighth day. Iversen died during early morning.

October 29th, Saturday. – One hundred and thirty-ninth day. Dressler died during night.

October 30th, Sunday. – One hundred and fortieth day. Boyd and Gortz died during night. Mr. Collins dying.

4 The Rapids of the Ogowé

MARY H. KINGSLEY

Mary Kingsley's Travels in West Africa, *first published in 1897, caused an immediate sensation. To understand the impact the book had, one has only to be reminded that it appeared in days when British women had scarcely any domestic rights – for example, at marriage their property automatically became their husbands'; they did not even obtain the vote until the 1920's. Quite apart from this, Mary Kingsley's journeys – largely in the French Congo, Gabon and the Cameroons – were an astonishing physical feat for a woman at any time, let alone in the days when Queen Victoria was celebrating her diamond jubilee. Here, with characteristic coolness and humour, Mary Kingsley describes a perilous voyage through the rapids of a tumultuous tropical river.*

I establish myself on my portmanteau comfortably in the canoe, my back is against the trade box, and behind that is the usual mound of pillows, sleeping mats, and mosquito-bars of the Igalwa crew; the whole surmounted by the French flag flying from an indifferent stick.

M. and Mme. Forget provide me with everything I can possibly require, and say, that the blood of half my crew is half alcohol; on the whole it is patent they don't expect to see me again, and I forgive them, because they don't seem cheerful over it; but still it is not reassuring – nothing is about this affair, and it's going to rain. It does, as we go up the river to Njole, where there is another risk of the affair collapsing, by the French authorities declining to allow me to proceed. On we paddled, M'bo the head man standing in the bows of the canoe in front of me, to steer, then I, the baggage, then the able-bodied seamen, including the cook also standing and paddling; and at the other extremity of the canoe – it grieves me to speak of it in this unseamanlike way, but in these canoes both ends are alike, and chance alone ordains which is bow and which is stern – stands Pierre, the first officer, also steering; the paddles used are all of the long-handled, leaf-shaped Igalwa type. We get up just past Talagouga Island and then tie up against the bank of M. Gazenget's plantation, and make a piratical raid on its bush for poles. A gang of his men come down to us, but only to chat. One of them, I notice, has had something happen severely to one side of his face. I ask M'bo what's the matter, and he answers, with a derisive laugh, 'He be fool man, he go for tief plantain and done got shot.' M'bo does not make it clear where the sin in this affair is exactly located; I expect it is in being 'fool man'. Having got our supply of long stout poles we push off and paddle on again. Before we reach Njole I recognize my crew have got the grumbles, and at once inquire into the reason. M'bo sadly informs me that 'they no got chop', having been provided only with plantain, and no meat or fish to eat with it. I promise to get them plenty at Njole, and contentment settles on the crew and they sing. After about three hours we reach Njole, and I proceed to interview the authorities. Dr. Pelessier is away down river, and the two gentlemen in charge don't understand English; but Pierre translates, and the letter which M. Forget has kindly written for me explains things, and so the palaver ends satisfactorily, after a long talk. First, the official says he does not like to take the responsibility of allowing me to endanger myself in those rapids. I explain I will not hold any one responsible but myself, and I urge that a lady has been up before, a Mme. Quinee. He says 'Yes, that is true, but Madame had with her a husband and many men, whereas I am alone and have only eight Igalwas and not Adoomas, the proper crew for the rapids, and they are away up river now with the convoy.' 'True, oh King!' I answer, but Madame Quinee went right up to Lestourville, whereas I only want to go sufficiently high up the rapids to get typical fish. And these Igalwas are great men at canoe work, and can go in a canoe anywhere that any mortal man can go' – this to cheer up my Igalwa interpreter – 'and as for the husband, neither the Royal Geographical Society's list, in their "Hints to Travellers", nor Messrs. Silver, in their elaborate lists of articles necessary for a traveller in tropical climates, make mention of husbands.' If they did, by the by, they would say he was to be green, but they don't say a word about one. However, the official ultimately says Yes, I may go, and parts with me as with one bent on self-destruction. This affair being settled I start off, like an old hen with a brood of chickens to provide for, to get chop for my men, and go first to Hatton and Cookson's factory. I find its white Agent is down river after stores, and John Holt's Agent says he has got no beef nor fish, and is precious short of provisions for himself; so I go back to Dumas', where I find a most amiable French gentleman, who says he will let me have as much fish or beef as I want, and to this supply he adds some delightful bread biscuits. M'bo and the crew beam with satisfaction; mine is clouded by finding, when they have carried off the booty to the canoe, that the Frenchman will not let me pay for it. Therefore taking the opportunity of his back being turned for a few minutes, I buy and pay for, across the store counter, some trade things, knives, cloth, &c. Then I say good-bye to the Agent. 'Adieu,

Mademoiselle,' says he in a for-ever tone of voice. Indeed I am sure I have caught from these kind people a very pretty and becoming mournful manner, and there's not another white station for 500 miles where I can show it off. Away we go, still damp from the rain we have come through, but drying nicely with the day, and cheerful about the chop.

The Ogowé is broad at Njole and its banks not mountainous, as at Talagouga; but as we go on it soon narrows, the current runs more rapidly than ever, and we are soon again surrounded by the mountain range. Great masses of black rock show among the trees on the hillsides, and under the fringe of fallen trees that hang from the steep banks. Two hours after leaving Njole we are facing our first rapid. Great gray-black masses of smoothed rock rise up out of the whirling water in all directions. These rocks have a peculiar appearance which puzzle me at the time, but in subsequently getting used to it I accepted it quietly and admired. When the sun shines on them they have a soft light blue haze round them, like a halo. The effect produced by this, with the forested hillsides and the little beaches of glistening white sand was one of the most perfect things I have ever seen.

We kept along close to the right-hand bank, dodging out of the way of the swiftest current as much as possible. Ever and again we were unable to force our way round projecting parts of the bank, so we then got up just as far as we could to the point in question, yelling and shouting at the tops of our voices. M'bo said 'Jump for bank, sar,' and I 'up and jumped', followed by half the crew. Such banks! sheets, and walls, and rubbish heaps of rock, mixed up with trees fallen and standing. One appalling corner I shall not forget, for I had to jump at a rock wall, and hang on to it in a manner more befitting an insect than an insect-hunter, and then scramble up it into a close-set forest, heavily burdened with boulders of all sizes. I wonder whether the rocks or the trees were there first? there is evidence both ways, for in one place you will see a rock on the top of a tree, the tree creeping out from underneath it, and in another place you will see a tree on top of a rock, clasping it with a network of roots and getting its nourishment, goodness knows how, for these are by no means tender, digestible sandstones, but uncommon hard gneiss and quartz which has no idea of breaking up into friable small stuff, and which only takes on a high polish when it is vigorously sanded and canvassed by the Ogowé. While I was engaged in climbing across these promontories, the crew would be busy shouting and hauling the canoe round the point by means of the strong chain provided for such emergencies fixed on to the bow. When this was done, in we got again and paddled away until we met our next affliction.

M'bo had advised that we should spend our first night at the same village that M. Allegret did: but when we reached it, a large village on the north bank, we seemed to have a lot of daylight still in hand, and thought it would be better to stay at one a little higher up, so as to make a shorter day's work for tomorrow, when we wanted to reach Kondo Kondo; so we went against the bank just to ask about the situation and character of the up-river villages. The row of low, bark huts was long, and extended its main frontage close to the edge of the river bank. The inhabitants had been watching us as we came, and when they saw we intended calling that afternoon, they charged down to the river edge hopeful with excitement. They had a great deal to say, and so had we. After compliments, as they say, in excerpts of diplomatic communications, three of their men took charge of the conversation on their side, and M'bo did ours. To M'bo's questions they gave a dramatic entertainment as answer, after the manner of these brisk, excitable Fans. One chief, however, soon settled down to definite details, prefacing his remarks with the silence-commanding 'Azuna! Azuna!' and his companions grunted approbation of his observations. He took a piece of plantain leaf and tore it up into five different-sized bits. These he laid along the edge of our canoe at different intervals of space, while he told M'bo things, mainly scandalous, about the characters of the villages these bits of leaf represented, save of course about bit A. which represented his own. The interval between the bits was proportional to the interval between the villages, and the size of the bits was proportional to the size of the village. Village number four was the only one he should recommend our going to. When all was said, I gave our kindly informants some heads of tobacco and many thanks. Then M'bo sang them a hymn, with the assistance of Pierre, half a line behind him in a different key, but every bit as flat. The Fans seemed impressed, but any crowd would be by the hymn-singing of my crew, unless they were inmates of deaf and dumb asylums. Then we took our farewell, and thanked the village elaborately for its kind invitation to spend the night there on our way home, shoved off and paddled away in great style just to show those Fans what Igalwas could do.

We hadn't gone 200 yards before we met a current coming round the end of a rock reef that was too strong for us to hold our own in, let alone progress. On to the bank I was ordered and went; it was a low slip of rugged confused boulders and fragments of rocks, carelessly arranged, and evidently under water in the wet season. I scrambled along, the men yelled and shouted and hauled the canoe, and the inhabitants of the village, seeing we were becoming amusing again, came, legging it like lamp-lighters, after us, young and old, male and female, to say nothing of the dogs. Some good souls helped the men haul, while I did my best to amuse the others by diving headlong from a large rock on to which I had elaborately climbed, into a thick clump of willow-leaved shrubs. They applauded my performance vociferously, and then assisted my efforts to extricate myself, and during the rest of my scramble they kept close to me, with keen competition for the front row, in hopes that I would do something like it again. But I refused the *encore*, because, bashful as I am, I could not but feel that my last performance was carried out with all the superb reckless *abandon* of a Sarah Bernhardt, and a display of art of this order should satisfy any African village for a year at least. At last I got across the rocks on to a lovely little beach of white sand, and stood there talking, surrounded by my audience, until the canoe got over its difficulties and arrived almost as scratched as I; and then we again said farewell and paddled away, to the great grief of the natives, for they don't get a circus up above Njole every week, poor dears.

Now there is no doubt that that chief's plantain-leaf chart was an ingenious idea and a credit to him. There is also no doubt that the Fan mile is a bit Irish, a matter of nine or so of those of ordinary mortals, but I am bound to say I don't think, even allowing for this, that he put those pieces far enough apart. On we paddled a long way before we picked up village number one, mentioned in that chart. On again, still longer, till we came to village number two. Village number three hove in sight high up on a mountain-side soon after, but it was getting dark and the water worse, and the hillsides growing higher and higher into nobly shaped mountains, forming, with their forest-graced steep sides, a ravine that, in the gathering gloom, looked like an alley-way made of iron, for the foaming Ogowé. Village number four we anxiously looked for; village number four we never saw; for round us came the dark, seeming to come out on to the river from the forests and the side ravines, where for some hours we had seen it sleeping, like a sailor with his clothes on in bad weather. On we paddled, looking for signs of village fires, and seeing them not. The *Erd-geist* knew we wanted something, and seeing how we personally lacked it, thought it was beauty; and being in a kindly mood, gave it us, sending the lovely lingering flushes of his afterglow across the sky, which, dying, left it that divine deep purple velvet which no one has dared to paint. Out in it came the great stars blazing high above us, and the dark round us was be-gemmed with fire-flies: but we were not as satisfied with these things as we should have been; what we wanted were fires to cook by and dry ourselves by, and all that sort of thing. The *Erd-geist* did not understand, and so left us when the afterglow had died away, with only enough starlight to see the flying foam of the rapids ahead and around us, and not enough to see the great trees that had fallen from the bank into the water. These, when the rapids were not too noisy, we could listen for, because the black current rushes through their branches with an impatient 'lish, swish'; but when there was a rapid roaring close alongside we ran into those trees, and got ourselves mauled, and had ticklish times getting on our course again. Now and again we ran up against great rocks sticking up in the black water – grim, isolated fellows, who seemed to be standing silently watching their fellow rocks noisily fighting in the arena of the white water. Still on we poled and paddled. About 8 p.m. we came to a corner, a bad one; but we were unable to leap on to the bank and haul round, not being able to see either the details or the exact position of the said bank, and we felt, I think naturally, disinclined to spring in the direction of such bits of country as we had had experience of during the afternoon, with nothing but the aid we might have got from a compass hastily viewed by the transitory light of a lucifer match, and even this would not have informed us how many tens of feet of tree fringe lay between us and the land, so we did not attempt it. One must be careful at times, or nasty accidents may follow. We fought our way round that corner, yelling defiance at the water, and dealt with succeeding corners on the *vi et armis* plan, breaking, ever and anon, a pole. About 9.30 we got into a savage rapid. We fought it inch by inch. The canoe jammed herself on some barely sunken rocks in it. We shoved her off over them. She tilted over and chucked us out. The rocks round being just awash, we survived and got her straight again, and got into her and drove her unmercifully; she struck again and bucked like a bronco, and we fell in heaps upon each other, but stayed inside that time – the men by the aid of their intelligent feet, I by clinching my hands into the bush rope lacing which ran round the rim of the canoe and the meaning of which I did understand when I left Talagouga. We sorted ourselves out hastily and sent her at it again. Smash went a sorely tried pole and a paddle. Round and round we spun in an exultant whirlpool, which, in a light-hearted, maliciously joking way, hurled us tail-first out of it into the current. Now the grand point in these canoes of having both ends alike declared itself; for at this juncture all we had to do was to revolve on our own axis and commence life anew with what had been the bow for the stern. Of course we were defeated, we could not go up any further without the aid of our lost poles and paddles, so we had to go down for shelter somewhere, anywhere, and down at a terrific pace in the white water we went. While hitched among the rocks the arrangement of our crew had been altered, Pierre joining M'bo in the bows; this piece of precaution was frustrated by our getting turned round; so our position was what you might call precarious, until we got into another whirlpool, when we persuaded nature to start us right end on. This was only a matter of minutes, whirlpools being plentiful, and then M'bo and Pierre, provided with our surviving poles, stood in the bows to fend us off rocks, as we shot towards them, while we midship paddles sat, helping to steer, and when occasion arose, which occasion did with lightning rapidity, to whack the whirlpools with the flat of our paddles, to break their force. Cook crouched in the stern concentrating his mind on steering only. A most excellent arrangement in theory and the safest practical one no doubt, but it did not work out what you might call brilliantly well; though each department did its best. We dashed full tilt towards high rocks, things twenty to fifty feet above water. Midship backed and flapped like fury; M'bo and Pierre received the shock on their poles; sometimes we glanced successfully aside and flew on; sometimes we didn't. The shock being too much for M'bo and Pierre they were driven back on me, who got flattened on to the cargo of bundles which, being now firmly tied in, couldn't spread the confusion further aft; but the shock of the canoe's nose against the rock did so in style, and the rest of the crew fell forward on to the bundles, me, and themselves. So shaken up together were we several times that night, that it's a wonder to me, considering the hurry, that we sorted ourselves out correctly with our own particular legs and arms. And although we in the middle of the canoe did some very spirited flapping, our whirlpool-breaking was no more successful than M'bo and Pierre's fending off, and many a wild waltz we danced that night with the waters of the River Ogowé.

Unpleasant as going through the rapids was, when circumstances took us into the black current we fared no better. For good all-round inconvenience, give me going full tilt in the dark into the branches of a fallen tree at the pace we were going then – and crash, swish, crackle and there you are, hung up, with a bough pressing against your chest, and your hair being torn out and your clothes ribboned by others, while the wicked river is trying to drag away the canoe from under you. I expect we should have been an amusing spectacle for hard-hearted onlookers; but onlookers there were none, neither could we form a co-operative society for consuming our own ridiculousness as we did when we had light to see it by. After a good hour and more of these experiences, we went hard on to a large black reef of rocks. So firm was the canoe wedged that we in our rather worn-out state couldn't move her so we wisely decided to 'lef 'em' and see what could be done towards getting food and a fire for the remainder of the night. Our eyes, now trained to the darkness, observed pretty close to us a big lump of land, looming up out of the river. This we subsequently found out was Kembe Island. The rocks and foam on either side stretched away into the darkness, and high above us against the star-lit sky stood out clearly the summits of the mountains of the Sierra del Cristal.

The most interesting question to us now was whether this rock reef communicated sufficiently with the island for us to get to it. Abandoning conjecture; tying very firmly our canoe up to the rocks, a thing that seemed, considering she was jammed hard and immovable, a little unnecessary – but you can never be sufficiently careful in this matter with any kind of boat – off we started among the rock boulders. I would climb up on to a rock table, fall off it on the other side on to rocks again, with more or less water on them – then get a patch of singing sand under my feet, then with varying suddenness get into more water, deep or shallow, broad or narrow pools among the rocks; out of that over more rocks, &c., &c., &c.: my companions, from their noises, evidently were going in for the same kind of thing, but we were quite cheerful, because the probability of reaching the land seemed increasing. Most of us arrived into deep channels of water which here and there cut in between this rock reef and the bank. M'bo was the first to find the way into certainty; he was, and I hope still is, a perfect wonder at this sort of work. I kept close to M'bo, and when we got to the shore, the rest of the wanderers being collected, we said 'chances are there's a village round here'; and started to find it. After a gay time in a rock-encumbered forest, growing in a tangled, matted way on a rough hillside, at an angle of 45 degrees, M'bo sighted the gleam of fires through the tree stems away to the left, and we bore down on it, listening to its drum. Viewed through the bars of the tree stems the scene was very picturesque. The village was just a collection of palm mat-built huts very low and squalid. In its tiny street, an affair of some sixty feet long and twenty wide, were a succession of small fires. The villagers themselves, however, were the striking features in the picture. They were painted ver-milion all over their nearly naked bodies, and were dancing enthusiastically to the good old rump-a-tump-tump-tump tune, played energetically by an old gentleman on a long, high-standing, white-and-black painted drum. They said that as they had been dancing when we arrived they had failed to hear us. M'bo secured a – well, I don't exactly know what to call it – for my use. It was, I fancy, the remains of the village club-house. It had a certain amount of palm-thatch roof and some of its left-hand side left, the rest of the structure was bare old poles with filaments of palm mat hanging from them here and there; and really if it hadn't been for the roof one wouldn't have known whether one was inside or outside it. The floor was trodden earth and in the middle of it a heap of white ash and the usual two bush lights, laid down with their burning ends propped up off the ground with stones, and emitting, as is their wont, a rather mawkish, but not altogether unpleasant smell, and volumes of smoke which finds its way out through the thatch, leaving on the inside of it a rich oily varnish of a bright warm brown colour. They give a very good light, provided some one keeps an eye on them and knocks the ash off the end as it burns gray; the bush lights' idea of being snuffed. Against one of the open-work sides hung a drum covered with raw hide, and a long hollow bit of tree trunk, which served as a cupboard for a few small articles. I gathered in all these details as I sat on one of the hard wooden benches, waiting for my dinner, which Isaac was preparing outside in the street. The atmosphere of the hut in spite of its remarkable advantages in the way of ventilation, was oppressive, for the smell of the bush lights, my wet clothes, and the natives who crowded into the hut to look at me, made anything but a pleasant combination. The people were evidently exceedingly poor; clothes they had very little of. The two head men had on old French military coats in rags; but they were quite satisfied with their appearance, and evidently felt through them in touch with European culture, for they lectured to the others on the habits and customs of the white man with great self-confidence and superiority. The majority of the village had a slight acquaintance already with this interesting animal, being, I found, Adoomas. They had made a settlement on Kembe Island some two years or so ago. Then the Fans came and attacked them, and killed and ate several. The Adoomas left and fled to the French authority at Njole and remained under its guarding shadow until the French came up and chastized the Fans and burnt their village; and the Adoomas – when things had quieted down again and the Fans had gone off to build themselves a new village for their burnt one – came back to Kembe Island and their plantain patch. They had only done this a few months before my arrival and had not had time to rebuild, hence the dilapidated state of the village. They are, I am told, a Congo region tribe, whose country lies south-west of Franceville, and, as I have already said, are the tribe used by the French authorities to take convoys up and down the Ogowé to Franceville, more to keep this route open than for transport purposes; the rapids rendering it impracticable to take heavy stores this way, and making it a thirty-six days' journey from Njole with good luck. The practical route is *via* Loango and Brazzaville. The Adoomas told us the convoy which had gone up with the vivacious government official had had trouble with the rapids and had spent five days on Kondo Kondo, dragging up the canoes empty by means of ropes and chains, carrying cargo that was in them along on land until they had passed the worst rapid and then repacking. They added the information that the rapids were at their worst just now, and entertained us with reminiscences of a poor young French official who had drowned in them last year – indeed they were just as cheering as my white friends. As soon as my dinner arrived they politely cleared out, and I heard the devout M'bo holding a service for them, with hymns, in the street, and this being over they returned to their drum and dance, keeping things up distinctly late, for it was 11.10 p.m., when we first entered the village.

While the men were getting their food I mounted guard over our little possessions, and when they turned up to make things tidy in my hut, I walked off down to the shore by a path, which we had elaborately avoided when coming to the village, a very vertically inclined, slippery little path, but still the one whereby the natives went up and down to their canoes, which were kept tied up amongst the rocks. The moon was rising, illuminating the sky, but not yet sending down her light on the foaming, flying Ogowé in its deep ravine. The scene was divinely lovely; on every side out of the formless gloom rose, the peaks of the Sierra del Cristal. Tomanjawki, on the further side of the river surrounded by his companion peaks, looked his grandest, silhouetted hard against the sky. In the higher valleys where the dim light shone faintly, one could see wreaths and clouds of silver-gray mist lying, basking lazily or rolling to and fro. Olangi seemed to stretch right across the river, blocking with his great blunt mass all passage; while away to the N.E. a cone-shaped peak showed conspicuous, which I afterwards knew as Kangwe. In the darkness round me flitted thousands of fire-flies and out beyond this pool of utter night flew by unceasingly the white foam of the rapids; sound there was none save their thunder. The majesty and beauty of the scene fascinated me, and I stood leaning with my back against a rock pinnacle watching it. Do not imagine it gave rise, in what I am pleased to call my mind, to those complicated, poetical reflections natural beauty seems to bring out in other people's minds. It never works that way with me; I just lose all sense of human individuality, all memory of human life, with its grief and worry and doubt, and become part of the atmosphere. If I have a heaven, that will be mine, and I verily believe that if I were left alone long enough with such a scene as this or on the deck of an African liner in the bights, watching her funnel and masts swinging to and fro in the great long leisurely roll against the sky, I should be found soulless and dead; but I never have a chance of that. This night my absent Kras, as my Fanti friends would call them, were sent hurrying home badly scared to their attributive body by a fearful shriek tearing through the voice of the Ogowé up into the silence of the hills. I woke with a shudder and found myself sore and stiff, but made hastily in the direction of the shriek, fancying some of our hosts had been spearing one of the crew – a vain and foolish fancy I apologize for. What had happened was that my men, thinking it wiser to keep an eye on our canoe, had come down and built a fire close to her and put up their mosquito-bars as tents. One of the men, tired out by his day's work, had sat down on one of the three logs, whose ends, pointed to a common centre where the fire is, constitute the universal stove of this region. He was taking a last pipe before turning in, but sleep had taken him, and the wretch of a fire had sneaked along in the log under him and burnt him suddenly. The shriek was his way of mentioning the fact. Having got up these facts I left the victim seated in a remedial cool pool of water and climbed back to the village, whose inhabitants, tired at last, were going to sleep. M'bo, I found, had hung up my mosquito-bar over one of the hard wood benches, and going cautiously under it I lit a night-light and read myself asleep with my damp dilapidated old Horace.

Woke at 4 a.m. lying on the ground among the plantain stems, having by a reckless movement fallen out of the house. Thanks be there are no mosquitoes. I don't know how I escaped the rats which swarm here, running about among the huts and the inhabitants in the evening, with a tameness shocking to see. I turned in again until six o'clock, when we started getting things ready to go up river again, carefully providing ourselves with a new stock of poles, and subsidizing a native to come with us and help us to fight the rapids.

The greatest breadth of the river channel we now saw, in the daylight, to be the S.S.W. branch; this was the one we had been swept into, and was almost completely barred by rock. The other one to the N.N.W. was more open, and the river rushed through it, a terrific, swirling mass of water. Had we got caught in this, we should have got past Kembe Island, and gone to glory. Whenever the shelter of the spits of land or of the reefs was sufficient to allow the water to lay down its sand, strange shaped sandbanks showed, as regular in form as if they had been smoothed by human hands. They rise above the water in a slope, the low end or tail against the current; the down-stream end terminating in an abrupt miniature cliff, sometimes six or seven feet above water; that they are the same shape when they have not got their heads above water you will find by sticking on them in a canoe, which I did several times, with a sort of automatic devotion to scientific research peculiar to me. Your best way of getting off is to push on in the direction of the current, carefully preparing for the shock of suddenly coming off the cliff end.

We left the landing place rocks of Kembe Island about 8, and no sooner had we got afloat, than, in the twinkling of an eye, we were swept, broadside on, right across the river to the north bank, and then engaged in a heavy fight with a severe rapid. After passing this, the river is fairly uninterrupted by rock for a while, and is silent and swift. When you are ascending such a piece the effect is strange; you see the water flying by the side of your canoe, as you vigorously drive your paddle into it with short rapid strokes, and you forthwith fancy you are travelling at the rate of a North-Western express; but you just raise your eyes, my friend, and look at that bank, which is standing very nearly still, and you will realize that you and your canoe are standing very nearly still too; and that all your exertions are only enabling you to creep on at the pace of a crushed snail, and that it's the water that is going the pace. It's a most quaint and unpleasant disillusionment.

Above the stretch of swift silent water we come to the Senegelade Islands, and the river here changes its course from N.N.W., to S.S.E. to north and south. A bad rapid, called by our ally from Kembe Island 'Unfanga', being surmounted, we seem to be in a mountain-walled lake, and keeping along the left bank of this, we get on famously for twenty whole restful minutes, which lulls us into a false sense of security, and my crew sing M'pongwe songs, descriptive of how they go to their homes to see their wives, and families, and friends, giving chaffing descriptions of their friends' characteristics and of their failings, which cause bursts of laughter from those among us who recognize the allusions, and how they go to their boxes, and take out their clothes, and put them on – a long bragging inventory of these things is given by each man as a solo, and then the chorus, taken heartily up by his companions, signifies their admiration and astonishment at his wealth and importance – and then they sing how, being dissatisfied with that last dollar's worth of goods they got from 'Holty's', they have decided to take their next trade to Hatton and Cookson, or *vice versa*; and then comes the chorus, applauding the wisdom of such a decision, and extolling the excellence of Hatton and Cookson's goods or Holty's. These M'pongwe and Igalwa boat songs are all very pretty, and have very elaborate tunes in a minor key. I do not believe there are any old words to them; I have tried hard to find out about them, but I believe the tunes, which are of a limited number and quite distinct from each other, are very old. The words are put in by the singer on the spur of the moment, and only restricted in this sense, that there would always be the domestic catalogue – whatever its component details might be – sung to the one fixed tune, the trade information sung to another, and so on. A good singer, in these parts, means the man who can make up the best song – the most impressive, or the most amusing; I have elsewhere mentioned pretty much the same state of things among the Ga's and Krumen and Bubi, and in all cases the tunes are only voice tunes, not for instrumental performance. The instrumental music consists of that marvellously developed series of drum tunes – the attempt to understand which has taken up much of my time, and led me into queer company – and the many tunes played on the 'mrimba and the orchid-root-stringed harp; they are, I believe, entirely distinct from the song tunes. And these peaceful tunes my men were now singing were, in their florid elaboration very different from the one they fought the rapids to, of – So sir – So Sur – So Sir – So Sur –Ush! So Sir, &c.

On we go singing elaborately, thinking no evil of nature, when a current, a quiet devil of a thing, comes round from behind a point of the bank and catches the nose of our canoe; wringing it well, it sends us scuttling right across the river in spite of our ferocious swoops at the water, upsetting us among a lot of rocks with the water boiling over them; this lot of rocks being however of the table-top kind, and not those precious, close-set pinnacles rising up sheer out of profound depths, between which you are so likely to get your canoe wedged in and split. We, up to our knees in water that nearly tears our legs off, push and shove the canoe free, and re-embarking return singing 'So Sir' across the river, to have it out with that current. We do; and at its head find a rapid, and notice on the mountain-side a village clearing, the first sign of human habitation we have seen today.

Above this rapid we get a treat of still water, the main current of the Ogowé flying along by the south bank. On our side there are sandbanks with their graceful sloping backs and sudden ends, and there is a very strange and beautiful effect produced by the flakes and balls of foam thrown off the rushing main current into the quiet water. These whirl among the eddies and rush backwards and forwards as though they were still mad with wild haste, until, finding no current to take them down, they drift away into the land-locked bays, where they come to a stand-still as if they were bewildered and lost and were trying to remember where they were going to and whence they had come; the foam of which they are composed is yellowish-white, with a spongy sort of solidity about it. In a little bay we pass we see eight native women, Fans clearly, by their bright brown faces, and their loads of brass bracelets and armlets; likely enough they have anklets too, but we could not see them, as the good ladies were pottering about waist-deep in the foam-flecked water, intent on breaking up a stockaded fish-trap. We pause and chat, and watch them collecting the fish in baskets, and I acquire some specimens; and then, shouting farewells when we are well away, in the proper civil way, resume our course.

The middle of the Ogowé here is simply forested with high rocks, looking, as they stand with their grim forms above the foam, like a regiment of strange strong creatures breasting it, with their straight faces up river, and their more flowing curves down, as though they had on black mantles which were swept backwards. Across on the other bank rose the black-forested spurs of Tomanjawki. Our channel was free until we had to fight round the upper end of our bay into a long rush of strong current with bad whirlpools curving its face; then the river widens out and quiets down and then suddenly contracts – a rocky forested promontory running out from each bank. There is a little village on the north bank's promontory, and, at the end of each, huge monoliths rise from the water, making what looks like a gateway which had once been barred and through which the Ogowé had burst.

For the first time on this trip I felt discouraged; it seemed so impossible that we, with our small canoe and scanty crew, could force our way up through that gateway, when the whole Ogowé was rushing down through it. But we clung to the bank and rocks with hands, poles and paddle, and did it; really the worst part was not in the gateway but just before it, for here there is a great whirlpool, its centre hollowed some two or three feet below its rim. It is caused, my Kembe islander says, by a great cave opening beneath the water. Above the gate the river broadens out again and we see the arched opening to a large cave in the south bank; the mountain-side is one mass of rock covered with the unbroken forest; and the entrance of this cave is just on the upper wall of the south bank's promontory; so, being sheltered from the current here, we rest and examine it leisurely. The river runs into it, and you can easily pass in at this season, but in the height of the wet season, when the river level would be some twenty feet or more above its present one, I doubt if you could. They told me this place is called Boko Boko, and that the cave is a very long one, extending on a level some way into the hill, and then ascending and coming out near a mass of white rock that showed as a speck high up on the mountain.

If you paddle into it you go 'far far', and then 'no more water live', and you get out and go up the tunnel, which is sometimes broad, sometimes narrow, sometimes high, sometimes so low that you have to crawl, and so get out at the other end.

One French gentleman has gone through this perform-ance, and I am told found 'plenty plenty' bats, and hedge-hogs, and snakes. They could not tell me his name, which I much regretted. As we had no store of bush lights we went no further than the portals; indeed, strictly between ourselves, if I had every bush light in Congo Français I personally should not have relished going further. I am terrified of caves; it sends a creaming down my back to think of them.

We went across the river to see another cave entrance on the other bank, where there is a narrow stretch of low rock-covered land at the foot of the mountains, probably under water in the wet season. The mouth of this other cave is low, between tumbled blocks of rock. It looked so sus-piciously like a short cut to the lower regions, that I had less exploring enthusiasm about it than even about its opposite neighbour; although they told me no man had gone down 'them thing'. Probably that much-to-be-honoured Frenchman who explored the other cave, allowed like myself, that if one did want to go from the Equator to

Hades, there were pleasanter ways to go than this. My Kembe Island man said that just hereabouts were five cave openings, the two that we had seen and another one we had not, on land, and two under the water, one of the sub-fluvial ones being responsible for the whirlpool we met outside the gateway of Boko Boko.

The scenery above Boko Boko was exceedingly lovely, the river shut in between its rim of mountains. As you pass up it opens out in front of you and closes in behind, the closely-set confused mass of mountains altering in form as you view them from different angles, save one, Kangwe – a blunt cone, evidently the record of some great volcanic outburst; and the sandbanks show again wherever the current deflects and leaves slack water, their bright glistening colour giving a relief to the scene.

For a long period we paddle by the south bank, and pass a vertical cleft-like valley, the upper end of which seems blocked by a finely shaped mountain, almost as conical as Kangwe. The name of this mountain is Njoko, and the name of the clear small river, that apparently monopolizes the valley floor, is the Ovato. Our peace was not of long duration, and we were soon again in the midst of a bristling forest of rock; still the current running was not dangerously strong, for the river-bed comes up in a ridge, too high for much water to come over at this season of the year; but in the wet season this must be one of the worst places. This ridge of rock runs two-thirds across the Ogowé, leaving a narrow deep channel by the north bank. When we got our canoe over the ridge, mostly by standing in the water and lifting her, we found the water deep and fairly quiet.

On the north bank we passed by the entrance of the Okana River. Its mouth is narrow, but, the natives told me, always deep, even in the height of the dry season. It is a very considerable river, running inland to the N.N.E. Little is known about it, save that it is narrowed into a ravine course above which it expands again; the banks of it are thickly populated by Fans, who send down a considerable trade, and have an evil reputation. In the main stream of the Ogowé below the Okana's entrance, is a long rocky island called Shandi. When we were getting over our ridge and paddling about the Okana's entrance my ears recognized a new sound. The rush and roar of the Ogowé we knew well enough, and could locate which particular obstacle to his headlong course was making him say things; it was either those immovable rocks, which threw him back in foam, whirling wildly, or it was that fringe of gaunt skeleton trees hanging from the bank playing a 'pull devil, pull baker' contest that made him hiss with vexation. But this was an elemental roar. I said to M'bo: 'That's a thunderstorm away among the mountains.' 'No, sir,' says he 'that's the Alemba.'

We paddled on towards it, hugging the right-hand bank again to avoid the mid-river rocks. For a brief space the mountain wall ceased, and a lovely scene opened before us; we seemed to be looking into the heart of the chain of the Sierra del Cristal, the abruptly shaped mountains encircling a narrow plain or valley before us, each one of them steep in slope, every one of them forest-clad; one, whose name I know not unless it be what is sometimes put down as Mt. Okana on the French maps, had a conical shape which contrasted beautifully with the more irregular curves of its companions. The colour down this gap was superb, and very Japanese in the evening glow. The more distant peaks were soft gray-blues and purple, those nearer, indigo and black. We soon passed this lovely scene and entered the walled-in channel, creeping up what seemed an interminable hill of black water, then through some whirlpools and a rocky channel to the sand and rock shore of our desired island Kondo Kondo, along whose northern side tore in thunder the Alemba. We made our canoe fast in a little cove among the rocks, and landed, pretty stiff and tired and considerably damp. This island, when we were on it, must have been about half a mile or so long, but during the long wet season a good deal of it is covered, and only the higher parts–great heaps of stone, among which grows a long branched willow-like shrub–are above or nearly above water. The Adooma from Kembe Island especially drew my attention to this shrub, telling me his people who worked the rapids always regarded it with an affectionate veneration; for he said it was the only thing that helped a man when his canoe got thrown over in the dreaded Alemba, for its long tough branches swimming in, or close to, the water are veritable life lines, and his best chance; a chance which must have failed some poor fellow, whose knife and leopard-skin belt we found wedged in among the rocks on Kondo Kondo. The main part of the island is sand, with slabs and tables of polished rock sticking up through it; and in between the rocks grew in thousands most beautiful lilies, their white flowers having a very strong scent of vanilla and their bright light-green leaves looking very lovely on the glistening pale sand among the black-gray rock. How they stand the long submersion they must undergo I do not know; the natives tell me they begin to spring up as soon as ever the water falls and leaves the island exposed; that they very soon grow up and flower, and keep on flowering until the Ogowé comes down again and rides roughshod over Kondo Kondo for months. While the men were making their fire I went across the island to see the great Alembo rapid, of which I had heard so much, that lay between it and the north bank. Nobler pens than mine must sing its glory and its grandeur. Its face was like nothing I have seen before. Its voice was like nothing I have heard. Those other rapids are not to be compared to it; they are wild, headstrong, and malignant enough, but the Alemba is not as they. It does not struggle, and writhe, and brawl among the rocks, but comes in a majestic springing dance, a stretch of waltzing foam, triumphant.

The beauty of the night on Kondo Kondo was superb; the sun went down and the afterglow flashed across the sky in crimson, purple, and gold, leaving it a deep violet-purple, with the great stars hanging in it like moons, until the moon herself arose, lighting the sky long before she sent her beams down on us in this valley. As she rose, the mountains hiding her face grew harder and harder in outline, and deeper and deeper black, while those opposite were just enough illumined to let one see the wefts and floating veils of blue-white mist upon them, and when at last, and for a short time only, she shone full down on the savage foam of the Alemba, she turned it into a soft silver mist. Around, on all sides flickered the fire-flies, who had come to see if our fire was not a big relation of their own, and they were the sole representatives, with ourselves, of animal life. When the moon had gone, the sky, still lit by the stars, seeming indeed to be in itself lambent, was very lovely, but it shared none of its light with us, and we sat round our fire surrounded by an utter darkness. Cold, clammy drifts of almost tangible mist encircled us; ever and again came cold faint puffs of wandering wind, weird and grim beyond description.

The individual names of the mountains round Kondo Kondo and above I cannot give you, though I was told them. For in my last shipwreck before reaching Kondo

Kondo, I had lost my pencil; and my note-book, even if I had had a pencil, was unfit to get native names down on, being a pulpy mass, because I had kept it in my pocket after leaving the Okana river so as to be ready for submergencies. And I also had several fish and a good deal of water in my pocket too, so that I am thankful I have a note left.

I will not weary you further with details of our ascent of the Ogowé rapids, for I have done so already sufficiently to make you understand the sort of work going up them entails, and I have no doubt that, could I have given you a more vivid picture of them, you would join me in admiration of the fiery pluck of those few Frenchmen who traverse them on duty bound. I personally deeply regret it was not my good fortune to meet again the French official I had had the pleasure of meeting on the *Eclaireur*. He would have been truly great in his description of his voyage to Franceville. I wonder how he would have 'done' his unpacking of canoes and his experiences on Kondo Kondo, where, by the by, we came across many of the ashes of his expedition's attributive fires. Well! he must have been a pleasure to Franceville, and I hope also to the good fathers at Lestourville, for those places must be just slightly sombre for Parisians.

Going down big rapids is always, everywhere, more dangerous than coming up, because when you are coming up and a whirlpool or eddy does jam you on rocks, the current helps you off – certainly only with a view to dashing your brains out and smashing your canoe on another set of rocks it's got ready below; but for the time being it helps, and when off, you take charge and convert its plan into an incompleted fragment; whereas in going down the current is against your backing off. M'bo had a series of prophetic visions as to what would happen to us on our way down, founded on reminiscence and tradition. I tried to comfort him by pointing out that, were any one of his prophecies fulfilled, it would spare our friends and relations all funeral expenses; and, unless they went and wasted their money on a memorial window, that ought to be a comfort to our well-regulated minds. M'bo did not see this, but was too good a Christian to be troubled by the disagreeable conviction that was in the minds of other members of my crew, namely, that our souls, unliberated by funeral rites from this world, would have to hover for ever over the Ogowé near the scene of our catastrophe. I own this idea was an unpleasant one – fancy having to pass the day in those caves with the bats, and then come out and wander all night in the cold mists! However, like a good many likely-looking prophecies, those of M'bo did not quite come off, and a miss is as good as a mile. Twice we had a near call, by being shot in between two pinnacle rocks, within half an inch of being fatally close to each other for us; but after some alarming scrunching sounds and creaks from the canoe, we were shot ignominiously out down river. Several times we got on to partially submerged table rocks, and were unceremoniously bundled off them by the Ogowé, irritated at the hindrance we were occasioning; but we never met the rocks of M'bo's prophetic soul – that lurking, submerged needle, or knife-edge of a pinnacle rock which was to rip our canoe from stem to stern, neat and clean into two pieces.

A comic incident happened to us one evening. The canoe jammed among a clump of rocks, and out we went anyhow into the water. Fortunately, there were lots of rocks about; unfortunately, we each chose different ones to perch on; mine was exceedingly inconvenient, being a smooth pillar affair, to which it was all I and the French flag, which always accompanied me in upsets, could do to hold on.

There was considerable delay in making up our party again, for the murkiness of the night only allowed each of us to see the foam which flew round our own particular rock, and the noise of the rapids made it difficult for us to interchange information regarding our own individual position and plan of action. However, owing to that weak-minded canoe swinging round broadside on to the rocks, she did not bolt down the river. When Pierre got to her she was trying to climb sideways over them, 'like a crab', he said. We seven of us got into her – number eight we could not find and were just beginning to think the Ogowé had claimed another victim when we heard the strains of that fine hymn 'Notre port est au Ciel', – which is a great favourite hereabouts owing to its noble tune – coming to us above the rapids' clamour in an agonized howl. We went joyfully and picked the singer off his rock, and then dashed downwards to further dilemmas and disasters. The course we had to take coming down was different to that we took coming up. Coming up we kept as closely as might be to the most advisable bank, and dodged behind every rock we could, to profit by the shelter it afforded us from the current. Coming down, fallen-tree-fringed banks and rocks were converted from friends to foes; so we kept with all our power in the very centre of the swiftest part of the current in order to avoid them. The grandest part of the whole time was coming down, below the Alemba, where the whole great Ogowé takes a tiger-like spring for about half a mile, I should think, before it strikes a rock reef below. As you come out from among the rocks in the upper rapid it gives you – or I should perhaps confine myself to saying, it gave me – a peculiar internal sensation to see that stretch of black water, shining like a burnished sheet of metal, sloping down before one, at such an angle. All you have got to do is to keep your canoe-head straight – quite straight, you understand – for any failure so to do will land you the other side of the tomb, instead of in a cheerful no-end-of-a-row with the lower rapid's rocks. This lower rapid is one of the worst in the dry season; maybe it is so in the wet too, for the river's channel here turns an elbow-sharp curve which infuriates the Ogowé in a most dangerous manner.

I hope to see the Ogowé next time in the wet season – there must be several more of these great sheets of water then over what are rocky rapids now. Just think what coming down over that ridge above Boko Boko will be like! I do not fancy however it would ever be possible to get up the river when it is at its height, with so small a crew as we were when we went and played our knock-about farce, before King Death, in his amphitheatre in the Sierra del Cristal.

5 The Troublesome Voyage

SIR JOHN HAWKINS

Like the account of Drake's Circumnavigation of the world, this story comes from the anthology of Richard Hakluyt – chaplain to Queen Elizabeth I's ambassador to France – who, riled by the gibes of foreigners at what they called English stay-at-homes, set out to collect accounts of the maritime achievements of his fellow-countrymen. Though anyone who voyaged across the oceans in the tiny ships of those days was indeed journeying into danger, Hawkins's purpose was a sordid one – the purchase of slaves in Africa and their sale in the West Indies to the Spaniards. From the days of this 'pioneer', the British slave trade grew to atrocious proportions, entailing untold human misery. Many respectable burgesses waxed fat on the trade and even ordinary people invested in it – almost as casually as nowadays people buy unit trusts.

The ships departed from Plymouth the second day of October in the year 1567 and had reasonable weather until the seventh day, at which time, forty leagues north of Cape Finisterre, there arose an extreme storm which continued for four days. It was of such strength that the fleet was dispersed, and all our great boats were lost, and the *Jesus of Lubeck*, our chief ship, was in such a plight that we thought her not able to serve the voyage. Therefore in the same storm we set our course homeward, determining to give over the voyage.

However, the eleventh day of the same month, the wind changed with fair weather, whereby we were animated to follow our enterprise, and so did, directing our course towards the Islands of the Canaries, where according to an order before prescribed, all our ships met at one of those islands, called Gomera, where we took water, and departed from thence the fourth day of November, towards the coast of Guinea, and arrived at Cape Verde the eighteenth of November.

Here we landed 150 men, hoping to obtain some negroes, but we got only a few – and those with great hurt and damage to our men, which chiefly proceeded from their envenomed arrows. Although in the beginning they seemed to be but small hurts, hardly anyone thus wounded but died in a strange manner, with their mouths shut some ten days before they died, and in spite of their wounds having healed. I myself had one of the greatest wounds, yet, thanks be to God, escaped.

From thence we passed the time upon the coast of Guinea, searching with diligence the rivers from Rio Grande, unto Sierra Leone, till the twelfth of January, in which time we had not gotten together a hundred and fifty negroes. However, there presently came to us a negro, sent from a king who was being oppressed by other kings. He desired our aid, promising us as many negroes as might be captured in the wars if we would help him. Whereupon we concluded to give aid, and sent 120 of our men, which, the 15th January, assaulted a town belonging to our ally's adversaries. It contained 8000 inhabitants and was strongly palisaded and fenced after their manner, and it was so well defended that our men prevailed not, losing six men and forty hurt.

So they sent forthwith to me for more help, whereupon, considering that the good success of this enterprise might further the object of our voyage, I went myself, and with the help of the king of our side, assaulted the town, both by land and by sea. Then, by the use of fire (their houses being covered with dry palm leaves) we obtained the town and put the inhabitants to flight. We took 250 persons, men, women and children, while our friend the king took 600 prisoners, whereof we hoped to have had our choice. But the negro king cheated us, for that night he removed his camp and his prisoners, so that we were fain to content us with those few which we had gotten ourselves.

Now we had obtained four or five hundred negroes, wherewith we thought it somewhat reasonable to seek the coast of the West Indies. There, for our negroes and other merchandize we hoped to obtain enough to show a profit. We proceeded with all diligence, furnishing our watering, took fuel, and departed the coast of Guinea the third of February, continuing at sea with a passage more hard than before hath been the custom till the 27th March. On that day we had sight of land, an island called Dominica, upon the coast of the West Indies, in fourteen degrees.

From thence we coasted from place to place, making our traffic with the Spaniards as we might – though with some difficulty, because the king had commanded all his governors in those parts not to suffer any trade to be done with us. Notwithstanding this we had reasonable trade, and courteous entertainment, from the isle of Margarita unto Cartagena. Nothing happened worth the noting, saving at Capo de la Vela, in a town called Rio de la Hacha (from whence come all the pearls), where the treasurer in charge would by no means agree to any trade or suffer us to take water. He had fortified his town with divers bulwarks in all places where it might be entered, and furnished himself with a hundred Hargabuziers (Harquebuses).

He thought by famine to force us to land our negroes and in this he would not have failed if we had not forcibly

entered the town. This we were obliged to do and with
two hundred men broke in upon their bulwarks and
entered the town with the loss only of two men – and no
hurt done to the Spaniards because after discharging one
volley of shot they fled.

Thus having the town with some circumstance, partly
through the Spaniards' desire of negroes and partly through
the friendship of the Treasurer, we obtained a secret trade.
The Spaniards resorted to us by night and bought of us
the number of two hundred negroes. In all other places
where we traded the Spanish inhabitants were glad of us
and traded willingly.

At Cartagena, the last town we thought to have seen on
the coast, we could by no means manage to deal with any
Spaniard, the governor being so strict. So, because our
trade was so near finished we thought it not worth the
while to try any other landing or to waste further time, but
in peace departed from thence the 24th July, hoping to
escape the time of their storms which would then soon after
begin to reign, and which they call Furicanos (Hurricanes).
But passing by the west end of Cuba, towards the coast of
Florida there happened to us the 12th day of August an
extreme storm which continued by the space of four days
and which so beat the *Jesus* that we cut down all her higher
buildings, her rudder was also sore shaken, and withal was
in so extreme a leak that we were rather upon the point of
leaving her than keeping her any longer.

Yet, hoping to bring all to a good pass, we sought the
coast of Florida, but there could find no place nor haven
for our ships because of the shallowness of the coast. We
were thus in greater despair and overtaken with a new
storm which continued another three days. We were thus
inforced to look for succour in the port which serveth the

city of Mexico called Saint John de Ullua, which standeth in 19 degrees. In seeking this port we took in our way three ships which carried passengers to the number of an hundred, which passengers we hoped should be a means for us the better to obtain victuals for our money and a quiet place for the repairing of our fleet.

Shortly after this, the 16th of September, we entered the port of Saint John de Ullua and in our entry the Spaniards, thinking us to be the fleet of Spain, the chief officers of the country came aboard us. But being disappointed of their expectation were greatly dismayed. However, immediately they saw our demand was nothing but victuals, they were recomforted.

I found also in the same port twelve ships which had in them by report two hundred thousand pound in gold and silver, all which (being in my possession, together with the king's island here and also the passengers before spoken of) I set at liberty, without the taking from them the weight of a groat. But because I did not wish to be delayed in my leaving, I held back two men of estimation* and sent post immediately to Mexico, which was two hundred miles from us, to the President and Council there, informing them of our arrival there by force of weather, and the necessity of the repair of our ships and victuals – which needs we required as friends to King Philip and to be paid for with our money. I begged also that the President and Council there should with all convenient speed take such necessary steps that at the arrival of the Spanish fleet, which was daily looked for, there might be no cause of quarrel between us and them and that for the better maintenance of amity their commandment might be made in that behalf.

This message being sent away the sixteenth of September

* Presumably as hostages.

at night, being the very day of our arrival, in the next morning we saw standing off the haven thirteen great ships and, understanding them to be the fleet of Spain, I sent immediately to advise the General of the fleet of my being there, giving him to understand that before I would suffer them to enter the port, there should pass between us some order of conditions for our safe-being there and the maintenance of peace.

Now it is to be understood that this port is made of a little island of stones not three foot above the water in the highest place, and but a bowshot of length any way. It standeth from the mainland two bowshots or more and it is to be understood also that there is not in all this coast any other place for ships to arrive in safety, because the north wind hath there such violence that unless the ships be very safely moored with the anchors fastened upon this island, there is no remedy for these north winds but death. Also the place of the haven was so little, that of necessity the ships must ride one alongside the other, so that we could not give place to them, nor they to us.

And here I began to bewail that which afterwards followed, for now, said I, I am in two dangers, and forced to receive one of them. That was, either I must keep out the fleet from entering the port – which with God's help I was very well able to do, – or else suffer them to enter in with their accustomed treachery, which they never fail to practise by one means or another.

If I had kept them out, then there had been present shipwreck of all the fleet which amounted in value to six millions, which was in value of our money 1,800000 li. which I considered I was not able to take responsibility for, fearing the Queen's Majesty's indignation in so weighty a matter. Thus debating the doubts, I thought it rather to abide the jutt or risk of the uncertainty than the certainty. The uncertainty was their treachery which a good policy I hoped might be prevented, and therefore as choosing the lesser mischief I proceeded to make conditions.

Now was our first messenger come and returned from the fleet with report of the arrival of a Viceroy who had authority, from the king of Spain, both in all this province of Mexico and on the sea. He sent us word that we should send our conditions which, for his part (for the better maintenance of amity between the Princes), he would favourably grant and faithfully comply with. He added many fair words of how, passing the coast of the Indies, he had learnt of our honest behaviour towards the inhabitants.

Thus to our demands which were – that we required victuals for our money, and licence to sell as much ware as might furnish our wants, and that there should be twelve gentlemen from either side as hostages for the maintenance of peace. Also that the island for our better safety should be in our own possession during our abode there, and such ordinance as was planted in the same island, which were eleven pieces of brass, should be held by us. Also that no Spaniard might land in the island with any kind of weapon.

These conditions at first he somewhat misliked, chiefly that of the island being under our guard – for if they had taken it we would soon have known our fare: for with the first north wind they would have cut our cables and our ships would have gone ashore. But in the end he acceded to our request, reducing the twelve hostages to ten, which with all speed of either part were received, with a writing from the Viceroy signed with his hand and sealed with his seal of all the conditions agreed. Forthwith a trumpet was blown with commandment that no one on either side should violate the peace upon pain of death.

Thus at the end of three days all was concluded and the fleet entered the port, saluting one another as the manner of the sea doth require. Thus as I said before, Thursday we entered the port, Friday we saw the Spanish fleet, and on Monday at night they entered the port. Then we laboured two days placing the English ships by themselves and the Spanish ships by themselves, the captains of each part and inferior men of their parts promising great amity of all sides.

This was meant with all fidelity for our part, but not so with the Spaniards. For from the mainland they had furnished themselves with a supply of men to the number of one thousand and meant next Thursday, being the 23rd of September, at dinnertime to set upon us on all sides. That same Thursday in the morning, the treachery being at hand, some signs of it were evident – such as the shifting of weapons from ship to ship, transferring of ordinance from the ships to the island, passing to and fro of companies of men and many other ill likelihoods, all of which caused us to have a vehement suspicion.

Therefore we sent to the Viceroy to enquire what was meant by all this, at which he immediately ordered these suspicious happenings to cease and gave his word as Viceroy to be our defence against all villainies. Yet, we being not satisfied with this answer, because we suspected a great number of men to be hid in a great ship of 900 tons which was moored next to our ship *Minion*. I sent again to the Viceroy the master of the *Jesus of Lubeck* who spoke Spanish tongue, and required to be satisfied if any such thing were or not.

The Viceroy now seeing that their treachery must be discovered, forthwith detained our master, blew the trumpet and on all sides set upon us. Our men who kept watch on shore being stricken with sudden fear, gave way, fled, and sought to recover safety in the ships. The Spaniards being previously ready for the purpose landed in all places in multitudes from their ships, which they were easily able to do without boats, and slew all our men who were on shore without mercy, except for a few who escaped aboard the *Jesus*.

The great ship which had by our reckoning three hundred men placed in her secretly, immediately fell aboard the *Minion*, but, by God's appointment, in the time since our suspicions were aroused, which was only half an hour, the *Minion* was made ready to move off, and so, loosing her headropes and warping her by her sternropes, we got her out. Thus with God's help she defended the first brunt of these three hundred men.

The *Minion* being safely away, they came aboard the *Jesus* and were only kept out at great trouble and the loss of many of our men. There were also two other Spanish ships that assaulted the *Jesus* at the same instant, so that it was hard getting her out, but when both the *Jesus* and the *Minion* were gotten about two ship's length from the Spanish fleet, the fight became so hot on all sides that within one hour the Admiral of the Spaniards was apparently sunk, their Vice-Admiral burned and one other of the principal ships sunk, so that the ships were little able to annoy us.

But it is to be understood that all the ordinance upon the island was in Spanish hands, which did us so great annoyance that it cut all the masts and yards of the *Jesus*, in such a way that there was no hope of saving her. Also it sank our small ships, whereupon we determined to place the *Jesus* on that side of the *Minion* that she might take all the battery from the land and so be a defence for the

Minion till night. Then we would take all the victuals and necessaries possible from the *Jesus* and abandon her.

As we were thus determining, and had placed the *Minion* away from the shot of the land, suddenly the Spaniards had set fire to two great ships and set them directly at us. We having no means to avoid the fire, it bred among our men a marvellous fear, so that some said, let us depart with the *Minion*, others said, let us see whither the wind will carry the fireships. But, in brief, the *Minion's* men, which always had their sails in a readiness, thought to make sure, and so without consent of the captain or master, they shaped their sail, so that with difficulty was I received into the *Minion*.

The most part of the men that were left alive in the *Jesus*, made shift and followed the *Minion* in a small boat. As for the rest which that little boat was not able to take, they were enforced to abide the mercy of the Spaniards (which I doubt was very little); so with the *Minion* only and the *Judith* – a small barque of 50 tons) we escaped, though that same barque forsook us that night in our great misery.

We were now removed with the *Minion* from the Spanish ships two bowshots, and there rode all night. The next morning we reached an island a mile from the Spaniards, where there took us a north wind. Being left with only two anchors and two cables (for in this conflict we lost three cables and two anchors) we thought always upon death which was ever present to drive us ashore, but God preserved us to a longer time.

The weather waxed reasonable, and the Saturday we set sail, and having a great number of men and little victuals, our hope of life waxed less and less. Some desired to yield to the Spaniards, some rather desired to find a place where

94

they might give themselves to the Infidels – and some had rather abide the mercy of God at Sea. So thus with many sorrowful hearts we wandered in an unknown sea by the space of 14 days, till hunger enforced us to seek land. For hides were thought very good meat, and rats, cats, mice and dogs, none escaped that might be gotten, parrots and monkeys also were thought very profitable if they served the turn for one dinner.

Thus in the end the 8 day of October, we came to the land in the bottom of the same bay of Mexico in 23 degrees and a half, where we hoped to find victuals and a place to repair our ship which was so sore beaten with shot from our enemies and bruised with shooting of our own guns, that our weak and weary arms were scarce able to cope. But all things happened to the contrary, for we found neither people, victuals, nor haven, but a place where even in fair weather we might land a boat only in peril. Our people being forced with hunger desired to be set on land, whereunto I consented.

And such as were willing to land I put them apart, and such were desirous to go homeward, I put apart, so that there were about a hundred of one side and a hundred of the other side. These hundred men we set on land with all diligence in this little place beforesaid, after which we determined to take in fresh water, and so with our little remain of victuals to take the sea.

The next day, having on land with me fifty of our hundred men for the speedier taking of water on board, there arose an extreme storm, so that in three days we could by no means return on board our ship. The ship also was in such peril that every hour we expected shipwreck.

But yet God again had mercy on us, and sent fair

weather. We got on board our water, and departed the sixteenth day of October, after which we had fair and prosperous weather till the sixteenth day of November, which day, God be praised, we were clear from the coast of the Indies, and out of the channel and gulf of Bahama, which is between the Cape of Florida and the Islands of Lucayo.

After this, growing near to the cold country, our men being oppressed with famine, they died continually, and they that were left grew into such weakness that we were scarce able to manage our ship. The wind being always ill for us to recover England, we determined to make for Galicia in Spain, with intent there to relieve our company and other extreme wants. And being arrived the last day of December in a place near unto Vigo called Ponte Vedra, our men with excess of fresh meat grew into miserable diseases, and died a great part of them.

This matter was borne out as long as might be, but in the end, although none of our men were allowed ashore, the Spaniards learned of our feebleness. Whereupon they sought all means to betray us, but with all speed possible we departed to Vigo, where we had some hope of certain English ships and twelve fresh men – and there we repaired our wants as we might, and departing the 20 day of January 1568, we arrived in Mounts Bay in Cornwall the 25 of the same month, praise be to God therefore.

If all the miseries and troublesome affairs of this sorrowful voyage should be perfectly and thoroughly written, it would need a diligent man with his pen – and as much time as he had that wrote the lives and deaths of the Martyrs.

6 To Hidden Depths

EGON LARSEN

As we saw in Exploration Earth, *underwater exploration has reached sophisticated proportions, not only regarding research into the sea-bed and its natural history but also in the realm of archaeology, with the raising of ancient ships such as the* Wasa – *the finding of scuptural master-pieces in the Mediterranean – and sunken villages in Lake Zurich. But before the last war, free-diving was not yet developed and conventional helmet-diving was very limited in its scope. The 'bathysphere' which Dr. Beebe and Otis Barton pioneered was a new departure in the exploration of the ocean depths and their first attempts were indeed hazardous adventures.*

At ten minutes to ten on the morning of 10 June 1930 two men squeezed through a little round hole into a steel ball measuring 4 feet 9 inches in diameter, with walls $1\frac{1}{4}$ inches thick, weighing 5,400 lb. A 400 lb. steel disc – the door – was hoisted and placed into the hole; it fitted over ten big steel bolts, and huge nuts were screwed on.

Thus began one of the craziest adventures any man has ever embarked upon. Crouching in that steel ball, these two were waiting to be dropped to nearly three times the depth to which human beings had ever penetrated into the ocean. If either of them had been nervous, those minutes when nut after nut was being fastened and the last contact with the outer world severed would have created in him a Poe-type nightmare of being sealed up alive. Yet even Edgar Allan Poe never thought of encasing the victims of his unfettered imagination in a narrow globe, dangling at the end of a thread-like cable, and lowered to a depth where the unshielded human body would be crushed to pulp by the immense pressure of the water.

Neither Dr. Charles William Beebe nor Mr. Otis Barton, however, was prone to nervous thoughts, and whatever anxieties they might have felt were blotted out by the overpowering desire to see what no man had seen before them. Dr. Beebe, 53-year-old Director of the Department of Tropical Research of the New York Zoological Society, had often gone down into the sea in diving-helmets and suits as far as he could, and had found it an irresistibly fascinating world: 'Until we have found our way to the surface of some other planet', he once said, 'the bottom of the sea will remain the loveliest and strangest place we can imagine.' So he had persuaded the Zoological Society to finance that weird expedition into the heart of the Atlantic Ocean, using the novel design of a 29-year-old Harvard graduate Otis Barton; a sphere of steel, later to be called 'bathysphere', with quartz windows, able to withstand pressures of more than 100 atmospheres, or about 1,500 lb. to the square inch. Only a ball could do this; any flat surface would be crushed unless it were impossibly thick.

There should have been three windows of fused quartz, 8 inches in diameter and 3 inches thick. Quartz is the strongest transparent substance which transmits the entire light spectrum. One of the quartz windows, however, cracked during a pressure test; it was not replaced, but the window opening filled with a steel plug. Behind one of the remaining windows was a powerful search-light.

A single steel cable, $\frac{7}{8}$-inch in diameter, was to be entrusted with the lives of the two men. It had a steel core and about 100 strands, and was 3,500 feet long; its entire weight was 2 tons when submerged, and it had been tested under a breaking-strain of 29 tons – equal to nearly a dozen bathyspheres. Still, it looked ridiculously frail as it was tightened by the winch, ready to heave the steel ball overboard into the mid-Atlantic abyss a few miles south of Nonsuch Island, in the Bermuda group. An electric cable with the light and telephone wires entered the bathysphere through a stuffing-box – a potential danger spot to which much thought had been given by the two scientists.

Air was supplied by oxygen tanks inside the sphere, and open trays with chemicals were to absorb the carbon dioxide of the used air. A sea-going tug took the bathysphere to the point where the descent was to be carried out, and a large, open-decked barge was furnished with a steam engine to drive two winches, one for raising and lowering the boom with the tackle for the main cable, and the other for operating the cable itself.

At the upper end of the telephone cable sat Miss Gloria Hollister, Dr. Beebe's secretary, earphones clipped to her head, pencil in hand, and notebook on her knee, to take down every word that would come up from the depths of the ocean.

Curled up on the cold hard bottom of the bathysphere, the two men felt their steel ball tremble and lift and swing out over the side of the barge. Now they were dangling in mid-air, slowly revolving. Then the descent began.

The bathysphere struck the surface of the water with a force that would have smashed a canoe to pieces. Foam and bubbles surged past the window, and while the steel ball was still revolving the hull of the barge came in view.

'We have just splashed below the surface', Miss Hollister noted down.

The keel of the barge passed upwards, and with it the last visible thing belonging to the upper world disappeared. Now it was all green outside the window. The explorers had tied a dead squid, wrapped in a cheesecloth, to a hook just underneath the observation window, a bait to attract fish. Dr. Beebe, his finger on the searchlight switch, felt that now the mysterious world of deep-sea creatures was at last within his grasp.

'285 feet . . . The *Lusitania* is resting at this level', came Otis Barton's voice over the telephone.

Suddenly, Barton called out and pointed to the door. A slow trickle of water was running down to the bottom of the sphere, where about a pint had already collected! Dr. Beebe watched it anxiously. The steel door was solid enough. There could not be any danger. But the inner pressure of the sphere was not yet great enough to keep the water out. He gave the signal: 'Descend quickly!'

The light green water had turned darker and darker. A 6-inch fish appeared, made for the squid bait, then peered into the window, curious to see what kind of creatures were invading its realm.

'525 feet . . . A diver in an armoured suit descended as far as this into a Bavarian lake – the deepest point which any live human has ever reached', Miss Hollister took down. And shortly afterwards came the words: '600 feet. Only dead men have sunk below this.'

Schools of jellyfish passed, then some vibrating notes which Dr. Beebe identified, after a while, as minute snails with wings. They were followed by lantern-fish – the first ever seen alive. They were ablaze with iridescence.

The two explorers were the first living men to see that

strangely illuminated world – stranger than their imagination could have anticipated. 'It was of an indefinable translucent blue quite unlike anything I have even seen in the upper world', Dr. Beebe later recalled, 'and it excited our optic nerves in a most confusing manner. We kept thinking and calling it "brilliant", and again and again I picked up a book to read the type, only to find that I could not tell the difference between a blank page and a coloured plate. I brought all my logic to bear, I put out of mind the excitement of our position in watery space and tried to think sanely of comparative colour, and I failed utterly. I flashed on the search-light, which seemed the yellowest thing I have ever seen, and let it soak into my eyes, yet the moment it was switched off, it was like the long vanished sunlight – it was as though it had never been – and the blueness of the blue, both outside and inside our sphere, seemed to pass materially through the eye into our very beings. This is all very unscientific; quite worthy of being jeered at by optician or physicist; but there it was. . . . I think we both experienced a wholly new kind of mental reception of colour impression.'

The leak at the door had not increased; in fact, it lessened. The temperature had dropped about 12° since the descent began. A large transparent jellyfish bumped against the window. The men could see its stomach filled with a glowing mass of luminous food. Then came an even more exciting visitor.

'Look! Quick!' cried Dr. Beebe. 'A hatchet-fish!'

It was a most unexpected and unique sight. This creature of the deep is covered with silver tinsel and has a number of lights to brighten its path; its enormous eyes can turn in almost any direction. More and more luminous fish – slowly moving coloured dots – passed the observation window, and when the search-light was turned on they proved to be a school of hatchet-fish; when it was switched off again the inky blue-black sea was alive with their silvery glow. Miss Hollister's voice came faintly through the ear-phones; to the two men it seemed as though the deck of the launching-barge was on another planet, perhaps in a world that had ceased to exist. They had reached a depth of 1,000 feet.

Was it safe to go down even deeper? The two men examined the danger spots of their minute home. The stuffing-box was standing up well to the pressure. The door was now perfectly dry. The oxygen cylinders were keeping the air sweet, and the men could make it circulate with their palm-leaf fans. The inner walls of the bathysphere were moist; the heat of the two bodies was condensing on the cold steel; but that did not matter at all. The chemicals did their job. Dr. Beebe and Barton shifted their arms and legs so as to be comfortable for the next stage of their fantastic journey.

'Let's go down', Miss Hollister heard over the telephone. She passed the order on to the officer in charge.

Twelve hundred feet: a golden-tailed serpent-dragon, an *idiacanthus*, swept into the search-light with eel-like motions, blinded and lured by the glare. Thirteen hundred feet: Dr. Beebe, who had tied his handkerchief over his mouth to keep his breath away from the quartz, recognized a number of *cyclothones*, or round-mouths, which he had often dragged up with the net, but never seen in their element. They were always heading upwards, and he saw only their profile with the thin lips and the small eyes.

Then there came a moment of complete silence in the faint bluish light that was still coming through the window.

The sphere stopped in its downward course, and swung quietly on its cable. Looking upward from the edge of the window, they could see a faint pale blue sheen; looking down, there was the black-blue abyss of the deep. This was as far as they had intended to go: 1,426 feet.

'A quarter of a mile down,' said Dr. Beebe into the telephone, 'and we're still alive.' The time was a quarter to eleven – 45 minutes after they had begun their journey. The pressure on the bathysphere was now more than six and a half million pounds. 'There is a pressure of over 650 pounds on every square inch of our window,' said Otis Barton and smiled. The least fracture of the quartz would have meant death: not, though, by drowning; for the first few drops of water would have shot through the men like machine-gun bullets.

'There came to me at that instant a tremendous wave of emotion', Dr. Beebe wrote later, 'a real appreciation of what was momentarily almost superhuman, cosmic, of the whole situation; our barge rolling high overhead in the blazing sunlight, like the merest chip in the midst of ocean, the long cobweb of cable leading down through the spectrum to our lonely sphere, where, sealed tight, two conscious human beings sat and peered into the abyssal darkness as we dangled in mid-water, isolated as a lost planet in outermost space. Here, under a pressure which, if loosened, in a fraction of a second would make amorphous tissue of our bodies, breathing our own home-made atmosphere, sending a few comforting words chasing up and down a string of hose – here I was privileged to peer out and actually see the creatures which had evolved in the blackness of a blue midnight which, since the ocean was born, had known no following day; here I was privileged to sit and try to crystallize what I observed through inadequate eyes and interpret with a mind wholly unequal to the task. To the ever-recurring question, "How did I feel?" I can only quote the words of Herbert Spencer: I felt like "an infinitesimal atom floating in illimitable space". No wonder my sole contribution to science and literature at the time was, "Am writing at a depth of a quarter of a mile. A luminous fish is outside the window." '

It took the bathysphere another three-quarters of an hour to return to the upper world. Dr. Beebe felt as if it were hitting a hard ceiling when it broke surface, and he unconsciously ducked. But there were only bubbles and foam; and there was, at last, the blue sky. The great enterprise, Man's deepest dive since he ventured into the sea, was over.

Yet what did it mean in terms of height and depth? Horizontally, a quarter of a mile is a distance we can walk in five minutes. Vertically, it means little more. An elevation of 1,400 feet can hardly be called a mountain; Mount Everest is nearly 30,000 feet high, aeroplanes had already reached 50,000 feet in 1930, and stratosphere balloons more than 70,000 feet. A mine in South Africa was being worked at a depth of 8,500 feet. The average depth of the ocean is 12,000 feet.

To call these figures into our mind does not mean an under-rating of Dr. Beebe's and Otis Barton's achievement with their first deep sea dive in the bathysphere. On the contrary; we must keep before our eyes the extreme difficulties of penetrating into the sea as compared with vertical travel up into the air or down into the earth. Yet once the possibility of using a steel chamber had been established by the two explorers, deeper and deeper dives were only a matter of improving the equipment, of painstaking calculations – and of immense courage.

Four years after reaching that quarter-mile, Dr. Beebe and Otis Barton succeeded in descending to a depth of 3,000 feet – half a mile; it was nearly the entire length of the cable on the winch. During this dive, the deepest Dr. Beebe ever made, he made a number of remarkable observations.

He saw a strange fish, entirely new to science: 2 feet long, slender, toothless, and without any iridescence; its small eyes could not possibly have seen anything in the jet-black abyss, yet it was 'watching' the scientists' steel ball quietly. In the search-light it had the colour of water-soaked flesh. It had hardly any tail, but enormous vertical fins above and beneath the body. Dr. Beebe called it the Pallid Sailfin, *bathyembryx istiophasma*. It was larger than any deep-sea fish he had ever dragged up in his net.

At 2,500 feet, when he turned on the search-light suddenly, he saw a strange quartet of fish which he could not fit into any known genus. They were about four inches long, slender and stiff, with long, pointed, bird-like beaks. They were 'standing' almost upright in a row, keeping equal distance from each other. The most surprising thing about them was their brilliant colouring, surely a wasted touch of beauty in the eternal night of the deep sea: their jaws and head were a bright scarlet, the part behind the gills a strong light-blue, merging into a clear yellow towards the tail.

Then there appeared what Dr. Beebe later called the Three-starred Anglerfish: 6 inches long, oval, black, with small eyes and short, even teeth. It had three long tentacles, each tipped with a strong yellow 'lamp'. 'No pioneer, peering at a Martian landscape, could ever have a greater thrill than I did at such an opportunity', Dr. Beebe wrote in his report. But he had hardly recovered from his excitement when a new and unbelievably beautiful creature floated into the search-light beam: a fish almost round, with big eyes and a snout-like mouth. Along its body were five lines of light – a horizontal one in the centre, and two slightly curved lines above as well as below; each line was made up of a series of wonderful golden-yellow lights, and each light was surrounded by a number of small purple lamps. Dr. Beebe named it the Five-lined Constellation-fish. 'In my memory it will live throughout the rest of my life as one of the loveliest things I have ever seen', he wrote.

But the important moment, to his mind, was one which occurred at a depth of about 1,700 feet – a mysterious occurrence, the display of some inexplicable habit which took place before his eyes, 'but which, like a sublimated trick of some master fakir, evades understanding', he confessed. He saw some creature, several inches long, dart towards the observation window, turn to the side, and . . . explode. This happened with a flash and flame so strong that they illuminated his face and the inner window sill, and their source was shown quite clearly: a great red deep-sea shrimp, which has this extraordinary power of defence – comparable with a flame-thrower, and much more effective, one would imagine, than the smoke-screen of the squid.

Fifteen years went by. The war interrupted the work and preparations of the deep-sea professors. Then, one August day in 1949, Otis Barton, in his late forties, squeezed through the door of another 5-foot steel ball, specially constructed for a one-man dive into the Pacific. He called it benthoscope, from the Greek words *benthus*, sea-bed, and *shopein*, to see. He was determined to go down as far as such a machine could be lowered at the end of a steel cable.

The spot he had chosen was a point off the coast of southern California, near Smugglers' Cove on the island of Santa Cruz.

'If I'm silent for more than five seconds, pull me up', he told his attendants on deck of the 80-foot barge, rented for him by his sponsors, the Hancock Foundation, A powerful crane operated the $\frac{5}{8}$-inch main cable. From the moment the benthoscope started its journey, the lonely man inside spoke and chattered without pause. When there was nothing to say he recited the alphabet, just to show that he was still alive. But on deck they would not have been surprised if the telephone had suddenly stopped, indicating that Otis Barton's calculations had, after all, been wrong; if some powerful undersea current had broken some vital link, and swept the steel sphere off into the deep from where there would be no return; or if the vast pressure had cracked the man-made shell like that of an egg, and left nothing but a piece of crumpled metal at the end of the cable.

'Getting darker', reported the telephone as the first few hundred feet of cable was unwinding. 'Nothing interesting yet . . .' Then, at 460 feet: 'There are a lot of lantern fish passing by now. They're jumping all over. Now the fireworks are really starting. There is a creature that looks like a long pipe with a row of lights along it. I don't know what it is . . . The tentacles of a jellyfish just dragged by the window and broke into a shower of sparks. . . .'

At 1,500 feet: 'The head 'phones are getting cold. It's just like sitting in an icebox. I'd hate to touch the walls here. . . . I'm wrapped in a blanket now.'

At 2,500 feet: 'I see a barrage of luminescent shrimp spiralling outside the window. They give off a flash when they hit . . . This is an unbelievable world. I wish Dr. Beebe were down here with me. He might know what some of these things are . . .' Then Barton passed the record set up by Beebe and himself in 1934.

A little later: 'Let's hold up here a while. There are so many things going by that it makes me dizzy . . .' At 4,100 feet, the light suddenly went out inside the steel ball. Otis Barton hesitated for a moment. Was this a warning? Should he return? 'Drop me down another 500 feet,' he said, and they could hear his teeth chattering.

A minute later his flashlight showed him that there was a puddle of water at his feet. After a few breathless seconds he realized that it was not from a leak, but from the condensation on the cold walls.

'I won't look at the window right now because it gives me rather an unsteady feeling . . . probably due to the rocking of the ball . . . I hear a continual crunching of the cable.'

Then came the deepest point – 4,500 feet, with a pressure of 2,000 lb. to the square inch. For eight minutes he stayed at this. 'I'll look now', came his words over the telephone. 'There's a triangular light with a glow behind it . . . A globular shape did a jig in front of the window . . . I'm freezing to death . . . If I had the lights on I'd go right down to 6,000 feet. But without lights it's pointless . . . Pull me up.'

They hauled him out of his sphere, exhausted, after his record-breaking dive, which took him two hours and nine-teen minutes. He had shown tremendous courage; he had proved how far a steel ball could descend with relative safety on a cable. But his scientific harvest was very small, and contributed hardly anything to the wealth of discoveries made by Dr. Beebe on their two-man dives of the early 'thirties. For Otis Barton was not a zoologist like Beebe; he was able to describe a few things he had seen, but he could not identify them except by comparing the photographs he had taken with the elaborate drawings made by Dr. Beebe's collaborators from the latter's observations. With Barton's dive of 1949, the period of deep-sea expeditions in cable-suspended globes came to an end.

7 'Horse Killer' – and other dangers

A. F. TSCHIFFELEY

Nearly forty years ago this Swiss adventurer rode ten thousand miles through the Americas, from the Argentine to Washington. The journey took him two and a half years and varied from the cold, barren 16,000 feet ranges of the Andes to the steaming jungles of Central America. He finished this arduous trek with the same two ponies he had started with – Mancha and Gato, who were sixteen and fifteen years of age respectively at the start. They were of the Argentine Criollo breed which has immense powers of resistance to the most adverse of conditions. Originally Mancha and Gato had belonged to a Patagonian Indian chief named Liempichun – 'I-have-feathers'. Here Tschiffeley recounts a few of the perils he met with during his ride.

In one of the small coastal towns a Spaniard introduced himself to me. He looked a pleasant sort of fellow, and told me he had lived quite a number of years in the Argentine. In the evening we chatted for some time, and during the course of conversation he said that no man's education was complete unless he had seen one of the low 'dance-halls' that exist in some of the small towns along the Peruvian coast, and when I expressed my willingness to see and learn he offered to act as guide. Soon we were on our way towards the place that was situated about a mile out of the little town. The dance-hall was merely a large adobe hut, and the interior was lit by two oil lamps. Along the walls were rough benches on which some dirty, ragged and barefooted men sat, whilst others were standing in front of a counter made of old packing-cases where alcohol was being despatched. The boss of the place was a fat and greasy mestizo woman with strands of black hair hanging over her face, hair that was coarse and wiry like a horse's mane. Several equally repulsive females were acting as 'dancing-partners' to any man who wished to pay ten cents for the pleasure of having one of them. I have seen some villainous faces in some of the 'western hair-raisers', but since I have been in that dance-hall it is obvious to me that the producers of these films have not been 'educated', as my Spanish guide would say. The type of villian we usually see in the 'movies' are mere cherubims compared to the men I saw that night. The majority were mestizos, or what I would like to call 'criss-cross breeds' between Indian, Spanish, Chinese and negro blood. One specimen was black, pock-marked, had Chinese slit eyes, and curly hair with a red tint!

Somehow our presence did not seem to please, and particularly one fellow kept casting nasty glances towards us, glances that said more than words could have done. When my companion became aware of it he took offence, and soon the inevitable happened; both jumping at each other like tigers. Some intervened and the two were separated, and then somebody suggested going outside to fight it out. The Spaniard took off his coat and handed it to me, and when we were outside the two started at each other. Owing to the darkness it was impossible to see what was happening, but after some quick shuffling, wrestling, fierce growling and many terrible oaths there was a piercing shriek, and then all was silence, a silence that was only broken by the heavy breathing of the two exhausted fighters. Presently I heard moans, and then somebody struck a match. The

Spaniard was standing over his opponent who was on the ground, and upon striking another match we noticed that the man who lay writhing on the ground had been stabbed in two places.

Only now did I begin to realize the seriousness of my situation, for here was I all alone with the Spaniard, who after all was only a chance acquaintance, and the others were many, and for all I knew they might try to avenge their badly-wounded friend, who was now moaning and rolling over on the ground. Whenever I was in a town or in a more or less decent village I never carried my fire-arms. for they were heavy, and the sight of them might offend people. On this occasion I had come out unarmed, and fearing the worst I thought I would try to get out of this ticklish situation by bluffing. I jumped on a low adobe wall that fenced off a field and shouted that if anybody moved I would shoot. Obviously somebody had long ago advised the police that there was trouble, for soon several terribly excited 'vigilantes' arrived on the scene, waving their arms, rifles and swords like actors in a stage version of the storming of the Bastille. One who had come with a lantern led the procession back towards the town, a few helping to carry the wounded man, who was evidently in a serious condition. Once at the police station the 'jefe' (chief) and a doctor were called, and everybody, except the Spaniard and myself were thrown into the filthy 'calabozo'. The jefe's language was most apologetic for what had happened to me, and the Spaniard, being a good friend of his, was told to embark on a sailing vessel that was to leave the little port next morning, for in case the wounded man should die it would be just as well if the guilty party could officially be announced as having escaped. When I saw the last of that little town, I promised myself never again to visit a 'dance-hall' in Peru, and I did not find it difficult to keep that promise!

Still following the hot, sandy coast, we came to a large sugar plantation, not far from which stands a fortress that was built by the ancient Chimu Indians. It is a colossal piece of work, entirely made of adobe and built in high terraces that appear like a square hill from the distance. Near the main fortress are high walls, and the way everything was built leaves no doubt that these ancients had a certain scientific knowledge of warfare. Some of the paint with which the walls were coloured still remains, neither weather nor centuries having been able to make it fade or to destroy it. The colours that exist are red, black and yellow, the same as are found on pottery that dates back to the Chimu period.

The fortress of Paramonga consists of two main strongholds. One of these is situated on a hill, the waves of the Pacific Ocean beating against its inaccessible cliffs which face west. The eastern side of that hill has a steep and sandy slope where numerous mummies, wrapped in coloured cloths, were buried and have now become uncovered by the shifting and sliding sands. The main fortress is roughly half a mile east from there, and the two were probably separated by a swamp in former times, but today the low flat stretch of land between the two is dry, and sugar-cane is successfully cultivated by a Japanese settler who entertained me splendidly when I happened to call at his place during my rambles among the ruins. Although subterranean passages and burial places exist here, the natives are afraid to explore them, for many strange tales and superstitions have been handed down from one generation to another. As I had not time enough, I could not do more than have a general look over these interesting relics of the past.

From Paramonga north there is a vast desert, close on a hundred miles from one river to the next, and as there is no water to be found there I was obliged to make the crossing in one journey. For this reason I had to wait for the full moon before I could, with a certain degree of safety, attempt this long ride.

There was an outbreak of bubonic plague whilst I was there, and quite a number of plantation workers died, whilst many more were ill. The authorities raided their filthy quarters, and it was a pathetic sight to see their owners howling and wailing as they walked behind their filthy belongings which were being carted out to be burnt, together with some ancient mummies that had been discovered near there in an old burial ground. I took every precaution against the horrible disease and was particularly careful never to lie down to rest unless I had previously sprinkled my bed with insect powder, for fleas and similar pests transmit the germs of bubonic plague. It was uncomfortable to have to remain in this place with the danger of catching the plague, but I was between the devil and the deep blue sea; for before attempting to cross the desert ahead of us I had to be careful to make my plans, and as I intended to start in the evening it was necessary to wait until the moon was at its brightest. I had heard many terrible stories about this sandy wilderness, its very name, 'Matacaballo' (Horse-killer), gave me food for reflection.

After four days' waiting I was ready to start, and as I did not intend to carry water for the horses, I was careful not to give them anything to drink the day before we left, for I wanted them to be thirsty and therefore not likely to refuse a good drink immediately before starting out. For myself I packed two bottles of lemon juice in the saddle-bags, and the only food I took with me were a few pieces of chocolate that had been in my pack for some days. Towards evening we were ready, and when the sun was setting we crossed the river, on the other side of which the rolling desert starts. I waited until the horses had finished their drink, and after they had pawed and played with the cool water I mounted, and soon we were on the soft and still hot sands that made a peculiar hissing sound under the hoofs of the animals. The indescribable colours of a tropical sunset were reflected on the glittering waves of the ocean, and the old Indian fortress assumed a tint of gold. Even the inhospitable sandy wastes had changed their dread and desolate appearance, for now the sand dunes and undulations were one mass of colour, from golden brown to dark purple, according to light and shadows. A few belated sea-birds were hurriedly flying towards their distant roosting-places on some rocky island; everything seemed to be different now, except the regular, eternal rolling of the breakers on the shore. No sooner had the last clouds ceased to glow like fading beacon fires than darkness set in, and after a while the moon rose over the mountain ranges in the far east, slowly, majestically; and more than welcome to me.

The sensation of riding on soft sand is a peculiar one at first, until the body becomes used to the peculiar springless motion of the horse. Knowing that such conditions mean a great strain on the animal I could not help moving in the saddle, uselessly endeavouring to assist my mount. We were twisting and winding our way through among high sand dunes and, whenever it was possible, I guided the animals down to the wet sand on the beach where I would urge them into a slow gallop. Often we came to rocky places or to land-points which stretched far out, and thus I was forced to make a detour inland again, frequently for considerable distances. For the first few hours I observed everything around me and admired the brilliance of the moon that made the ocean glitter like silver, and gave the often strange sand formations a ghostly appearance. Soon even all this became monotonous to me, and every time I stopped to rest the horses for a while or to adjust the saddles, I lit a cigarette to help pass the time away. Shortly before dawn I had to halt for quite a long time, for the moon had gone down behind some clouds and we were left in darkness; it would not have been wise to continue lest I should take the wrong direction or lead the horses into places where the sand is so soft that they would sink in up to their bellies.

My instinct for finding the direction had developed to a notable degree by this time, probably because I had not very much to think about besides keeping the horses' noses facing the right way, but even when I knew exactly which way to go, fogs or darkness on several occasions made me think it wiser to wait until I could see.

The first rays of the morning sun were hot, and I rightly anticipated that the day was going to be a 'scorcher'. The horses plodded along as if they realized that they were in the midst of a serious test, and when it was about one hour after noon I noticed that they lifted their heads and sniffed the air. Immediately after they hurried their steps, and I believe they would have broken into a gallop if I had permitted them to do so. I was wondering why the horses were so keen to hurry along, and within an hour I knew the reason, for we arrived at the river, and I am certain that the animals had scented water long before I could see it; obviously Mancha and Gato still possessed the instincts of the wild horse.

Great were my feelings of relief when we left the Mata-caballo desert behind us and, in spite of my already high

opinion of the horses' resistance, I admired the splendid
behaviour they had shown during so long and trying a
journey – a journey that would have killed most horses
unaccustomed to such conditions. After I had unsaddled
them they had a good drink, and then I gave them a much-
needed bath. When this had been done I turned them loose
in a small field with good grass, and after both had rolled,
stretched and shaken themselves, they started to eat, and
anybody might have believed they had only just returned
from a short canter. I only realized how tired and played
out I was when I sat down on my saddles whilst a woman
in a hut prepared some food for me, and I thought I had
only dozed off to sleep for a few moments when I awoke in
the evening. The good woman, knowing that I needed sleep
more than food, had kept my meal warm for me, and once
I had the first taste of it I did not stop until the last grain
of rice and the last bean had disappeared. It had taken us
exactly twenty hours to cross the desert, and I have no
desire ever to make another such ride.

All the coastal villages are much alike, equally depressing, hot and miserable. A few houses and huts, a couple of
uneven and sandy roads, sometimes a tumbledown adobe
church, hens and pigs roaming about in search of refuse
that is simply thrown out of the houses into the street, and
on the roofs a few mournful-looking 'gallinazos' (buzzards)
waiting to pick up bits of filth at which other animals refuse
even to look. At the doors of some houses, and particularly
in front of the 'palacio municipal', a primitive construction
that is no better than the rest of the dilapidated houses,
men can be seen loitering all day and, although they never
seem to work, they always appear to have money enough
to buy alcohol, and once they are stimulated by its temporarily elevating effects they talk in such sums of money

that even the most powerful Wall Street magnates would prick up their ears. Rich mines, large estates, social reform, are discussed and debated, and once the bottle is empty and the men full, they again fall into silence or shuffle home, happy and satisfied after a good day's work.

Malaria is very common in some of the regions along the rivers, and Indians who come from the mountains to work in the cotton and sugar plantations invariably fall victims to this tropical fever. Once the effects of malaria have rendered them unfit for work, the landowners simply dismiss them, the existing law that is supposed to protect the unfortunate semi-slaves against this crime hardly ever being observed.

Whilst I was riding along in company of a native who was on his way to another village, we had a most unpleasant experience with a snake. On a sandy plain we had dismounted to have a short rest, when suddenly the man shouted to me in a very excited manner. A small snake had crawled under his mule, probably in order to take advantage of the only shady spot within miles. The frightened man said that this was a particularly venomous reptile, and that its bite would without doubt kill his mule. We tried to tease the snake away by throwing pebbles at it, and fortunately the mule was very tame and did not move. However, instead of coming away from under the beast, the snake tried to climb up one of its legs, and I held my breath, expecting the mule to move or stamp, but somehow it did not seem to feel anything. We were lucky to be able to attract the snake away at last, and I immediately killed it with a leather strap I had ready for that purpose.

I had sometimes hired guides to take me through bad

and tricky parts, but most of these men were so useless, lazy and impertinent that I much preferred to travel alone, and leave the rest to chance.

We had crossed another long and weary stretch of sandy desolation in which walls and other remains of the old Indians could be seen, and when we arrived at the river it was already dark. I knew that a village was not far from the opposite banks of the river, and as I had eaten nothing all day I was keen on crossing in spite of the prevailing darkness. I rode along the bank until I thought I had found a suitable place to cross, and there I made the horses wade out. I had not expected to find such a strong current and began to wonder if it would not be wiser to turn back, and just then the horse I was riding was swept off its feet. Very foolishly I still had the pack-animals tied to the wide girth of my mount, the usual manner in which lead-horses are taken along the pampas. Before I had time to think, the three of us were swept down-stream, and it was due more to luck than to ability that we landed safely back on the shore from which we had started. Besides having had a longer drink than I had bargained for, I rightly suspected in what a mess I would find the contents of my saddle-bags next day. I had no desire to make a second attempt to cross the river that night, so I resigned myself to fate and prepared to wait for daylight. I let the horses look after themselves among the coarse grass near the river, whilst I went to spread my soaked blankets at the foot of a sandy hill close by, for there it would not be damp, and the sand was still comfortably warm after the day's terrific heat. In spite of my raving appetite and my wringing wet clothes I was soon fast asleep, but during the night I was several times awakened by a strange noise that sounded like the beating of drums, or as if a motor launch were travelling on the river. As I could see nothing I continued to sleep, and only awoke when the sunrays were beginning to be hot. When I looked about, I found that I had slept near a 'gentilar' as the ancient Indian burial-grounds are called. There are many of these along the Peruvian coast and, after seeing a few, one takes hardly any more notice of all the skulls and bones that lie about on the sand, which has shifted with the passing centuries. The horses must have had a good feed, for they were waiting for me, and when all was ready we crossed the river without much difficulty, and when we arrived in the village I fully made up for arrears in the food line.

While conversing with some people I told them about my nasty experience in the river the night before, and when they heard where I had slept all wanted to know if I had heard the 'manchang'. This word sounding rather like Chinese to me I asked them what it meant, whereupon they all started to explain in chorus that the sandhill where I had slept was haunted, and that the dead Indians of the 'gentilar' danced every night to the beating of drums. So many terrible superstitious stories did they tell me about the 'manchang' that I began to think I was lucky to be still alive. Later I had occasion to speak to an educated gentleman who had come to visit me, and he said that both Baron von Humboldt and Raimondi had once upon a time investigated the strange phenomenon of that hill, and that they had expressed the opinion that the peculiar sounds that are frequently heard during the night were due to underground waters which moved as the temperature changed. Another theory that has been brought forward is that when the sea breezes blow from a certain direction and the air hits the sandy ripples on the slopes of the hill, it will produce this strange sound. Somehow both explanations appealed to me as being sensible, but I feel inclined to think that the former is more likely to be correct.

After all these trying journeys I rested for two days, for there was plenty of grass for the horses, and I, for a change was able to even enjoy a few decent meals again.

One evening I thought I would pass a couple of hours away by going to see some moving pictures which were announced for that night. The 'teatro' was merely a large shed with a tin roof, and the films shown were old and worn out, but yet the audience seemed delighted with the show. All of a sudden everybody made a rush for the door; there were a few shrieks from women, and the whole place shook. Before I had even time to think what was happening the place was empty, only myself and two women who had fainted remaining there. Even then I could not make out what had happened, but when I went outside I was told that there had been an earthquake. I had been under the impression that the trampling and rushing crowd had shaken up the place. Luckily nobody was hurt in that stampede for the open, but a few had sustained minor bruises and knocks and the rest had come out of it with only a good fright. No one seeming keen on going back, the management announced the show as having terminated; much to my surprise nobody protested or asked for 'money back'.

Earthquakes are very common occurrences along the Peruvian coast, but as the houses and huts are so lightly built, and the roofs being merely light covers to protect against the fierce sun, it is rarely that much harm is done. As I have mentioned before, rains are practically unknown in these regions, and so the houses are simply covered with bamboo canes, mud and straw.

Fording some of the wide and usually slow-flowing rivers

was not without its dangers, treacherous quicksands lurking where one least expects to find them. If anybody happened to live near a river I had to ford, I always offered a good reward if he were willing to show me the best place where to cross, but often I had to try my luck alone.

One evening, after a long day's riding, I came to a solitary hut near the mouth of a river where a fisherman and his family lived. I was very hungry and thirsty, and looked forward to a change of diet, for I had lived on sardines and biscuits for some days. Two children were playing in the sand outside the hut, and as it was always my policy to make friends with the youngsters in order more easily to approach the parents, I thought I would do the same here, and so gave them my last biscuits and the remaining tin of sardines. I thought this was a good investment and a safe gamble to get something more agreeable to my taste from the grateful parents later on, but to my bitter disappointment I was told that they had run out of supplies and that there would be nothing to eat until next morning when the man was going out fishing. I was given some hot water with which I brewed myself some tea, and even this I had to drink without sugar, my supply having come to grief whilst crossing a river. The next journey being a long one I had to start early, and so I had to do another day's hard riding on an empty stomach, and it can easily be imagined how I blessed those children and how pleased I was with myself for having given them that tin of sardines and the biscuits.

After a few hours we came to a river that had a very bad reputation for quicksands, and so I rode up-stream until I came to a hut where another fisherman lived. He was willing to help me across. He had a pony which, he told me, served to drag his net through the shallow water along the beach. Mounted on this animal he came to show me the way, but he only did this after having received five *soles* (Peruvian standard currency) in advance for his services. We had nearly reached the other side of the shallow but wide river when suddenly his pony's hindlegs sank into the sand. Knowing what this meant, I hurried my horses along, made a semi-circle around my guide, and was fortunate enough to reach the dry shore. Without losing a moment I untied the lasso I always had handy, and then cautiously waded back to where the man was still sitting on his animal, which was sinking deeper and deeper. As soon as I had thrown him the lasso he put it around the pony's neck; then he jumped off and came towards me, all the time holding on to the lasso in case he also should sink in. Whenever a horse sinks into a quicksand hindlegs first, it is of no use to try to pull him out from in front, but to save him one has to pull in such a manner as to make him fall on his side. This frees his hindlegs and gives him buoyancy, and then one can usually rescue him. Should the animal be left alone he will gradually sink in and finally drown, and the more he struggles and fights the quicker will he sink. Working like Trojans we finally rescued the guide's pony, and in case the same thing should happen to him again I waited until he had safely reached the home shore.

In riding across such rivers it is advisable to wear spurs and to have something ready to whip the horses with, for if they step into a quicksand and are hurried along, it will often prevent them from getting stuck.

8 'White men, you are trespassers!'

ERNEST GILES

*Once Columbus had in 1492 accidentally 'discovered' the
New World in the shape of the West Indies (and insisted
to the end of his life they were part of Asia), a spate of
exploration followed, with Vasco de Gama reaching India
in 1498 and Magellan's ship the* Victoria *circumnavigating
the world in 1519–22. But it was many generations before
Europeans became aware of a vast continent in the far
south. Even after Cook and Flinders had charted the coast-
line, it was much later that the interior was explored by
men such as Sturt – Kennedy – the Gregory Brothers –
Stuart and McKinley – Burke and Wills. Giles himself
made five expeditions from 1872–76 through Central South
Australia and Western Australia. The last sentence in this
present extract from his journals has an ironic ring in view
of the fate of the aborigines he talks about – a fate that
differs from that of the American Indians only in the
numbers involved.*

Perils there were in plenty and not least from the
aboriginals. One day, for example, we saw two natives looking most intently at our outgoing horse tracks, along which
they were slowly walking, with their backs towards us.
They neither saw nor heard us until we were close upon
their heels. Each carried two enormously long spears, two-
thirds mulga wood and one-third reed at the throwing end,
of course having the instrument with which they project
these spears, often called a wommerah.

This is in the form of a flat ellipse, elongated to a sort of tail at the holding end; a kangaroo's claw or wild dog's tooth is firmly fixed by gum and gut-strings. The projectile force of this implement is enormous, and these spears can be thrown with the greatest precision for more than a hundred yards. They also had narrow shields, three to four feet long, to protect themselves from hostile spears, with a handle cut out in the centre.

These two natives had their hair tied up in a kind of chignon at the back of the head, the hair being dragged back off the forehead from infancy. This mode gave them a wild though somewhat effeminate appearance; others, again, wear their hair in long thick curls reaching down the shoulders, beautifully elaborated with iguanas' or emus' fat and red ochre. This applies only to the men; the women's hair is worn either cut with flints or bitten off short.

So soon as the two natives heard, and then looking round saw us, they scampered off like emus, running along as close to the ground as it is possible for any two-legged creature to do. One was quite a young fellow, the other full grown. They ran up the side of the hills, and kept travelling along parallel to us; but though we stopped and called, and signalled with boughs, they would not come close, and the oftener I tried to come near them on foot, the faster they ran.

They continued alongside us until we reached a certain creek, where we rested the horses for an hour. We soon became aware that a number of natives were in our vicinity, our original two yelling and shouting to inform the others of our advent, and presently we saw a whole nation of them coming from the glen or gorge to the south-west, where I had noticed camp-fires.

The new people were also shouting and yelling in the

most furious and demoniacal manner; and our former two, as though deputed by the others, now approached us much nearer than before, and came within twenty yards of us, but holding their spears fixed in their wommerahs, in such a position that they could use them instantly if they desired. The slightest incident might have induced them to spear us, but we appeared to be at our ease, and endeavoured to parley with them.

The men were not handsome or fat, but were very well made, and, as is the case with most of the natives of these parts, were rather tall, viz. five feet eight and nine inches. When they had come close enough, the elder began to harangue us, and evidently desired us to know that we were trespassers, and were to be off forthwith, as he waved us away in the direction we had come from. The whole host then took up the signal, howled, yelled, and waved their hands and weapons at us. Fortunately, however, they did not actually attack us; we were not very well prepared for attack, as we had only a revolver each, our guns and rifles being left with Robinson. As our horses were frightened and would not feed, we hurried our departure, when we were saluted with rounds of cheers and blessings – i.e. yells and curses in their charming dialect, until we were fairly out of sight and hearing.

But on a later occasion, when we were preparing to camp in the same area, we suddenly perceived that the whole region seemed alive with aborigines, men, women and children running down from the highest points of the mountain to join the tribe below, where they all congregated. The yelling, howling, shrieking, and gesticulating they kept up was, to say the least, annoying.

When we began to unpack the horses, they crowded

closer round us, carrying their knotted sticks, long spears, and other fighting implements. I did not notice any boomerangs among them – and I did not request them to send for any! They were growing very troublesome, and evidently meant mischief. I rode towards a mob of them and cracked my whip, which had no effect in dispersing them. They made a sudden pause, and then gave a sudden shout or howl. It seemed as if they knew, or had heard something, of white men's ways, for when I unstrapped my rifle, and holding it up, warning them away, to my great astonishment they departed; they had probably wanted to find out if we possessed such things, and I trust they were satisfied, for they gave us up apparently as a bad lot.

We were by no means rid of them, however. When I was searching for water I saw a single native leisurely walking along in front of me with a guana in his hand, taking it home for supper. He carried several spears, a wommerah, and a shield, and had long curled locks hanging down his shoulders. My horse's nose nearly touched his back before he was aware of my presence, when, looking behind him, he gave a sudden start, held up his two hands, dropped his guana and his spears, uttered a tremendous yell as a warning to his tribe, and bounded up the rocks in front of us like a wallaby.

I then passed under a eucalyptus-tree, in whose foliage two ancient warriors had hastily secreted themselves. I stopped a second and looked up at them, they also looked at me; they presented a most ludicrous appearance. A little further on were several rows of wurleys or dwellings, and I could perceive the men urging the women and children away, as they doubtless supposed many more white men were in company with me, never supposing I could possibly be alone.

While the women and children were departing up the rocks, the men snatched up spears and other weapons, and followed the women slowly towards the rocks. The glen had here narrowed to a gorge, the rocks on either side being not more than eighty to a hundred feet high. It is no exaggeration to say that the summits of the rocks on either side of the glen were lined with natives: they could almost touch me with their spears.

I did not feel quite at home in this charming retreat, although I was the cynosure of a myriad eyes. The natives stood upon the edge of the rocks like statues, some pointing their spears menacingly towards me, and I certainly expected that some dozens would be thrown at me. Both parties seemed paralyzed by the appearance of the other. I scarcely knew what to do; I knew if I turned to retreat that every spear would be launched at me. I was, metaphorically, transfixed to the spot, but thought the only thing to do was to brave the situation out.

I was choking with thirst, though in vain I looked for a sheet of water; but seeing where they had dug out some sand, I advanced to one or two wells in which I could see water, but without a shovel only a native could get any out of such a funnel-shaped hole. In sheer desperation I dismounted and picked up a small wooden utensil from one of the wurleys, thinking if I could only get a drink I should summon up pluck for the last desperate plunge. I could only manage to get up a few mouthfuls of dirty water, and my horse was trying to get in on top of me.

So far as I could see, there were only two or three of these places where all those natives got water. I remounted my horse, one of the best and fastest I have. He knew exactly what I wanted because he wished it also – and that was to be gone. I mounted slowly with my face to the enemy, but the instant I was up he sprang round and was away with a bound that almost left me behind; then such demoniacal yells greeted my ears as I had never before heard and do not wish to hear again; the echoes of the voices of these now indignant and infuriated creatures reverberating through the defiles of the hills, and the uncouth sounds of the voices themselves smote so discordantly on my own and my horse's ears that we went out of that glen faster, oh! ever so much faster than we went in.

I heard a horrid sound of spears, sticks, and other weapons striking violently upon the ground behind me – but I did not stop to pick up any of them, or even to look round to see what caused it!

The next time I encountered natives, they were burning the grass along a creek. I was in company with Mr. Tietkens and we had ridden ahead of our company to reconnoitre; we went nearly three miles, when we came to running water. At the same time we evidently disturbed a considerable number of natives, who raised a most frightful outcry at our sudden and unexpected advent amongst them. Those nearest to us walked slowly into the reeds, rushes, tea-trees, and high salt bushes, but deliberately watching our every movement. While watering our horses a great many from the outskirts ran at us, poising and quivering their spears, some of which were over ten feet long; of these every individual had an extraordinary number.

When they saw us sitting quietly – but not comfortably – on our horses, which became very frightened and impatient, they renewed their horrible yells and gesticulations, some waving us away, others climbing trees, and directing their spears at us from the branches. Another lot on the opposite side of the creek now came rushing up with spears advanced and ensigns spread, and with yells and cries encouraged those near to spear us. They seemed, however, to have some doubts on the nature or vulnerability of our horses.

At the head of our new assailants was one sophisticated enough to be able to call out, 'Walk, white fellows, walk'; but as we still remained immobile he induced some others to join in making a rush at us, and they hurled their jagged spears at us before we could get out of the way. It was fortunate indeed that we were at the extreme distance that these weapons can be projected, for they struck the ground right amongst our horses' hoofs, making them more restive than ever.

I now let our assailants see we were not quite so helpless as they might have supposed. I unslipped my rifle, and the bullet, going so suddenly between two of these worthies and smashing some boughs just behind them, produced silence amongst the whole congregation, at least for a moment. All this time we were anxiously awaiting the arrival of two others of our band, as my instructions had been that if we did not return in a given time, they were to follow after us. But these valiant retainers, who admitted they heard firing, preferred to remain out of harm's way, leaving us to kill or be killed, as the fortunes of war might determine; and we at length had to retreat from our sable enemies, and go and find our white friends.

We got the mob of horses up (we had brought several to water them), but the yelling of these fiends in human form, the clouds of smoke from the burning grass and bushes, and the many disagreeable odours incident to a large native village, and the yapping and howling of a lot of starving dogs, all combined to make us and our horses exceedingly restless. They seemed somewhat overawed by the number of the horses, and though they crowded round from all directions, for there were more than two hundred of them, the women and children being sent away over the hills at our first approach, they did not then throw any more spears.

I selected as open a piece of ground as I could get for the camp, which, however, was very small, back from the water, and nearly under the foot of a hill. When they saw us dismount, for I believe they had previously believed ourselves and our horses to form one animal, and begin to unload the horses, they proceeded properly to work themselves up for a regular onslaught. So long as the horses remained close, they seemed disinclined to attack, but when the horses were hobbled and went away, the enemy made a grand sortie, rushing down the hill at the back of the camp where they had congregated, towards us in a body with spears fitted in pose and yelling their war cries.

Our lives were in imminent danger; we had out all the firearms we could muster; these amounted to two rifles, two shot guns and five revolvers. I watched with great keenness the motion of their arms that gives the propulsion to their spears, and the instant I observed that, I ordered a discharge of the two rifles and one gun, as it was no use waiting to be speared first. I delayed almost a second too long, for at the instant I gave the word several spears had left the enemy's hands, and it was with great good fortune we avoided them.

Our shots as I had ordered, cut up the ground at their feet, and sent the sand and gravel into their eyes and faces; this and the noise of the discharge, made the great body of them pause. Availing ourselves of this interval, we ran to attack them, firing our revolvers in quick succession as we

ran. This, with the noise and to them extraordinary phenomenon of a projectile approaching them which they could
not see, drove them up into the hills from which they had
approached us, and they were quiet for nearly an hour,
except for their unceasing howls and yells, during which
time we made an attempt at getting some dinner.

That meal, however, was not completed when we saw
them stealing down on us again. Again they came more
than a hundred strong, with heads held back, and arms at
fullest tension to give their spears the greatest projective
force, when, just as they came within spear shot, for we
knew the exact distance now, we gave them another volley,
striking the sand up just before their feet; again they
halted, consulted one another by looks and signs, when the
discharge of Gibson's gun (two other of our companions
had now joined us), with two long-distance cartridges,
decided them, and they ran back, but only to come again.
In consequence of our not shooting any of them, they
began to jeer and laugh at us, slapping their backsides at
us and jumping about in front of us, and indecently daring
and deriding us. These were evidently some of those lewd
fellows of the baser sort, in the words of Acts xvii. 5.

We were at length compelled to send some rifle bullets
into such close proximity to some of their limbs that at
last they really did believe we were dangerous folk after
all. Towards night their attentions ceased, and though they
camped just on the opposite side of the creek, they did not
trouble us any more. I was very gratified to think afterwards that no blood had been shed, and that we had got
rid of our enemies with only the loss of a little ammunition.

This, however, was not always the case. One evening the
cheery voice of the expedition cook had called us to our

evening meal; as usual we sat down in peaceful contentment, not dreaming that death or danger was lurking near, but nevertheless, outside this peaceful scene a mighty preparation for our destruction was being made by an army of unseen and unsuspected foes.

> *The hunting tribes of air and earth*
> *Respect the brethren of their birth;*
> *Man only mars kind Nature's plan,*
> *And turns the fierce pursuit on man.*

Our supper was spread, by chance or Providential interference, a little earlier than usual. Mr. Young, having finished his meal first, had risen from his seat. I happened to be the last at the festive board. In walking towards the place where his bedding was spread upon the rocks, he saw close to him, but above on the main rock, and at about the level of his two eyes, a couple of unarmed natives making signs to the two quiet and inoffensive ones who had earlier come to visit our camp – and instantaneously after he saw the front rank of a grand and imposing army approaching, guided by the two scouts in advance.

I had not much time to notice them in detail, but I could see that these warriors were painted, feathered, and armed to the teeth with spears, clubs and other weapons, and that they were ready for instant action. Mr. Young gave the alarm, and we had only just time to seize our firearms when the whole army was upon us. At a first glance this force was most imposing; the coup d'œil was really magnificent; they looked like what I should imagine a body of Comanche Indians would appear when ranged in battle line. The men were closely packed in serried ranks, and it was evident they formed a drilled and perfectly organized force. Immediate action became imminent, and as most fortunately they had thought to find us seated at supper, and to spear us as we sat in a body together, we had just time, before fifty, sixty, or a hundred spears could be thrown at us, as I immediately gave the command to fire, to have the first discharge at them.

Had it been otherwise not one of us could possibly have escaped their spears – all would certainly have been killed, for there were over a hundred of the enemy, and they approached us in a solid phalanx of five or six rows, each row consisting of eighteen or twenty warriors. Their project was no doubt that so soon as any of us was speared by the warriors, the inoffensive spies (our visitors) in the camp were to tomahawk us at their leisure, as we rolled about in agony from our wounds; but, taken by surprise, their otherwise exceedingly well-organized attack, owing to a slight change in our supper-hour, was a little too late, and our fire caused a great commotion and wavering in their legion's ordered line.

One of the quiet and inoffensive spies in the camp, as soon as he saw me jump up and prepare for action, ran and jumped on me, put his arms round my neck to prevent my firing, and though we could not get a word of English out of him previously, when he did this, he called, clinging on to me, with his hand on my throat, 'Don't, don't!' I don't know if I swore, but I suppose I must, as I was turned away from the thick array with most extreme disgust. I couldn't disengage myself; I couldn't attend to the main army, for I had to turn my attention entirely to this infernal encumbrance; all I could do was to yell out 'Fire! Fire for your lives.' I intended to give the spy a taste of my rifle first, but in consequence of his being in such close quarters to me, and my holding my rifle with one hand, while I endeavoured to free myself with the other, I could not point the muzzle at my assailant, and my only way of clearing myself from his hold was by battering his head with the butt end of the weapon with my right hand, while he still clung round my left side.

At last I disengaged myself and he let go suddenly, and slipped instantly behind one of the thick acacia bushes, and got away, just as the enemy in front was wavering. All this did not occupy many seconds of time, and I believe my final shot decided the battle. The routed army, carrying their wounded, disappeared behind the trees and bushes beyond the bare rock where the battle was fought, and from whence not many minutes before they had so gallantly emerged. This was the best organized and most disciplined aboriginal force I ever saw. They must have thoroughly digested their plan of attack, and sent not only quiet and inoffensive spies into the camp but a pretty little girl also, to lull any suspicion of their evil intentions we might have entertained.

Once during the day the little girl sat down by me and began a most serious discourse in her own language, and as she warmed with her subject she got up, gesticulated and imitated the action of natives throwing spears, pointed towards the natives' camp, stamped her foot on the ground close to me, and was no doubt informing me of the intended onslaught of the tribe. Unfortunately, as I did not understand a word she said I failed to realize the warning she was evidently giving.

That was not the last of the attacks. Travelling along in the cool of the next morning we surprised some natives hunting. Their wonderfully acute perceptions of sight, sound and scent almost instantly apprised them of our presence, and as is usual with these persons, the most frantic yells rent the air. Signal fires were immediately lighted in all directions, in order to collect the scattered tribe, and before we had gone a mile we were pursued by a multitude of howling demons.

A great number came running after us, making the most unearthly noises, screeching, rattling their spears and other weapons, with the evident intention of not letting us depart out of their coasts. They drew around so closely and so thick that they prevented our horses from going on, and we were compelled to get out our revolvers for immediate use; we had at that moment no rifles with us.

A number from behind threw a lot of spears; we were obliged to let the pack-horse go – one spear struck him and made him rush and jump about. This drew their attention from us for a moment; then, just as another flight of spears was let fly at us, we plunged forward on our horses and fired our revolvers. I was horrified to find that mine would not go off, something was wrong with the cartridges and, though I snapped it four times, not a single discharge took place. Fortunately Mr. Tietkens's went off all right, and what with that and the pack-horse rushing wildly about, trying to get up to us, we drove the wretches off, for a time at least.

They seemed far more alarmed at the horses than at us, of whom they did not seem to have any fear whatever. We induced them to retire for a bit, and we went on, after catching the pack-horse and breaking about forty of their spears. I believe a wild Australian native would almost as soon be killed as have his spears destroyed.

Nine miles from where we had encountered that band we stopped to eat our dinner when Mr. Tietkens gave the alarm that the enemy was upon us again, and instantly we heard their discordant cries. The horses began to gallop off although they were hobbled. These wretches now seemed determined to destroy us, for, having considerably augmented their numbers, they swarmed around us on all sides.

Two of our new assailants were of commanding stature, each being nearly tall enough to make two of Tietkens if not of me. These giants were not, however, the most forward in the onslaught. The horses galloped off a good way, with Tietkens running after them: in some trepidation lest my revolver should again play me false, though of course I had cleaned and re-loaded it, I prepared to defend the camp. The assailants immediately swarmed round me, those behind running up, howling, until the whole body were within thirty yards of me, then they came on more slowly.

I could now see that aggression on my part was the only thing for it; I must try to carry the situation with a coup. I walked up to them very fast and pointed my revolver at them. Some, thinking I was only pointing my finger pointed their fingers at me. They all had their spears ready and quivering in their wommerahs, and I am sure I should in another instant have been transfixed with a score or two of spears, had not Tietkens, having tied up the horses, come running up, which caused a moment's diversion, and both our revolvers going off properly this time, we made our foes retreat at a better pace than they had advanced.

Some of their spears were smashed in their hands; most of them dropped everything they carried and went scudding away over the rocks as fast as fear and astonishment would permit. We broke all the spears we could lay our hands on – nearly a hundred – and then finished our dinner.

That done, we departed, leaving the aboriginal owners of this splendid piece of land in the peaceful possession of their beautiful hunting grounds, and travelled on our way.

9 On the Verge of Starvation

DR. FREDERICK A. COOK

The Cook-Peary controversy over who truly reached the North Pole first, if at all, was one that divided the world in pre-World War I days. Either you firmly supported Peary or you gave your allegiance to Dr. Cook. Violent quarrels ensued, dozens of books and learned papers were published on the subject; charges of liar and fraud were bandied to and fro between the rival camps. Cook had started off as ethnologist in Peary's Greenland Expedition of 1892, while four years later he was surgeon to a Belgian Antarctic expedition. In 1907 he set out on his own polar expedition and it was unquestionably a splendid adventure, at least as told by Cook in his My Attainment of the Pole, *but much of his evidence was later refuted, while his reputation for veracity had not been helped by his earlier claim to have climbed the 21,000 feet Mount McKinley in Alaska whereas in fact it was proved that he had got no higher than 11,000 feet.*

The stormy sea rose with heavy swells. Oceanward, the waves leaped against the horizon tumultuously. Pursuing our vain search for food along the southern side of Jones Sound, early in September, we had been obliged to skirt rocky coves and shelves of land on which we might seek shelter should harm come to the fragile craft in which we braved the ocean storms and the spears of unseen ice beneath water.

We had shaped crude weapons. We were prepared to attack game. We were starving; yet land and sea had been barren of any living thing.

Our situation was desperate. In our course it was often necessary, as now, to paddle from the near refuge of low-lying shores, and to pass precipitous cliffs and leaping glaciers which stepped threateningly into the sea. Along these were no projecting surfaces, and we passed them always with bated anxiety. A sudden storm or a mishap at such a time would have meant death in the frigid sea. And now, grim and suffering with hunger, we clung madly to life.

Passing a glacier which rose hundreds of feet out of the green sea, heavy waves rolled furiously from the distant ocean. Huge bergs rose and fell against the far-away horizon like Titan ships hurled to destruction. The waves dashed against the emerald walls of the smooth icy Gibraltar with a thunderous noise. We rose and fell in the frail canvas boat, butting the waves, our hearts each time sinking.

Suddenly something white and glittering pierced the bottom of the boat! It was the tusk of a walrus, gleaming and dangerous. Before we could grasp the situation he had disappeared, and water gushed into our craft. It was the first walrus we had seen for several weeks. An impulse, mad under the circumstances, rose in our hearts to give him chase. It was the instinctive call of the hungering body for food. But each second the water rose higher; each minute was imminent with danger. Instinctively Ah-we-lah pressed to the floor of the boat and jammed his knee into the hole, thus partly shutting off the jetting, leaping inrush. He looked mutely to me for orders. The glacier offered no stopping place. Looking about with mad eagerness, I saw, seaward, only a few hundred yards away, a small pan of drift-ice. With the desire for life in our arms, we pushed toward it with all our might. Before the boat was pulled to its slippery landing, several inches of water flooded the bottom. Once upon it, leaping in the waves, we breathed with panting relief. With a piece of boot the hole was patched. Although we should have preferred to wait to give the walrus a wide berth, the increasing swell of the stormy sea, and a seaward drift forced us away from the dangerous ice cliffs.

Launching the boat into the rough waters, we pulled for land. A triangle of four miles had to be made before our fears could be set at rest. A school of walrus followed us in the rocking waters for at least half of the distance. Finally, upon the crest of a white-capped wave, we were lifted to firm land. Drawing the boat after us, we ran out of reach of the hungry waves, and sank to the grass, desperate, despairing, utterly fatigued, but safe.

Now followed a long run of famine luck. We searched land and sea for a bird or a fish. In the boat we skirted a barren coast, sleeping on rocks without shelter and quenching our thirst by glacial liquid till the stomach collapsed. The indifferent stage of starvation was at hand when we pulled into a nameless bay, carried the boat on a grassy bench, and packed ourselves in it for a sleep that might be our last.

We were awakened by the glad sound of distant walrus calls. Through the glasses, a group was located far off shore, on the middle pack. Our hearts began to thump. A stream of blood came with a rush to our heads. Our bodies were fired with a life that had been foreign to us for many moons. No famished wolf ever responded to a call more rapidly than we did. Quickly we dropped the boat into the water with the implements, and pushed from the famine shores with teeth set for red meat.

The day was beautiful, and the sun from the west poured a wealth of golden light. Only an occasional ripple disturbed the glassy blue through which the boat crept. The pack was about five miles northward. In our eagerness to reach it, the distance seemed spread to leagues. There was not a square of ice for miles about which could have been sought for refuge in case of an attack. But this did not disturb us now. We were blinded to everything except the dictates of our palates.

As we advanced, our tactics were definitely arranged. The animals were on a low pan, which seemed to be loosely run into the main pack. We aimed for a little cut of ice open to the leeward, where we hoped to land and creep up behind hummocks. The splash of our paddles was lost in the noise of the grinding ice and the bellowing of walrus calls.

So excited were the Eskimos that they could hardly pull an oar. It was the first shout of the wilderness which we had heard in many months. We were lean enough to appreciate its import. The boat finally shot up on the ice, and we scattered among the ice blocks for favorable positions. Everything was in our favor. We did not for a moment entertain a thought of failure, although in reality, with the implements at hand, our project was tantamount to attacking an elephant with pocket knives.

We came together behind an unusually high icy spire only a few hundred yards from the herd. Ten huge animals were lazily stretched out in the warm sun. A few lively babies tormented their sleeping mothers. There was a splendid line of hummocks, behind which we could advance under cover. With a firm grip on harpoon and line, we started. Suddenly E-tuk-i-shook shouted 'Nannook!' (Bear.)

We halted. Our implements were no match for a bear. But we were too hungry to retreat. The bear paid no attention to us. His nose was set for something more to his liking. Slowly but deliberately, he crept up to the snoring herd while we watched with a mad, envious anger welling up within us. Our position was helpless. His long neck reached out, the glistening fangs closed, and a young walrus struggled in the air. All of the creatures woke, but too late to give battle. With dismay and rage, the walruses sank into the water, and the bear slunk off to a safe distance, where he sat down to a comfortable meal. We were not of sufficient importance to interest either the bear or the disturbed herd of giants.

Our limbs were limp when we returned to the boat. The sunny glitter of the waters was now darkened by the gloom of danger from enraged animals. We crossed to the barren shores in a circuitous route, where pieces of ice for refuge were always within reach.

On land, the night was cheerless and cold. We were not in a mood for sleep. In a lagoon we discovered moving things. After a little study of their vague darts they proved to be fish. A diligent search under stones brought out a few handfuls of tiny finny creatures. With gratitude I saw that here was an evening meal. Seizing them, we ate the wriggling things raw. Cooking was impossible, for we had neither oil nor wood.

On the next day the sun at noon burned with a real fire – not the sham light without heat which had kept day and night in perpetual glitter for several weeks. Not a breath of air disturbed the blue glitter of the sea. Ice was scattered everywhere. The central pack was farther away, but on it rested several suspicious black marks. Through the glasses we made these out to be groups of walruses. They were evidently sound asleep for we heard no calls. They were also so distributed that there was a hunt both for bear and man without interference.

We ventured out with a savage desire sharpened by a taste of raw fish. As we advanced several other groups were noted in the water. They gave us much trouble. They did not seem ill-tempered, but dangerously inquisitive. Our boat was dark in color and not much larger than the body of a full-sized bull. To them, I presume, it resembled a companion in distress or asleep. A sight of the boat challenged their curiosity, and they neared us with the playful intention of testing with their tusks the hardness of the canvas. We had experienced such love taps before, however, with but a narrow escape from drowning, and we had no desire for further walrus courtship.

Fortunately, we could maintain a speed almost equal to theirs, and we also found scattered ice-pans, about which we could linger while their curiosity was being satisfied by the splash of an occasional stone.

From the iceberg we studied the various groups of walruses for the one best situated for our primitive methods of attack. We also searched for meddlesome bears. None was detected. Altogether we counted more than a hundred grunting, snorting creatures arranged in black hills along a line of low ice. There were no hummocks or pressure lifts, under cover of which we might advance to within the short range required for our harpoons. All of the walrus-encumbered pans were adrift and disconnected from the main pack. Conflicting currents gave each group a slightly different motion. We studied this movement for a little while.

We hoped, if possible, to make our attack from the ice. With the security of a solid footing, there was no danger and there was a greater certainty of success. But the speed of the ice on this day did not permit such an advantage. We must risk a water attack. This is not an unusual method of the Eskimo, but he follows it with a kayak, a harpoon and line fitted with a float and a drag for the end of his line.

Our equipment was only a makeshift, and could not be handled in the same way.

Here was food in massive heaps. We had had no breakfast and no full meal for many weeks. Something must be done. The general drift was eastward, but the walrus pans drifted slightly faster than the main pack. Along the pack were several high points, projecting a considerable distance seaward. We took our position in the canvas boat behind one of these floating capes, and awaited the drift of the sleeping monsters.

Their movement was slow enough to give us plenty of time to arrange our battle tactics. The most vital part of the equipment was the line. If it were lost, we could not hope to survive the winter. It could not be replaced, and without it we could not hope to cope with the life of the sea, or even that of the land. The line was a new, strong sealskin rawhide of ample length, which had been reserved for just such an emergency. Attached to the harpoon, with the float properly adjusted, it is seldom lost, for the float moves and permits no sudden strain.

To safeguard the line, a pan was selected only a few yards in diameter. This was arranged to do the duty of a float and a drag. With the knife two holes were cut, and into these the line was fastened near its center. The harpoon end was taken into the boat, the other end was coiled and left in a position where it could be easily picked from the boat later. Three important purposes were secured by this arrangement – the line was relieved of a sudden strain; if it broke, only half would be lost; and the unused end would serve as a binder to other ice when the chase neared its end.

Now the harpoon was set to the shaft, and the bow of our little twelve-foot boat cleared for action. Peeping over the wall of ice, we saw the black-littered pans slowly coming toward us. Our excitement rose to shouting point. But our nerves were under the discipline of famine. The pan, it was evident, would go by us at a distance of about fifty feet.

The first group of walruses were allowed to pass. They proved to be a herd of twenty-one mammoth creatures, and, entirely aside from the danger of attack, their unanimous plunge would have raised a sea that must have swamped us.

On the next pan were but three spots. At a distance we persuaded ourselves that they were small – for we had no ambition for formidable attacks. One thousand pounds of meat would have been sufficient for us. They proved, however, to be the largest bulls of the lot. As they neared the point, the hickory oars of the boat were gripped – and out we shot. They all rose to meet us, displaying the glitter of ivory tusks from little heads against huge wrinkled necks. They grunted and snorted viciously – but the speed of the boat did not slacken. E-tuk-i-shook rose. With a savage thrust he sank the harpoon into a yielding neck.

The walruses tumbled over themselves and sank into the water on the opposite side of the pan. We pushed upon the vacated floe without leaving the boat, taking the risk of ice puncture rather than walrus thumps. The short line came up with a snap. The ice-pan began to plough the sea. It moved landward. What luck! I wondered if the walrus would tow us and its carcass ashore. We longed to encourage the homing movement, but we dared not venture out. Other animals had awakened to the battle call, and now the sea began to seethe and boil with enraged, leaping red-eyed monsters.

The float took a zigzag course in the offing. We watched the movement with a good deal of anxiety. Our next meal and our last grip of life were at stake. For the time being nothing could be done.

The three animals remained together, two pushing the wounded one along and holding it up during breathing spells. In their excitement they either lost their bearings or deliberately determined to attack. Now three ugly snouts pointed at us. This was greatly to our advantage, for on ice we were masters of the situation.

Taking inconspicuous positions, we awaited the assault. The Eskimos had lances, I an Alpine axe. The walruses dove and came on like torpedo boats, rising almost under our noses, with a noise that made us dodge. In a second two lances sank into the harpooned strugglers. The water was thrashed. Down again went the three. The lances were jerked back by return lines, and in another moment we were ready for another assault from the other side. But they dashed on, and pulled the float-floe, on which we had been, against the one on which we stood, with a crushing blow.

Here was our first chance to secure the unused end of the line, fastened on the other floe. Ah-we-lah jumped to the floe and tossed me the line. The spiked shaft of the ice-axe was driven in the ice and the line fixed to it, so now the two floes were held together. Our stage of action was enlarged, and we had the advantage of being towed by the animals we fought.

Here was the quiet sport of the fisherman and the savage excitement of the battle-field run together in a new chase. The struggle was prolonged in successive stages. Time passed swiftly. In six hours, during which the sun had swept a quarter of the circle, the twin floes were jerked through the water with the rush of a gunboat. The jerking line attached to our enraged pilots sent a thrill of life which made our hearts jump. The lances were thrown, the line was shortened, a cannonade of ice blocks was kept up, but the animal gave no signs of weakening. Seeing that we could not inflict dangerous wounds, our tactics were changed to a kind of siege, and we aimed not to permit the animal its breathing spells.

The line did not begin to slacken until midnight. The battle had been on for almost twelve hours. But we did not feel the strain of action, nor did our chronic hunger seriously disturb us. Bits of ice quenched our thirst and the chill of night kept us from sweating. With each rise of the beast for breath now, the line slackened. Gently it was hauled in and secured. Then a rain of ice blocks, hurled in rapid succession, drove the spouting animals down. Soon the line was short enough to deliver the lance in the captured walrus at close range. The wounded animal was now less troublesome, but the others tore about under us like submarine boats, and at the most unexpected moments would shoot up with a wild rush.

We did not attempt to attack them, however. All our attention was directed to the end of the line. The lance was driven with every opportunity. It seldom missed, but the action was more like spurs to a horse, changing an intended attack upon us to a desperate plunge into the deep, and depriving the walrus of oxygen.

Finally, after a series of spasmodic encounters which lasted fifteen hours, the enraged snout turned blue, the fiery eyes blackened, and victory was ours – not as the result of the knife alone, not in a square fight of brute force, but by the superior cunning of the human animal under the stimulus of hunger.

During all this time we had been drifting. Now, as the battle ended, we were not far from a point about three miles south of our camp. Plenty of safe pack-ice was near. A primitive pulley was arranged by passing the line through slits in the walrus' nose and holes in the ice. The great carcass, weighing perhaps three thousand pounds, was drawn onto the ice and divided into portable pieces. Before the sun poured its morning beams over the ice, all had been securely taken ashore.

With ample blubber, a camp fire was now made between two rocks by using moss to serve as a wick. Soon, pot after pot of savory meat was voraciously consumed. We ate with a mad, vulgar, insatiable hunger. We spoke little. Between gulps, the huge heap of meat and blubber was cached under heavy rocks, and secured – so we thought, from bears, wolves and foxes.

When eating was no longer possible, sleeping dens were arranged in the little boat, and in it, like other gluttonous animals after an engorgement, we closed our eyes to a digestive sleep. For the time, at least, we had fathomed the depths of gastronomic content, and were at ease with ourselves and with a bitter world of inhuman strife.

At the end of about fifteen hours, a stir about our camp suddenly woke us. We saw a huge bear nosing about our fireplace. We had left there a walrus joint, weighing about one hundred pounds, for our next meal. We jumped up, all of us, at once, shouting and making a pretended rush. The bear took up the meat in his forepaws and walked off, manlike, on two legs, with a threatening grunt. His movement was slow and cautious, and his grip on the meat was secure. Occasionally he veered about, with a beckoning turn of the head, and a challenging call. But we did not accept the challenge. After moving away about three hundred yards on the sea-ice, he calmly sat down and devoured our prospective meal.

With lances, bows, arrows, and stones in hand, we next crossed a low hill, beyond which was located our precious cache of meat. Here, to our chagrin, we saw two other bears, with heads down and paws busily digging about the cache. We were not fitted for a hand-to-hand encounter. Still, our lives were equally at stake, whether we attacked or failed to attack. Some defense must be made. With a shout and a fiendish rush, we attracted the busy brutes' attention. They raised their heads, turned, and to our delight and relief, grudgingly walked off seaward on the moving ice. Each had a big piece of our meat with him.

Advancing to the cache, we found it absolutely depleted. Many other bears had been there. The snow and the sand was trampled down with innumerable bear tracks. Our splendid cache of the day previous was entirely lost. We could have wept with rage and disappointment. One thing we were made to realize, and that was that life here was now to be a struggle with the bears for supremacy. With little ammunition, we were not at all able to engage in bear fights. So, baffled, and unable to resent our robbery, starvation again confronting us, we packed our few belongings and moved westward over Braebugten Bay to Cape Sparbo.

10 The Flight from Mexico

BERNAL DIAZ DEL CASTILLO

The sixteenth century Spaniards who invaded Mexico, land of the Aztecs and their king Montezuma, were simultaneously explorers and conquerors. They went not only in search of gold but also as crusaders: they regarded the Aztec religion as horribly decadent, but their own deeds included massacre, torture, and forcible conversion to Christianity. In this passage, from a book written by a member of the 1519 expedition of Hernando Cortes, the invaders are in great danger and forced to retreat – though only for the time-being. Ironically, much of the treasure plundered from the Aztecs was in turn captured by a French privateer when it was being shipped across the Atlantic – and ended up in the coffers of the King of France.

When dawn broke we commended ourselves to God and sallied forth with strong timber towers which we had constructed, each capable of sheltering twenty-five men, and provided with apertures and loopholes which were to be manned by musketeers and crossbowmen. The cannon, muskets, and crossbows went ahead, and the horsemen made charges. But it was to no purpose. Although we killed many of them we could not drive them back. Bravely though they had fought on the previous two days, they were much more vigorous on this occasion and brought up even greater forces. Nevertheless we were determined, even at the cost of our lives, to advance with our towers as far as the great *cue* of Huichilobos.

I will not give a full account of the fighting in one fortified house, or tell how they wounded our horses, which were useless to us. For though they charged the enemy bands, they received so many arrows, darts, and stones that, well-armoured though they were, they could not break the enemy's ranks. If they caught up with any Mexicans, these warriors would quickly jump for safety into the canals or the lake, besides which they had raised fresh walls against the horsemen. There many other Indians were stationed with very long lances to finish them off. If our horses were useless, it was equally useless to turn aside and burn or demolish a house. For they all stood in the water with drawbridges between them. To swim across the gap was very dangerous, for they had so many rocks and stones on their fortified flat roofs that it meant certain destruction to attempt it. In addition to this, when we did set fire to some houses, a single one would take all day to burn, and one did not catch light from the other, because their roofs were flat and because of the water between. It was no good our risking our lives in this direction, therefore, so we made for the great *cue*.

Suddenly more than four thousand warriors ascended it, to reinforce the bands already posted there with long lances and stones and darts. Then all of them together took up a defensive position, and for a long time prevented our ascending the steps. Neither our towers, nor our cannon or crossbows, nor our muskets were of any avail; and although our horsemen tried to charge, the horses lost their foothold and fell down on the great slippery flagstones with which the whole courtyard was paved. While those on the steps of the *cue* prevented our advance, we had so many of the enemy also on both our flanks that although ten or fifteen of them might fall to one cannon-shot, and many others were killed by sword-thrusts and charges, the hosts against us were overwhelming. For a long time we could not ascend the *cue*, although we most persistently pressed home our attacks. We did not take the towers, for they were already destroyed, but in the end we reached the top.

Here Cortes showed himself the brave man he was! The battle was fierce and the fighting intense. It was a memorable sight to see us all streaming with blood and covered with wounds; and some of us were slain. It pleased Our Lord that we should reach the place where the image of Our Lady used to stand, but we did not find it there. It appears, as we afterwards learnt, that the great Montezuma paid devotion to it, and he had ordered it to be kept safe. We set fire to their idols, and a large part of the hall in which Huichilobos and Tezcatlipoca stood was burnt down. In all this we received great help from the Tlascalans. And when we reached the top, some of us fighting and some of us lighting the fire, the *papas* who belonged to that great *cue* were a sight to see! As we retired, however, four or five thousand Indians, every one a leading warrior, tumbled us down steps, six or ten at a time. Then there were some enemy bands posted on the battlements and in the embrasures of the *cue*, who shot so many darts and arrows at us that we could face neither one group of squadrons nor the other. So we resolved, with much toil and risk of our lives, to return to our quarters. Our towers had been destroyed, all of us were wounded, we had lost sixteen men, and the Indians constantly pressed on our flanks and rear. We captured two of their chief *papas* in this battle, whom Cortes told us to bring back with great care.

The Mexican bands continued to attack our quarters most obstinately and tenaciously all the time we were fighting outside. On our laborious return, indeed, we found as many of the enemy in the fortress as in the force that was pursuing us. They had already demolished some walls to force an entry, but they broke off their attacks when we arrived. Nevertheless during what remained of the day they never ceased to fire darts, stones, and arrows, and during the night they not only fired them but yelled also.

We spent the night dressing the wounded and burying the dead, preparing for going out to fight next day, strengthening and adding parapets to the walls they had pulled down and the breaches they had made, and discussing some method of fighting which would cost us less in dead and wounded. But much though we talked we found no remedy at all.

To return to our story, we came to the conclusion that we must ask for peace, in order that we might retire from Mexico. As soon as it was dawn many more bands of warriors arrived and very effectually surrounded our quarters on every side. The stones and arrows fell even thicker than before, the howls and whistles were even louder, and new bands endeavoured to force an entrance in new places. Cannon and musket were of no avail, though we did them plenty of damage.

In view of this situation, Cortes decided that the great Montezuma must speak to them from the roof and tell them that the attacks must cease, since we wished to leave the city. When they went to give this message to the prince, it is reported that he said in great grief: 'What more does Malinche want of me? Fate has brought me to such a pass because of him that I do not wish to live or hear his voice again.' He refused to come, and he is even reported to have said that he would not see Cortes again, or listen to any more of his false speeches, promises and lies. Then the Mercedarian friar and Cristobal de Olid went and talked to him most respectfully and tenderly, and Montezuma answered! 'I do not believe that I can do anything towards ending this war, because they have already chosen another lord, and made up their minds not to let you leave this place alive. I believe therefore that all of you will be killed.'

While the fighting continued, Montezuma was lifted to a battlement of the roof with many of us soldiers guarding him, and began to speak very lovingly to his people, telling them that if they stopped their attacks we would leave Mexico. Many of the Mexican chiefs and captains recognized him and ordered their people to be silent and shoot no more darts, stones, or arrows, and four of them, coming to a place where Montezuma could speak to them and they to him, addressed him in tears: 'Oh, lord, our great lord, we are indeed sorry for your misfortune and the disaster that has overtaken you and your family. But we must tell you that we have chosen a kinsman of yours as our new lord.' And they named Cuitlahuac, the lord of Iztapalapa – for it was not Guatemoc, who was lord soon after. They said moreover that the war must be carried on, and that they had promised their idols not to give up until we were all dead. They said they prayed every day to Huichilobos and Tezcatlipoca to keep him free and safe from our power, and that if things ended as they hoped, they would undoubtedly hold him in greater regard as their lord than they had done before. And they begged for his forgiveness.

Barely was this speech finished when a sudden shower of stones and darts descended. Our men who had been shielding Montezuma had momentarily neglected their duty when they saw the attack cease while he spoke to his chiefs. Montezuma was hit by three stones, one on the head, one on the arm, and one on the leg: and though they begged him to have his wounds dressed and eat some food and

spoke very kindly to him, he refused. Then quite unex-
pectedly we were told that he was dead.

Cortes and all of us captains and soldiers wept for him,
and there was no one among us that knew him and had
dealings with him who did not mourn him as if he were
our father, which was not surprising, since he was so good.
It was stated that he had reigned for seventeen years, and
was the best king they ever had in Mexico, and that he had
personally triumphed in three wars against countries he
had subjugated.

I have spoken of the sorrow we all felt when we saw that
Montezuma was dead. We even blamed the Mercedarian
friar for not having persuaded him to become a Christian,
but he excused himself by saying that he had not supposed
that Montezuma would die of these wounds, though he
deaden the pain. After much discussion Cortes ordered a
ought to have ordered them to give him something to
papa and a chief from among our prisoners to go to tell the
chief Cuitlahuac and his captains that the great Montezuma
was dead, and that they had seen him die, and of the
manner of his death and the wounds he had received from
his own people. They were to say how grieved we all were,
and that they must bury him like the great king that he
was, and raise his cousin who was with us to be king in
his place, since the inheritance was rightfully his; or else
one of his sons, for the prince they had chosen had no right
to the succession; and that they should negotiate a peace,
so that we could leave the city. Failing that, our messengers
were to say that we would sally out to fight them and burn
all their houses and do them great damage, since only our
respect for Montezuma had prevented us from destroying
their city, and he was now dead.

To convince them of Montezuma's death, Cortes ordered

six Mexicans, all important men, and the rest of the *papas* whom we held prisoner, to carry him out on their shoulders and hand him over to the Mexican captains, to whom they were to convey Montezuma's orders at the time of his death. For those who carried him out had been present at his deathbed, and they told Cuitlahuac the whole truth, that his own people had killed the prince with three stones.

When they saw Montezuma dead they wept, as we could see, very bitterly, and we clearly heard their shrieks and lamentations. But for all this their fierce attack did not cease; darts, stones and arrows continued to fly, and they came on again with greater force and fury, crying: 'Now you shall indeed pay for the death of our king and lord, and for your insults to our gods. As for the peace you ask for, come out here and we will settle the terms!'

They said much else that I cannot now remember, about how they had chosen a brave king, who could not be so faint-hearted as to be deceived by false speeches like their good Montezuma. As for his burial, we need not trouble about that, but about our own lives, for in two days not one of us would be left to send them any more messages. With these words came loud yells and whistles and showers of stones, darts and arrows; and other bands continued their attempts to set fire to our quarters in many places.

In face of all this, Cortes and the rest of us agreed that we would all come out of our camp next day and attack in another direction, where there were many houses on dry land. Then, doing them all the damage we could, we would make for the causeway. First, however, our horsemen would break through their bands, and spear them or drive them into the lake, even at the cost of losing the horses. This plan was made in the hope that the death and wounds we should inflict on them might make them abandon their attack, and arrange some sort of peace that would let us go free without more destruction. But though we all fought bravely next day and killed many of the enemy, and burnt some twenty houses and almost reached the mainland, it was all to no purpose because of the heavy casualties we suffered. We could not hold a single bridge, for they were all half broken down. Many Mexicans charged down on us, and they had set up walls and barricades in the places which they knew our horses could reach. Great though our trials had been before, we found much greater ones ahead of us.

But let us turn from the subject and repeat that we decided to get out of Mexico.

Now we saw our forces diminishing every day, and the Mexicans increasing in numbers. Many of our men had died, and all the rest were wounded. Though we fought most valiantly, we could not drive back the many bands which attacked us by night and day, or force them to a standstill. We became short of powder, and then of food and water. We had sent to ask them for a truce, and because of Montezuma's death they would not leave us in peace. In fact we stared death in the face, and the bridges had been raised. It was therefore decided by Cortes and all of us captains and soldiers that we should depart during the night, choosing the moment when their warriors were most careless. And to put them off their guard, on that very afternoon we sent one of their *papas* whom we had captured, a man of great importance among them, with some other prisoners, to propose that they should let us retire within eight days, leaving them all our gold. But this was only in order to distract their attention, so that we could get out that night.

In our company was a soldier called Botello, who seemed

a very decent man and knew Latin and had been in Rome. He was reputed, however, to be a sorcerer. Some said that he had a familiar spirit, others called him an astrologer. Now, four days before, this Botello had claimed to have learnt, by casting lots or by astrology, that if we did not leave Mexico on that particular night, but delayed our departure, not one of us would escape with his life. He had said also, on other occasions, that Cortes was to suffer many hardships and lose both position and honour, but that he would afterwards become a great lord, rich in wealth and reputation. He made other prophecies as well. But enough of Botello, whom I shall mention again later on.

An order was now given that a bridge should be made of very strong beams and planks. This we were to carry with us and use in the places where the bridges had been broken. Four hundred Tlascalans and a hundred and fifty soldiers were chosen to carry this bridge and place it in position, to guard the passage until the army and all the baggage had crossed. Two hundred Tlascalans and fifty soldiers were chosen to carry the cannon, and Gonzalo de Sandoval and Diego de Ordaz to lead the men and do the fighting, while a company of a hundred picked and valiant young soldiers under Francisco de Saucedo and Francisco de Lugo were to march in two equal companies and rush to any place where there was a heavy attack. Cortes himself, Alonso de Avila, Cristobal de Olid and other captains were to go in the middle, and Pedro de Alvarado and Juan Velazquez de Leon in the rear, behind two of Narvaez' captains and their soldiers. Finally the three hundred Tlascalans and thirty soldiers were ordered to guard the prisoners and Dona Marina and Dona Luisa. By the time these dispositions had been made it was already night, and the gold could be divided among those who were to carry it.

Cortes ordered Cristobal de Guzman his steward, and other soldiers who were his servants, to have all the gold and jewels and silver brought out. He gave them many Tlascalans to do the work, and it was all placed in the hall. Cortes then told the King's officials, Alonso de Avila and Gonzalo Mejia, to take charge of the royal portion. He gave them seven wounded and lame horses and one mare and more than eighty of our Tlascalan allies, and they loaded men and animals alike with as much as each could carry. It was, as I have said, made up in the hall. Then Cortes called his secretary, and others who were the King's notaries, and said: 'Bear witness for me that I can do no more with this gold. Here in this hall we have more than seven hundred thousand pesos' worth, and as you have seen, it cannot be weighed or brought to safety. I now give it over to any soldiers who care to take it. Otherwise we shall lose it to these dogs.'

On hearing this, many of Narvaez' men and some of ours loaded themselves with it. I had no desire, I assure you, but to save my life. Nevertheless I picked up four *chalchihuites* from the little boxes in which they lay, and quickly stowed them in my bosom, under my armour. The price of them afterwards served to cure my wounds and buy me food.

As soon as we knew Cortes' plan that we should escape during the night, we prepared to move towards the bridges. Since it was rather dark and there was some mist and drizzle, we began before midnight to transport the bridge and the baggage; and the horses, the mare and the Tlascalans who were carrying the gold started on their way. The bridge was quickly put in place, and Cortes crossed over with those of the leading detachment and many of the horses. While this was happening the shouts and cries and whistles of the Mexicans rang out, and they called in their language to the people of Tlatelolco: 'Bring out your canoes at once. The *Teules* are departing. You must cut them off, so that not one remains alive.' Then all of a sudden we saw many bands of warriors descending on us, and the whole lake so thick with canoes that we could not defend ourselves, since many of our men had already crossed the bridge. While we were in this position, a great crowd of Mexicans charged down on us to remove the bridge and kill and wound our men, who could not help one another. And since misfortune is cruel at such times, one disaster followed another. Because of the rain two of the horses slipped and fell in the lake. Just as we saw this, I and some others of Cortes' detachment struggled to the other side of the bridge, but we were borne down on by so many warriors that, hard though we fought, no further use could be made of it. The channel, or water-gap, was soon filled up with dead horses, Indians of both sexes, servants, bundles and boxes.

Fearing that we should inevitably be killed, we pushed ahead along the causeway, where we found many bands with long spears awaiting us. They shouted abuse at us. 'Villians,' they cried, 'are you still alive?' Although six of my companions were wounded, we cut and hacked our way through. They seemed to have concocted some accursed plan, just as we had. For though Cortes and the captains and soldiers who rode first spurred along the causeway, and did not fail to reach dry land and save their lives, and the horses with the gold and the Tlascalans reached safety also, I declare that if the horsemen had waited for the soldiers at each bridge, it would have been the end of us all: not one of us would have survived. For as we passed along the causeway, charging the Mexican bands, the water was on one side of us and flat roofs on the other, and the lake was full of canoes. There was nothing we could do. Moreover all the muskets and crossbows had been left behind at the bridge, and it was night. What more could we have attempted than we did, which was to charge and deal sword-thrusts at those who tried to seize us, and push ahead till we were off the causeway?

Had it been day-time things would have been even worse. Those of us who escaped only did so by the grace of God. It must be terrifying merely to read of the hosts of warriors who descended on us that night, and the canoes that bore down to seize our soldiers. As we advanced along the causeway towards the town of Tacuba, which Cortes had already reached with Gonzalo de Sandoval, Cristobal de Olid and the other horsemen who had gone ahead, there were cries of: 'My lord Captain, let us halt here. They say that we are running away and leaving them to die at the bridges. Let us go back and help them, if any of them survive and cannot get away.' But Cortes replied that it was a miracle that any of us had escaped. He turned back, however, with the horsemen and those soldiers who were unwounded. But they did not go far, for Pedro de Alvarado soon met them, badly wounded, on foot and with a spear in his hand, since they had killed his sorrel mare. With him he brought four soldiers as badly wounded as himself and eight Tlascalans, all of them pouring from many wounds.

While Cortes was on the causeway with the other captains, we took refuge in the square at Tacuba. Many bands had already reached there from Mexico and were shouting orders to the people of that town and another called Atzopotzalco. Then they began to hurl darts, stones and arrows at us, and to attack us with their long lances. We engaged them several times, attacking them and defending ourselves.

To return to Pedro de Alvarado. When Cortes and the other captains met him and saw that no more soldiers were coming down the causeway, tears sprang to their eyes. Pedro de Alvarado told them that Juan Velasquez de Leon lay dead at a bridge, with many other gentlemen both of Narvaez' company and our own, more than eighty in all. He said that he and the four soldiers had crossed the bridge in great peril after their horses had been killed, treading on the dead men, horses and boxes with which the approach to it was choked. He said also that all the bridges and causeways were crowded with warriors. That unhappy bridge was afterwards called Alvarado's Leap. But no soldier stopped at the time, I assure you, to see whether his leap was long or short. We had enough to do to save our lives, for so many Mexicans were charging down on us that we were in great danger of death.

While we remained in Tacuba, many Mexican warriors from the lakeside towns gathered and killed three of our soldiers. So we decided to leave the place as quickly as possible, and five Tlascalans, who found a path to Tlascala without following the road, guided us with great precautions until we reached some small houses built on a hill, and beside them a fortress-like *cue* that was their shrine. Here we halted.

During our retreat we were followed by the Mexicans, who hurled arrows and darts at us, and stones from their slings. The way they surrounded us and continually attacked us was most terrifying. I have already said this many times, and am tired of repeating myself, but my readers must not think me prolix, for each time they attacked and wounded us I am forced to speak of it again.

Let us tell how we defended ourselves. We took refuge in that fortified *cue* and attended to our wounded, and made many fires, but there was not so much as a morsel to eat. Later on, after the great city of Mexico was finally captured, we built a church on the site of that *cue*, which is called Nuestra Senora de los Remedios, and is now much visited. Many citizens and ladies of Mexico go there on pilgrimages, and to make *novenas*.

Let me now say that it was pitiable to see our wounds dressed and bandaged with cotton cloths, for being both chilled and swollen they were very painful. But more deplorable was the loss of the gentlemen and brave soldiers who were missing, namely Juan Velasquez de Leon, Francisco de Saucedo, Francisco de Morla, Lares 'the good rider' and many others of Cortes' followers. I mention these few only, since it would be a long business to write down the names of our many missing comrades. Of Narvaez' company, the majority fell at the bridge, weighed down with gold.

I will now speak of Botello the astrologer. His astrology did not help him, for he too died there with his horse. But let me go on to say that after we got to safety some papers, bound together like a book, were found in his box, marked with figures, lines, notes and symbols: and beside them were the words: 'Whether I shall die in this wretched war, murdered by the Indians.' And further on there were other lines and figures, beside which it said: 'You will die.' But beside others it said: 'You will not die.' In another place were the words. 'Whether they will kill my horse,' and a little further on it said: 'They will kill him.' There were other figures in these papers, apparently for fortune-telling, and other pairs of contradictory statements. Also in the box was an object four inches long and made of leather, in the shape of a man's genitals. The resemblance was remarkable, and it was stuffed with flock.

Among those who perished at the bridge were the sons and daughter of Montezuma, the prisoners we were bringing with us, and Cacamatzin, lord of Texcoco, also some other provincial rulers. But enough of our disasters. We were thinking of the prospect before us. We were all wounded, only twenty-three horses survived, we had saved no muskets, cannon, or powder, and had very few crossbows. These we promptly mended with cord, however, and we made new arrows. But the worst thing of all was that we did not know in what state of mind we should find our Tlascalan allies. Moreover, once darkness fell we were continually surrounded by shouting Mexicans who fell on us with their darts, arrows and slings. So we decided to leave the place at midnight, with the Tlascalans as guides, and taking every precaution. We then placed the wounded in the middle and provided the lame with staffs; and those who were very ill and could not walk went on the croups of such horses as were lame and unfit for fighting. Those horsemen who were not wounded went ahead, or in bands on one flank or the other. The wounded Tlascalans walked in the middle of our squadron, and the rest of them who were unwounded faced the enemy with us.

The Mexicans continually harassed us with loud shouts and cries and whistlings. 'You are going to a place where you will perish to a man,' they shouted. Not one of us, they shouted would remain alive that day. They would sacrifice our hearts and blood to their gods, and with our legs and arms they would have enough to glut themselves at their feasts. They would throw our bodies for the tigers, lions, vipers and serpents to gorge on; and for that reason orders had been given that for the last two days the beasts in their cages should be given no food. As for the gold we had, we would get little pleasure from that, or from all our cloth;

and as for the Tlascalans who were with us, they would put them into cages to fatten, so that their bodies could be offered one by one as sacrifices.

To continue the story of our march, that day we reached some farms and isolated houses belonging to a large town named Cuauhtitlan (after the capture of Mexico these were awarded to Alonso de Avila), and though the Mexicans yelled and shouted at us, hurling stones, darts and arrows, we withstood it all. From there we went past some houses and shacks with the Mexicans still following us, and, as many of them had now collected, they endeavoured to slaughter us. Beginning to surround us, they hurled stones from their slings and darts and arrows; and at a difficult pass they attacked us with their broad-swords, killing two of our soldiers and one horse, and wounding almost all the rest. But with cut and thrust we killed several of them, and our horsemen accounted for several more. Having slept in these houses and eaten the horse they killed, we resumed our march early next morning, sending half the horsemen ahead. But when we reached a plain about three miles further on and were beginning to think we could march on in safety, our scouts rode back from the country they had reconnoitred to tell us that the fields were full of Mexican warriors who were lying in wait for us. Alarmed though we were by this news, we were not dismayed. Ready to meet them and fight them to death, we halted for a little, while orders were given to the cavalry that they must charge and return rapidly, aiming at the enemies' faces until they had broken their ranks, and to us soldiers that we must drive our swords into their bellies and so most thoroughly avenge our dead and wounded comrades. Then, if God willed it, we should escape with our lives.

We saw them beginning to surround us. Our horsemen,

charging in bands of five, broke their ranks. And then, commending ourselves most heartily to God and the Blessed Mary, and calling on the name of our patron St. James, we charged them, all together.

It was a destructive battle, and a fearful sight to behold. We moved through the midst of them at the closest quarters, slashing and thrusting at them with our swords. And the dogs fought back furiously, dealing us wounds and death with their lances and their two-handed swords. And, the field being level, our horsemen speared them at their pleasure, charging and retiring and charging again. Although both they and their horses were wounded, they never stopped fighting, like the brave men they were. As for the rest of us who had no horses, we seemed all to be given double strength. For although we were wounded and now received fresh wounds, we did not stop to bind them up, for there was no time, but most courageously closed with the enemy, to stab them with our swords. I should like to describe the actions of Cortes, Cristobal de Olid, Gonzalo de Sandoval, Gonzalo Dominguez and a certain Juan de Salamanca, who rode from one part of the field to the other breaking the enemy's ranks, although themselves badly wounded, and to record Cortes' instructions to us who were in the thick of the enemy that we must aim our cuts and thrusts at distinguished chieftains, who all wore great golden plumes and rich armour and devices.

We were marvellously encouraged also by the brave and bold Sandol, who cried: 'Today, gentlemen, is the day on which we are certain to win. Trust in God, and we shall come out of this alive, and to some purpose!' I must say once more that they killed and wounded many of our soldiers.

Now by God's grace, Cortes and the captains who rode

with him came to the place where the commander-in-chief of the Mexicans marched with his banner displayed, in rich golden armour and high silver plumes, followed by his great band of warriors. And when Cortes saw him and other Mexican chieftains, all with high plumes, he said to his captains: 'Now gentlemen, let us cut our way through them, and leave none of them without a wound!' Then, commending themselves to God, our horsemen charged, and Cortes, riding straight for the Mexican commander, made him drop his banner, while the other captains succeeded in breaking the large bands of Indians who followed him. Cortes' charge had not thrown the Mexican down, but Juan de Salamanca, who rode beside our captain on a piebald mare, dealt him a lance-thrust and snatched his rich plume. This he afterwards gave to Cortes, saying that it was his by right, since he had charged him first and made him drop his banner, thus depriving his followers of the courage to fight. However, three years afterwards His Majesty gave it to Salamanca as his coat of arms, and his descendants carry it on their saddle-cloths.

Let us return to the battle. When the Mexican commander and many other chiefs had been killed, it pleased the Lord that their attack should slacken. Then all our horsemen followed them, and we felt neither hunger nor thirst. It was as if we had suffered no disaster and undergone no hardships; we followed up our victory, dealing death and wounds, and our allies the Tlascalans became like very lions. With their swords, their two-handed blades and other weapons which they had just captured, they fought most valiantly and well.

When our horsemen returned from following up our victory, we all gave great thanks to God for our escape from this mighty host. For never had there been seen throughout the Indies so many warriors assembled for any battle. All the flower of Mexico, of Texcoco, of all the towns around the lake, and of many others in the neighbourhood, was present, and the men of Otumba, Tepetezcuco and Saltocan, who all came in the belief that this time we should be totally destroyed. Their armour moreover was extremely rich, and decorated with much gold and many plumes and devices, and nearly all of them were chieftains or important persons. Near the spot where this famous and sternly contested battle was fought – for indeed it can be so described, since only by God's grace did we escape with our lives – stood the town of Otumba.

Interested readers will remember that when we went to the relief of Pedro de Alvarado in Mexico, we numbered in all thirteen hundred soldiers, including ninety-seven horsemen, eighty crossbowmen and as many musketeers. In addition we had more than two thousand Tlascalans and we brought in many cannon. Now the day of our entry into Mexico was Midsummer Day 1520, and we escaped on 10 July of the same year; the battle of Otumba, as it was called, being fought on 14 July. But now, within a matter of days, in the battle of Mexico and on the bridges and causeways, and all the engagements, including that of Otumba and those on the road, more than eight hundred and sixty soldiers were killed and sacrificed, and seventy-two more, together with five Spanish women – all belonging to Narvaez' company – at the town of Tuztepec, also a thousand Tlascalans. And if we come to consider it, none of us had much luck with his share of the gold we received, for if more of Narvaez' men than those of Cortes' fell at the bridges it was because they were so weighed down by the stuff that they could neither run nor swim.

We marched along very cheerfully towards Tlascala,

eating some gourds that they call *ayotes*, and the Mexican bands did not dare to collect and attack us from the small towns, although they still shouted at us from places where we could not get at them, and hurled stones, darts and arrows at us, until we took refuge first in some farm buildings and then in a small town, where there was a good *cue* and a strong house in which we could spend the night. Here we dressed our wounds and got some rest. We were still followed by Mexican bands, however. But they dared not draw close, and those who came nearest seemed to say: 'There you go, out of our country!' From this small town where we rested we could see the hills above Tlascala, and the sight was as welcome to our eyes as if we had seen home. But how could we be sure that the Tlascalans would be loyal to us? What did we know of their attitude, or of the fate of the settlers at Villa Rica, whether they were alive or dead? Cortes said to us that although we were so few, only four hundred and forty of us surviving, with twenty horses, twelve crossbowmen, and seven musketeers – almost the same number as had followed him into Mexico in the first place – and though we had no powder and were all wounded, lamed and maimed, we could clearly see that it had been Jesus Christ's pleasure to spare our lives, and that we must always give Him great thanks and honour.

11 Andrée's Folly

ROBERT DE LA CROIX

Nowadays aircraft over the North Pole – or submarines under it, for that matter – are taken for granted. But as long ago as 1896, a Swedish scientist, Salomon August Andrée, tried to reach it by balloon. In company with Nils Strindberg and Knut Fraenkel, he set off in the Eagle *from Spitzbergen on what seemed a crazy adventure. But Andrée was no fool; he was a courageous visionary, a generation ahead of his time in being so air-minded. His expedition ended in tragedy: the* Eagle *crash-landed on the ice and Andrée and his companions began a hopeless march in search of food-caches two hundred miles away in Franz Josef Land. Inevitably they perished, but the same ice that killed them also preserved them and, by a freak chance, their bodies and journals were discovered thirty-three years later.*

Andrée's idea was to get to the North Pole within a few days, two days if he was lucky. Yet it was only after twenty years of preparation and reconnaissance – and many setbacks – that the American polar explorer Commander Robert Peary succeeded in reaching the Pole. After an unsuccessful attempt the previous year, he finally reached the Pole by sled accompanied by a few Eskimos on April 6, 1909.

'That's a wonderful present', observed President Taft when he received Peary's telegram announcing his success, 'but what can I do with it?' Public opinion had come to regard the feat as impossible – worse still, useless. But now that it had been done, Peary's triumph was greeted with acclaim as a magnificent exploit, a sporting achievement, if without much practical value. And that had been very much President Taft's first reaction.

Only the polar explorers themselves knew how much it had really cost. Many men and many expeditions had contributed to Peary's final success, and the way to the Pole was dotted with the bodies of men who had died in the attempt. Their frozen corpses were being carried along endlessly by the polar drift, their graves were unknown, their fate a matter of gloomy speculation. And such thoughts led once again to perhaps the most mysterious affair of all: the disappearance of Andrée, Strindberg, Fraenkel and their balloon.

Nothing further had been heard of them since that day in 1896 when the seamen of the Swedish warship *Svenskund* had cut the moorings of the balloon and cheered the aeronauts on their way. The names of Andrée and his companions were occasionally mentioned in geographical and other scientific journals, and in connection with Peary's triumph they were mentioned once again. On foot and with sleds and dogs was obviously the only way to reach the Pole. The idea of flying over it was clearly Utopian and condemned to failure, perhaps tragedy, from the start.

Silence fell again around the three names.

But one man sometimes thought of Andrée and his venture and that was Roald Amundsen, the man who had first sailed through the North-West Passage that Franklin and M'Clure had discovered between them. Amundsen had planned to be the first to reach the North Pole, but Peary forestalled him. He then turned his attention to the South Pole and two years later, in 1911, he succeeded in reaching it – six weeks before Captain Scott and his ill-fated Antarctic Expedition.

The polar regions were now no longer unknown, but the price of penetrating into them to the poles was a terrible one. Peary had reached the North Pole and Amundsen had reached the South Pole, but behind them both were the frozen bodies of many gallant men who had been less fortunate. Perhaps the method of sleds and dogs was not the best after all? The rigours of such an expedition were arduous, the preparations great and the time required so long that the achievement must always remain isolated and exceptional. Perhaps Andrée was right after all? Perhaps the only practicable and easy route to the Pole was by air, and in that case Andrée was not an impetuous crank, but a pioneer ahead of his time?

Many years passed and in the meantime the world experienced a still greater tragedy, the First World War. Then in 1926, as a few Swedes who still remembered the fate of their unfortunate countrymen held a memorial meeting on the twenty-ninth anniversary of Andrée's take-off, the shadow of a dirigible passed over the North Pole. It was the *Norge*, and from its gondola three pieces of bunting fluttered slowly down on to the ice, the flags of the United States, Norway and Italy. In the gondola were Ellsworth the American, Amundsen the Norwegian and Nobile the Italian.

The *Norge* reached the Pole in seventy-one hours. Its voyage was a difficult one, but it was successful and the airship suffered no serious damage. After circling the Pole twice it flew across the as yet unexplored Arctic Basin to Point Barrow in Alaska and finally landed safely on May 14 at Teller on the Bering Sea.

Only a few hours previously, on May 9, Commander Richard Byrd, another American explorer, had flown from Spitzbergen accompanied by co-pilot Floyd Bennet in the hydroplane *Josephine Ford*. They reached the North Pole at nine o'clock in the morning, circled it several times and then returned safely to their base. This was a simple to and fro hop which took only sixteen hours. The flight of the *Norge*, a semi-rigid dirigible built in Italy, was the first real aerial exploration of the Arctic regions. Above all it had demonstrated that to reach the North Pole need no longer be an isolated and exceptional exploit, but could be repeated indefinitely. In the not too distant future it would be a timetable affair of everyday occurrence.

In July 1930, the polar explorer, Theodor Grodhal, set off – without much hope incidentally – to look for the remains of the airship *Italia* which had disappeared two years previously with a part of its crew.* He landed on White Island, a small barren hump of land, usually covered with ice, in the Spitzbergen group. Finding nothing of any interest there beyond a few ancient tins scattered around in the snow he left again.

A few weeks later, in August, a ship, taking advantage of ice-free water, anchored at White Island. It was the *Bratvag* carrying members of the scientific mission sent out by the Norwegian Society for Polar Exploration under the leadership of Dr. Gunnar Horn to Franz Josef Land, now known as Fritjof Nansen Land, after the great polar explorer.

That summer the weather was exceptionally warm, and the ice with which White Island was normally completely covered had melted in places. Large patches of earth were visible and yellow flowers were showing here and there amidst the sombre green of moss and lichen.

Sailors and seal-hunters went ashore from the *Bratvag*.

* In the original rescue-search for the *Italia*, Amundsen himself had lost his life.

The weather was extraordinarily warm, and two of the men, Olav Salen and Karl Tusvik, felt so very thirsty they searched around for fresh water, and, seeing a small stream in the distance, they made their way towards it. Suddenly they noticed something shining in the sun, and going to investigate they discovered that it was the aluminium lid of a cooking-pot. They looked at each other in astonishment. How on earth had such a thing got on to this uninhabited island? Neither could think of any explanation, but their interest was aroused and they now looked around more carefully. Salen was the first to spot a black object in the distance, and he drew his companion's attention to it.

'Good Lord, it looks like a boat!' exclaimed Tusvik.

It proved to be a canvas boat, containing a variety of objects: kitchen utensils, tins of food, oars and navigational instruments embedded in slush. Greatly excited now the two fetched Captain Eliassen of the *Bratvag* to see their find. The captain was soon infected by their excitement, and he began to examine the contents of the boat in detail. They offered very little clue to their origin until he found a canvas bag, which he examined carefully, trying to decipher the lettering on the worn material. Then abruptly he took it back with him to where the *Bratvag* lay at anchor in the calm sea to show it to the members of the polar mission.

'What's the matter, captain?' demanded Gunnar Horn.

'I think we've come across something very interesting,' the captain replied. 'Take a look at this,' and he handed Gunnar Horn the canvas bag.

On it, just decipherable, were the words 'Andrée's Polar Expedition 1896'.

'It looks as though we had accidentally come across Andrée's last camp,' said the captain.

Gunnar Horn went ashore and hurried eagerly towards the spot where the boat had been found. There he carefully removed object after object from the slushy mass of wet snow in the boat. They found two rifles, an anometer, a sailor's holdall, more kitchen utensils . . .

Then suddenly Gunnar Horn straightened himself. He was very pale. He had found a body under the half-melted ice and snow. It was the corpse of a man, and the bare knees showed through torn trousers. Assisted by Captain Eliassen he carefully freed it from the snow and together they lifted it out of the boat.

'Look!' exclaimed Horn. 'There's an initial on this jacket. It's an A! No doubt about it; it's an A! Eliassen, we've found Andrée's body.'

They continued the search. About twenty yards away they found what proved to be a tomb built in Eskimo fashion. A body had been laid on the ground and covered with a cairn of stones. This corpse was covered with an overcoat on which an S was just distinguishable. It was the tomb of young Strindberg.

The search went on. More tins of food were found and an oil stove. Horn tried to light it. He succeeded and a blue flame burned distinctly, thirty-three years after that stove had last been lit.

An hour later a boat pulled towards *Bratvag* and was hoisted aboard by the davits. It contained the bodies of Andrée and his companion Strindberg. The mystery surrounding their end had at last been solved.

At first Horn was uncertain of what he ought to do. Should he proceed on the voyage or return to Norway at once? Finally he decided to continue the mission he had been entrusted to carry out. After all, what did it matter if the world waited another month or so before learning of their find? The *Bratvag* therefore hoisted anchor and went on its way. It had only low-powered wireless apparatus of very limited range and it was not until the *Terningen* of Tromsö met her at Franz Josef Land and returned to Europe first that the world learned the news.

'Yes, I saw Andrée's body perfectly preserved in the ice,' declared the captain of the *Terningen*. 'And Gunnar Horn told me that he had made highly interesting discoveries.'

This information naturally caused something of a sensation in Sweden, and the authorities were astonished that Horn had not returned at once instead of carrying the bodies of Andrée and Strindberg off with him. By wireless he was immediately instructed to make as soon as possible for Tromsö where he would find the *Michael Sars* waiting to take official possession of the remains of the two polar explorers.

When the *Bratvag* received this message Horn was a little astonished at its peremptory tone. What was the matter with them? Did they think he was trying to keep all the credit for the find to himself? After all, he had carried on in good faith, believing that to be his primary duty. Now, of course, he must obviously obey these new instructions.

On September 2 the *Bratvag* arrived in Tromsö harbour, and the well-meaning and conscientious Gunnar Horn found himself the object of lively reproaches.

'What about Fraenkel's body? And what did you do with the canvas boat and the things you found in it? Why didn't you search carefully for Andrée's log-book or some record of his flight? Are you quite certain there's nothing more to be found on the island? It may be years before such a warm summer occurs again, and in the meantime the ice will close in and rob us of all chance of finding anything, perhaps for ever, and we may never know exactly what happened to Andrée's balloon.'

Horn replied that he had not been instructed to do anything of the sort, and that he had therefore carried out the instructions he had been given. Anything further was a matter for the government.

In the meantime others had taken action without waiting for the government. A powerful sealer, the *Isbjörn*, was chartered by two newspapers, and a party of journalists, led by Knut Stubbendorf, set off for White Island with instructions to go through the place with a fine toothcomb and bring back everything to be found at Andrée's camp, and, in particular, to move heaven and earth to find his diary or log-book or any written account of his adventure.

At first Stubbendorf and his party found nothing of any importance: just instruments, cartridges and so on, so he began to search farther afield. As he found nothing elsewhere he decided that Fraenkel had probably died together with Andrée, and so the search was resumed at the spot where the other two bodies had been found. His theory was correct, and before long the body of Fraenkel was also found.

But Stubbendorf found something still more important – a notebook with pages stuck together and damaged by water, containing observations made by Andrée during his disastrous voyage. Stubbendorf had every reason to be satisfied with himself. The experts would certainly be able to decipher what Andrée had written, and then the mystery surrounding the fate of the balloon and its crew which had defied the curiosity of the world for thirty-three years would be solved at last.

Stubbendorf had found something else, and he was guarding it jealously. It was a black box: Andrée's camera – intact! Who knew what it might not reveal? If it contained exposed plates – and there was every reason to suppose that it would – then, with a bit of luck, they could still be developed. The pictures taken by the dead explorer shortly before his end might still see the light.

While Stubbendorf's search was proceeding, a first-class scandal had blown up in Sweden. Gunnar Horn's strange behaviour had given rise to all sorts of speculations. People were irritated. They suspected a journalistic trick, and voices were soon raised denouncing the whole affair as a put-up job and a disgraceful scandal. 'What proof is there that the alleged bodies really are those of Andrée and Strindberg?' they asked. 'And there were three explorers, not two. It's a publicity swindle, nothing more.'

Poor Gunnar Horn was the centre of the storm. His story was derided and those who had believed him were ridiculed. The contradictory accounts which had been circulating for months had made people suspicious and unwilling to believe anything. The icy phantom of Andrée rising suddenly from the Arctic wastes after thirty-three years too closely resembled an imaginative thriller to be credible. Obviously, the two bodies were those of unfortunate seal-hunters who had perished there.

Then suddenly the polemic was cut short by a long and detailed wireless message from Stubbendorf on board the *Ibsjörn*. The evidence he provided established the identity of the bodies beyond all question; and now the body of Fraenkel had also been found. One of Stubbendorf's finds was a letter written to Strindberg and found on his body. It was from his brother Tore, now grown up and a member of the Tromsö meteorological service.

On September 16 Stubbendorf arrived on board the *Ibsjörn* and presented his valuable discoveries to the authorities and the general public: there was Andrée's notebook, the log-book of the *Oern* (*Eagle*), various other documents, and – photographs!

A voice from the tomb now took up the long silenced story, and for the first time the world heard the details of the strangest of all polar tragedies.

On July 11, 1897, Andrée's balloon had passed over Dutch Point, the extreme northern point of Danes Island, about ten minutes after its take-off, when even then it had looked as if the balloon would be wrecked on the hillside. As the crew of the *Svenskund* watched in dismay, it just skimmed the top and grew smaller and smaller until it finally disappeared against the blue sky.

Though they did not realize it, Andrée and his companions had already passed into legend.

Now below them lay Vogelsang Island, flat and sombre. It was here that Strindberg dropped a brass tube containing his last letter. It was addressed to his fiancée. After that a mist gathered and the aeronauts could see nothing. At five o'clock in the afternoon there was a break in the mist, and they looked back to see if they could catch a glimpse of the land they had left behind. There was nothing to be seen but the grey sea, hidden from their view here and there by motionless banks of heavy mist. Civilization was now behind them; ahead of them was the unknown. From now on they were alone, completely dependent on their own devices, without hope of aid. This moment when they realized that they were out of sight of land was the real beginning of their adventure.

They were flying at a height of about 1,600 feet. The

only sign of life was a gull winging away below them. Half an hour later the *Oern* began to lose height until they were only about eight hundred feet above the water. The thing that impressed all three of them, even more than their loneliness, was the enormous silence, and they therefore welcomed the least sound that came to their ears: the hissing of the balloon valve, the cry of a sea bird and the occasional sound of the sea rising up to them. They began to talk to each other, raising their voices as though the conversation of civilized men was a link with the world they had left behind them.

To keep their minds occupied they concentrated on their observations and they were careful to limit the entries in the log to figures and facts, and, in particular, the record of their course.

It was absolutely necessary that they should travel northwards, that being the essential condition of rapid success. Unfortunately at first the balloon began to sail definitely westward, but then, to their relief, it gradually turned northward. Their joy, however, was short-lived. The northward course was not maintained, and when Andrée asked Strindberg to prepare their first meal the wind was blowing the balloon off its course towards the north-east.

Strindberg prepared soup, macaroni and sandwiches, and they ate with a good appetite. By this time they were beginning to get accustomed to their surroundings though their nerves were still taut. The unknown affected them eerily, and their reactions were primitive and rather child-like.

'We are gliding along so lightly and mysteriously,' wrote Strindberg, 'that we find it difficult not to hold our breath for fear of upsetting the equilibrium of our featherlight balloon.'

To their right a long stretch of grey land appeared. It

was North-East Land and their course was mainly northward as they desired, but at two o'clock in the morning
when Andrée awoke to take his watch he was informed
by Fraenkel that the balloon had veered round and was
sailing back the way it had come!

Andrée refused himself to be unduly disturbed.

'It's nothing to worry about,' he said confidently. 'Such
changes, of course, are due to local winds.'

But there was something which was not so easy to shrug
off: the balloon was steadily losing height. Mist and humidity, the two dangers against which they were able to do
nothing, now threatened them. They dared not think what
a forced landing on the drift ice below them would mean.
They were many days distant from inhabited land or food
depots. No help could be expected and there would be
nowhere for them to winter.

It was twenty-four hours since the *Oern* had taken off
from Danes Island. Carrier pigeons had been released at
intervals with short messages recording their position, the
temperature and the course being flown, all ending with
the ritual observation: 'All goes well on board.'

That was true enough at the time the messages were
written, but now the slowness of their progress, their lack
of adequate height, their position and the wind direction
combined to suggest that before long things would be going
very far from well.

They were flying through miserable weather, half-mist,
half-drizzle, which was not unexpected. It was well known
to polar explorers for its depressing effect on the spirits.
The world was grey in grey, the sky above them and the
ice below were dull and toneless. The only colour they saw
was a sudden patch of brilliant red on the ice below, no
doubt the blood of some bear's victim.

At three o'clock in the afternoon on July 12 Andrée, Strindberg and Fraenkel, now very anxious men, felt a series of bumps that heralded the coming disaster. The gondola was bumping and scraping along the ice.

Hurriedly they pitched sacks of ballast overboard and as this had no effect, they cast off most of the remaining guide ropes, and for a moment or two this seemed to be effective. The *Oern* rose once more, but soon began to lose height again. This up-and-down movement was both exhausting and dangerous, for at any moment the gondola could crash for good on the treacherous ice. By some means the balloon had to be lightened: it was a matter of life and death. Desperately Andrée looked around for something weighty to cast overboard.

Cases of food? Boxes of cartridges? Their sledge? To abandon any of them would be madness. What then? There was the great buoy which was to be dropped over the Pole, as a symbol of their triumph. That could go; it was useless to them now. A moment or two later the aeronauts heard the heavy cracking thud as it crashed to the ice. It was a symbolical act. Andrée felt as though his own dreams had been destroyed.

'We have had to throw a good deal of ballast overboard today', he noted in his diary. 'The constant bumps have made it quite impossible for us to take food or rest. It can't go on much longer like this. All three of us desperately need sleep. At 11.30 I ordered Strindberg and Fraenkel to turn in. I shall let them rest if possible until six or seven in the morning. I hope to keep awake that long myself. After that I will try to get a little sleep. I wonder if they have been taxed too much. What would happen if one of them died?'

For the first time Andrée let himself give way to depression – and not without good cause.

When the balloon finally rose again one of the remaining guide ropes caught round a block of ice and held them. The balloon floated motionless, heavy, soaked and dripping with water.

Andrée was alone now, alone with his ambitions.

'How strange it is to sail like this over the polar night', he wrote. 'To be the first men to fly over these unknown and unexplored regions. How long will it be before other men follow in our path? Or shall we be looked upon as fools whose example is not to be followed? I cannot conceal the fact that we are filled with pride, all three of us. It is quite clear that we are risking our lives, that we may never return. But if we die it will be in doing what we set out to do.

'I ask myself whether what we feel now has its source perhaps in a feeling of exalted individualism which makes us unwilling to be a mere link in an ordinary chain, unconsidered by present and future generations. Perhaps this is what people call ambition. The dragging of our remaining guide ropes through the snow, the flapping of the sails and the soughing of the wind in the wickerwork are the only sounds that break the silence.'

At dawn on July 13 the *Oern* was still held fast. As it happened this was not a bad thing at all because the wind was now blowing steadily from the north-west, and if the balloon had been free it would have sailed back towards its point of departure – to failure. But also to life and an opportunity to try again. The destiny of the aeronauts was in the balance.

Andrée was well aware of this, and he hesitated. Should he cut the guide rope and release the balloon? To do so would be to surrender all possibility of directing it. He decided that they would have to wait with as much patience as they could muster until the balloon freed itself.

In the morning the mist cleared to some extent and large patches of blue were visible in the sky. Then the sun came out at last. Andrée checked the tension of the guide rope anxiously. Suddenly it relaxed, the balloon changed position and then, almost imperceptibly, it broke free. It had been held fast for more than thirteen hours.

The aeronauts celebrated their liberty with a good meal: soup, chateaubriand, chocolate, biscuits, raspberry juice and bottled beer. Their joy did not last long. After a while the up-and-down nightmare began once more and three hours later the *Oern* was again scraping and bumping along the ice.

Made desperate, Andrée began to pitch other articles overboard besides ballast, including even food – a really despairing choice. For the moment it had some effect once more. The *Oern* began to rise again. It even rose freely, and under sail it attained quite a high speed. From the depths Andrée too rose to the heights. He was optimistic and enthusiastic again.

'This is splendid!' he exclaimed, and his satisfaction was increased by Strindberg's calculation that they had penetrated northward to the extent of a degree and a half of latitude. It was the last satisfaction Andrée was to experience, for hardly had they had time to congratulate themselves when the mist began to gather again, spongy and threatening. Andrée knew what that meant. Before long the dragging, scraping and bumping over the ice would begin again.

Occasionally the *Oern* seemed to pause almost like an animal out of breath and forced to rest, and all around there was dead silence and not the slightest sign of any life.

'We are experiencing shock after shock', recorded Andrée. In the end he realized that there was no further chance for them in the balloon and they began to keep their eyes open for a suitable place at which to descend to the ice. At eight o'clock in the morning of July 14 they scrambled out of the gondola and jumped to the ground. To the ground? To the ice which spread away endlessly in all directions. Their flight had lasted 66 hours and 14 minutes. If Andrée's calculations had proved correct, and if good luck had been with them, they would have reached the Pole twenty hours before and would now have been well on their way to Alaska on the return journey. Instead they were still about five hundred miles away from the Pole.

But as they stood by the *Oern*, whose half-distended envelope stretched over the ice like the body of a dying animal, they realized only too well that the North Pole no longer mattered. What did matter was the fact that they were something like two hundred miles from the food depots in North-East Land and Franz Josef Land, and to reach them they would have to drag their sledge laboriously over terribly broken ice, full of fissures and crevasses, ice, which, ironically, was drifting in the opposite direction to that in which they would have to go.

They were doomed men. But it was three months before the ice finally conquered their high spirit – and a third of a century before it yielded up its secrets.

It was September 30, 1930. Seventy-five thousand people were waiting in the harbour of Göteborg. In the white light of the electric-lamp standards and the red glow of many torches the dark hull of a naval vessel slid slowly through the reflections in the lapping water towards its moorings. Many of the older people in the crowds were deeply moved as memories of their youth came back to them. Thirty-three years before, this very ship had moored in the same place. That had been in the spring. On board it had carried Andrée, Strindberg and Fraenkel, the three men who were to fly over the North Pole in a balloon. In their minds the older spectators could see them again as they stood on deck, smiling and waving to the cheering crowds.

The Swedish authorities had never been able to decide to send the old *Svenskund* to the breaker's yard because its name was so closely connected with the names of the three Swedish polar heroes. The little vessel had been obsolete for a long time, but she had been kept in commission almost as though one day she was to perform one more service before she finally left the stage, an undefined and mysterious service that no one could describe. . . .

That day had arrived. The *Svenskund* had accompanied Andrée, Strindberg and Fraenkel to Danes Island in preparation for their polar flight. The *Svenskund* now carried their bodies home in the glory of their tragic failure. All along the coasts of Norway the church bells tolled at her passing.

The *Svenskund* lay at anchor now, the gangway was brought up and hauled into place, and a white-haired officer went on board to lay a wreath on each of the three coffins in the name of the Swedish Government. It was Colonel Swedenborg, the man who thirty-three years before had volunteered to step into the breach and fly with the expedition if either Strindberg or Fraenkel had for any reason been compelled to step down. But for chance, fate, call it what you like, his body would have occupied one of those coffins now lying on the deck of the *Svenskund* and covered with the Swedish flag.

After the ceremony the *Svenskund* continued its funeral journey to Stockholm escorted by other naval vessels, to the accompaniment of the sound of tolling bells, the reverberations of salutes from guns and the dropping of wreaths from aeroplanes. In the capital the King of Sweden was waiting to receive the coffins, after which the remains of the three brave men would be buried and memorial services and commemorative meetings held up and down the country.

The main outlines of the tragedy were known to the world at last, only the final moments of the stranded aeronauts remained shrouded in a mystery that would now never be dissipated. One thing was certain: young Strindberg, the cheerful and robust Strindberg, must have died first, for his companions had given him a proper resting-place. As for Andrée and Fraenkel, left behind with the knowledge that they too must soon follow, it was to be hoped that the cold had taken them in their sleep gently and that they had slid as easily into death as the *Oern* had sailed into the grim skies of the Arctic it had set out so bravely to conquer.

12 Dark Waters

NORBERT CASTERET

*Since the great Martel, pioneer spelaeologist of the nine-
teenth century, the French have had a long tradition of
underground exploration, partly because of their immense
opportunities in the shape of the superb caves that exist in
France – not only those made famous by prehistoric paint-
ings, such as Lascaux, but profound caverns like the Puits
Berger, nearly 3,000 feet deep, or the Gouffre St. Martin
of 2,400 feet. But caving is one of the most dangerous forms
of exploration, especially because of the swirling, unpre-
dictable waters that rage beneath the earth's crust – as
Casteret – most distinguished of modern cavers – shows in
his account of subterranean tragedies and escapes.*

The presence of water underground is recognized as a
serious obstacle to the exploration of a cave, and adds considerably to that discomfort and those innumerable snares
to which the spelaeologist is already exposed. Navigation
of even the smallest subterranean stream gives rise to prob-
lems concerning the choice and transport of boats. No less
crucial is the question of ensuring a supply of light and
some means of escape in the event of shipwreck.

The first explorers of underground lakes and water-
courses used either rafts constructed of such material as
was available, or boats that were generally cumbersome
and heavy. It was Martel who introduced the small canvas
craft. The latter was superceded by a collapsible rubber
boat which, though lighter and more manageable, had the
one grave defect of being very easily damaged.

In his pioneering days Martel had a number of accidents, some of which might easily have proved fatal. The first of these occurred in 1895 when he was exploring the subterranean lake at Padirac. He and two companions had embarked in a small overloaded craft which suddenly capsized. All three fell into the water; their candles were extinguished, and each man had to grope his own way to safety as best he could. Delclaux and Pradine were fortunate and quickly reached the bank. Martel suffered a longer ordeal which he describes as follows: 'I had been thrown out on the opposite side, and had no idea in what direction to swim. The weight of my boots and clothes was beginning to drag me down when all at once I felt the boat surfacing beneath me: it was upside-down, but it still floated. I climbed astride and thought myself safe, but a moment later I was thrust back into the water by the projecting roof which had caused the accident. Again the boat sank and left me once more swimming for dear life. I did not count the strokes, but I know that I became slowly exhausted and began to lose control. I was out of my depth and clearly remember shouting: 'Help! I'm drowning.' My companions, safe on dry land, were now able to call back and give me my bearings; but I must have travelled half-way round the lake, for their welcome cry, "This way; we're on a rock over here", reached me from a considerable distance.'

As soon as Martel was out of the water and established on a small ledge he remembered having candles in his pocket. 'But the matches,' he tells us, 'were soaked; our only hope lay in my secret store. The latter consisted of two metal boxes, wrapped in oilcloth and carried one in each breast pocket of my flannel shirt. They accompany me on every expedition, and have often proved a godsend.

It may be imagined with what care I extracted those precious boxes from my saturated clothes. The first was full of water and its contents were useless, but the second was quite dry and almost at the first attempt yielded the spark of deliverance. The sun himself can never have received a more joyous salute than did that flickering flame that lifted from us the heavy weight of darkness. Without delay we lit several candles and set them in their own wax on the rock. A first look round showed me that we had nothing to fear. The boat was lying under the projecting roof; we had only to swim across and recover it.'

The shipwreck in Padirac occurred in water of 57° F., and Martel has more than once been immersed at far lower temperatures. On one occasion he and a forester were exploring an underground torrent in the cavern of Brudoux. As they walked along the cornice overhanging the stream they heard the noise of a waterfall and tried to reach it. 'We were propped insecurely against the rocky wall of the left bank, convinced that it was impossible to go farther without a boat. To attempt swimming in water as cold as this would be really dangerous. However, I was very keen to obtain at least a glimpse of the cascade which was hidden from us just round the next corner. I believed we might reach it by laying an expanding ladder across the channel. The ends had to rest on narrow ledges which it was impossible to widen; indeed the whole contrivance looked most unsafe. The ladder was extended to its full length and sagged in an alarming fashion. My companion was holding down one end with his foot, and I told him that, as I was sure to fall in, he should dig in his heels so as not to be shaken off the ledge. He was also to plant two candles in a niche, for without light there was no hope of escape. My prediction were fulfilled. At my fourth step the ladder sagged yet more beneath my weight, both ends slid from the ledges, and I fell straight in. The water was 41° F., I had never felt so cold, and decided at once to postpone operations. I had not gazed upon that waterfall, whose voice seemed to mock us, but my only desire was to regain the surface and change my clothes.'

On 12th August 1902, two German tourists, Dr L. of Dresden and Dr. W. of Nassau, tried to repeat Martel's successful voyage in the Austrian cave at Adelsberg and even to carry it a stage farther. They were accompanied by two of Martel's own guides, Anton Sibenik and Joseph Vilhar. Having only one small canvas boat, they had to work an inconvenient series of relays. First, Sibenik escorted Dr. W. through the hazardous passage called the Mousetrap and as far as the first natural dam. He landed his passenger and went back to fetch the other two members of the party. Now when Vilhar and Dr. L. had been waiting three hours, the former became so anxious that he left the cave to summon help. Since there was no boat, he was obliged to swim across a pool more than twenty yards wide. Returning with his brother, they built a makeshift raft from a few planks, on which Vilhar and Dr. L. embarked. After passing the Mousetrap they saw a light, called out, and received an answer. It seemed, then, that the others were alive. But on reaching Dr. W. they learned that he had spent nine hours waiting for Sibenik. It is not difficult to imagine the return journey: three men on their frail craft, peering into recesses in the walls and into the depths of the dark waters until four o'clock in the morning. They found only two laths and an oar from the canvas boat, and reached the entrance of the cave utterly exhausted. Next afternoon a rescue party under Dr. L., specially equipped with a wooden boat and grappling-irons, recovered the boat and Sibenik's corpse just below the Mousetrap. The body was enmeshed in a long rope, and there were slight wounds on the forehead.

It was only too easy to see what had happened. While on his way back (possibly in too great a hurry) through the narrow, winding tunnel of the Mousetrap, Sibenik may have struck his forehead against one of those sharp edges of rock that come right down into the water, fallen into the tiny boat, and capsized it. Or perhaps the boat itself struck a rock and sank. Struggling under water, the hapless guide must have become hopelessly entangled in the rope which, as it were, paralyzed his limbs. The tragedy must have occurred at some point beyond reach or hearing of the other three, who could have had no suspicion of what was happening.

In April 1905, Mulhofer, Martin and Ceh resumed the exploration of the Adelsberg cave and progressed another 650 yards. They, too, suffered shipwreck: their boat was destroyed, and they had the greatest difficulty in swimming to safety.

The moment one embarks on a subterranean waterway, the nature of one's surroundings and the hazardous conditions of navigation cannot but increase the danger. Two young men whose misadventure I shall now relate had ample time in which to learn that truth: they were imprisoned underground for no less than sixty-five hours in circumstances reminiscent of a nightmare rather than of sober fact.

On Sunday, 15th October 1946, Marcel Monnayeur and Roger Jaquin, both good sportsmen but without much experience, decided to explore the underground river of La Verna near Crémieux in Isère. They had a two-seater rubber canoe, a couple of acetylene lamps, and one rope.

Embarking at 10 a.m. they paddled as far as the third water level where, because of the trouble of unloading, of overland transport, and reloading, they most foolishly decided to leave behind one of the lamps and so obtain more freedom of movement. They reached the fifth level without incident. To leave it, however, required no small agility, for at this point the ceiling comes down to within a foot or so of the water. They had partially to deflate their canoe in order to pass and reach the sixth level, where they were stopped by a siphon or submerged tunnel.

'It was only midday,' says Monnayeur, 'and we were pleased with ourselves for having covered a distance of about 1,100 yards in two hours.' But no sooner had they started back than a sharp rock tore a hole in the canoe, which instantly collapsed, depositing its occupants in the water. Their one remaining lamp sank like a stone, and they were in total darkness. Jaquin dived again and again in a fruitless attempt to recover the lamp. Monnayeur clutched at the wall in the hope of saving the matches which he alone carried. But he lost his hold and slipped back into the water; the matches were soaked and of no further use.

There followed a desperate battle for life, which lasted for two days and nights, or perhaps I should say for four nights because the drama was unfolded in impenetrable darkness. Here is Monnayeur's account of what took place: 'We swam about for a long time, perhaps for three hours or more, trying to find some way out. In fact we were going round and round a single column of rock which appeared to support the roof of this final chamber. We had fortunately been able, in spite of the darkness, to effect some temporary repairs to our canoe by binding the torn edges with our lead-line. It was very hard work: I wedged myself firmly in a cleft and supported Jaquin in the water while he began the job. We relieved one another at intervals, but finished with hands covered with blood, for the fine cord bit into our flesh as we drew it tight.'

Although exhausted, they continued to swim, looking for some place where they might land and rest but colliding time after time with the vertical walls. At last their groping fingers found a ledge 3 feet long by 4 inches wide, on which they managed to perch clear of the water. The two youths now entered upon a long vigil which must have seemed to them like some hideous dream. Their one idea was to hold on at all costs until a rescue party arrived; they had no doubt that one must eventually come, since the innkeeper at La Verna, at whose place they had breakfasted, knew of their destination.

Time passed slowly, so slowly that minutes seemed like hours: weariness, cold, and hunger were added torments. They became drowsy and took turns to sleep, one holding the other to prevent him falling off the ledge. Once they dozed off together, only to be plunged immediately into an icy bath.

'We sat there for hours with chattering teeth, haunted by the fear of pneumonia, and rubbed one another as vigorously as our comfortless situation allowed. I have not Jaquin's endurance, and suffered all the while from a sharp pain in the lower part of my back, which worried me considerably.'

They were indeed in a sorry plight, alone by that underground lake some three-quarters of a mile from the light of day. Miniature waterfalls trickled all around them, whispering, as it were, with many voices which their strained nerves interpreted as human calls, blasts of a whistle, or snatches of conversation. Extreme weariness also helped to deceive both ear and eye. At every moment it seemed that a rescue party was approaching; effects similar to those of a mirage deluded them. First the walls, then the roof of the gallery appeared faintly illuminated: 'We thought we saw a light of some kind, hardly perceptible at first, but growing stronger and stronger until it became a blinding glare. Then it vanished. The hallucination repeated itself in the same form whenever our nerves were set on edge by those strangely human voices of the waterfalls. Suddenly, however, a shout, a real shout, sounded far away. We grasped each other's hands and let out a joyful yell. What a moment that was! A flood of emotion swept through our minds and filled our hearts. We were beside ourselves with joy as the rescue party approached and we asked them an absurd question: 'Have you a light?' As long as we live we shall remember the vision of that light: a pale gleam at first, which increased until we discerned the smiling face of Théolère, a brave, sturdy young fellow who brought us deliverance and life.'

They reached the open air three hours later: the worst was over, but they were in a state of exhaustion which no words can describe. They had passed sixty-five hours in the cavern of La Verna which had so nearly been their last resting-place.

The two lads had been cruelly punished for their negligence; but their reaction to the ordeal was in every sense admirable, exemplary. Comment on my part would only lessen the force of those wise and courageous words in which they have embodied their thoughts after a most terrible experience. 'We have learned a great deal. We had not realized just how dangerous spelaeology can be; we should like to warn intending "troglodytes" not to follow our example, but to start their careers in the company of more experienced men. We understand now the risk of depending on a single hand-lamp, and for all future expeditions we shall provide ourselves with some kind of watertight electric torch. We might have expected that this adventure, which came so near to disaster, would finally deter us from exploring caves. On the contrary, we are more than ever resolved to bear our torches through the underworld of France.'

Inexcusable carelessness and total lack of experience are the causes of numerous accidents and perilous situations that overtake the novice in spelaeology. It is plain madness to undertake the survey of a cave with too few or unreliable lamps. Such, however, may be the starting-point of many a harrowing ordeal similar to that of Jaquin and Monnayeur at La Verna.

On 25th May 1943, J. Pittard and J. Della Santa entered the Grotte de Grange-Lens near Saint-Léonard in Switzerland and descended an escarpment of shale to a great sheet of water. Pittard, the historian of this journey, has described what happened:

' This was to have been merely a reconnaissance, because our supply of light was insufficient for a detailed examination of the cave. As there were numerous reefs in the lake, we did not take our boat for fear it should be damaged. We intended as far as possible to cling to the walls and to avoid getting drenched, for the water there is extremely cold. The light coming through the opening was reflected in the water, and we took advantage of it to make our preparations. One of our acetylene lamps had been damaged on the previous day; the other, which we had with us, was not in perfect order, nor was our single box of matches watertight.

'We set off, clinging to the rock, and at first all went well.

Soon, however, we were obliged to step into the water to obtain a foothold. Presently we had to go yet deeper, until the water was waist-high. After some time we reached a small island, from which we could see a still larger lake extending westwards and communicating with the first by a rocky channel. Immediately in front of us was a long causeway of piled-up rocks, whether a peninsula or not we were unable to say. We decided to make for it: but in places the water was chest-high. We came at last to a bank of loose rocks which involved a stiff climb as our heavy boots were full of water and our soaking overalls clung to our bodies. The wide roof stretched upwards far above us, and we could see that the cave extended farther to a third lake connected with the second. There was the sound of falling water in the distance. Should we go on? Reason said no: our matches were wet; our one lamp was already in that spasmodic phase that threatens extinction; the cave was of immense size and full of pitfalls. "We'll go as far as that promontory; the water looks quite shallow and there seems to be a ford of sorts between the second and third lakes.' "Very well, just to see if it goes on much farther. Then we'll come back; it's certainly a bit risky, considering our equipment and the bitter cold."

'We paddled through the ford with no difficulty whatsoever, and came to a tumbled heap of rocks. Next we picked our way slowly along the edge of the lake: it gradually changed to a sheet of almost liquid mud, in which we were nearly engulfed. After that, the ground rose slightly and the harder mud bore our weight as we followed the course of a small stream which seemed slightly ferruginous. It looked like the end of the cave, but we were mistaken. Low down in the enormous vault there was an opening; the stream, in fact, came out of a tunnel through which we might have passed by bending down and crawling about twenty yards. It was possible, therefore, to go farther, but the lamp was behaving badly. We had to get back as quickly as we could, and postpone a more thorough exploration. We began retracing our steps along the small watercourse, and soon approached the lake. "Here's the mud, mind we don't get stuck!" At that moment the lamp flickered and went out.

'There were no dry matches left. A horrible darkness closed around us, and we were on hostile ground! For a moment or two nothing broke the oppressive silence save the tiny cascade falling from rock to rock. Something had to be done.

' "Can you hear the waterfall?"

' "Yes. It must be quite near, on our right."

' "We must get to the stream without sticking in the mud, follow it to the lake, and then try to find the ford."

'Much easier said than done! We went forward step by step, holding hands and trying to keep our sense of direction. We guided ourselves by the noise of the falling water, but very soon realized that there was a slight echo which made things extremely difficult.

' "Do you think we've reached the lake?"

' "I'll have a look. No, I'm in soft mud: give me a pull!"

'Water at last; but where was the ford? We started to go through it: splash! Della Santa was in deep water and swimming out of his depth. I called him back, but it was some time before we found ourselves together again on a small mound. Our wet clothes were saturated, the water in them was icy; we were horribly cold. . . .

' "Now listen: the peninsula should be somewhere in front of us; we shall never find the ford; I'm going to swim over and reconnoitre. You stay here and keep talking to me so that I shan't lose my bearings. As soon as I get to the far side I'll call you and you can swim across to me: the sound of my voice will guide you."

' "Right you are."

'He started; I could hear him gasping in the icy water, and did my best to cheer him up. The lake was quite invisible, the tiny waves made a gentle lapping noise, the darkness was full of terrors. Our acetylene lamp, now useless, was abandoned: its gas expired with a soft, derisive whistle. . . . Ah! he's made it. . . .

' "I'm here; but it's not a bit like the peninsula: I'm up against a wall of rock. Still, come on."

'So I swam over, his voice keeping me on my course. Where were we? We clambered up, barking our shins on sharp projections of rock, and arrived at the top of an unfamiliar slope. We had to crawl down the far side; the leader slipped and fell into a hole full of water. Was it yet another lake? We listened for the sound of the waterfall; it sounded much fainter and seemed now to be in front of us.

' "We've simply turned face about!"

'Bruised, battered and frozen, we felt momentarily exhausted.

' "No, it must be either an echo or water dripping somewhere else."

'What was to be done? Keep straight ahead? If this were a second lake, whose end we had not yet seen, we might easily be lost.

' "We can't stay here and trust to luck that someone will find us. No one knows where we are, and this cave is unexplored."

' "No; we shall have to move on."

'We decided therefore to follow the water's edge as far as possible, and the journey was a veritable nightmare. We had to clamber over unstable rocks and even at times to swim in that grim lake which was hidden from our eyes.

' "Wait a moment! If we're on an island there's nothing to prevent us going round and round in a circle. In this chaos of rock, too, it's hard to get one's bearings when touch is the only means of identifying anything. One of us had better go on ahead: we'll keep in touch by calling to one another."

'I set off, stumbling from one obstacle to the next, falling into holes, but always managing somehow to struggle out again. At long last, far away on my right there appeared the faintest glimmer. Was it just another hallucination, like the many we had already seen? No, it was the real thing.

' "Look! There's a light! Come on!"

'Della Santa stumbled after me until he reached my side, and stood gazing intently at this new phenomenon. So there was, after all, a means of escape. We started moving towards that light, swimming in single file, cutting our knees on invisible rocks. The cold made breathing difficult, and our teeth chattered. But nothing mattered now except to reach the light. It grew steadily stronger and proved at length to be a patch of sky showing through an opening in the cliff and faintly reflected in the water.

'Eventually we reached the lake shore looking like drowned rats, badly battered, and completely exhausted. As we arrived at the top of the last slope and emerged into daylight we noticed that the sun was setting. So that we must have spent five hours wandering in total darkness. An hour later, and we should never have found the entrance: by then night would have fallen. . . .'

One of the most striking instances of dangerous underground waters happened in 1950 when the Trou de la

Creuze at Blamont in Doubs acquired grim distinction as the scene of the worst catastrophe ever recorded in the annals of spelaeology. The Blamont disaster, as it is generally called, involved six deaths by drowning and shocked the whole of France.

A whole set of quite exceptional circumstances, in which luck seems to have been against them from start to finish, combined to destroy these men. On 11th November 1950, at 3.15 p.m., eight spelaeologists from Lure and Belfort made their way into the cave known as the Trou de la Creuze, paddling in the shallow water of a subterranean river that flows through it. This was not, strictly speaking, an exploring party; its main purpose was to study the habits of water insects that live in caves.

Before he had gone far through those low-ceilinged corridors young Fréminet, who was only seventeen years old, became scared. The icy water, too, made him feel unwell; he turned back and left the cave. The other seven walked on, dragging after them two rubber boats, through water that was nowhere deep enough to allow their use. They had gone about half a mile when the waterway became too narrow and they had to return. On their way back they noticed the water rising, slowly at first, then more rapidly. It had been raining when they entered the cave, as it had done unceasingly for a week, and they awoke to their peril. They began to hurry back as fast as they could, so fast indeed that the leader of the expedition, Dr. Mairey of Lure, was left behind by his companions, whose alarm steadily increased until they could not or would not hear his appeal for discipline. The doctor had entered the cave first and therefore brought up the rear on the return journey; but he managed to overtake Claude Vien as they came to a tunnel that was flooded almost to the roof.

'There's a siphon here, I'm going to dive.' That was all Dr. Mairey heard as he saw his companion disappear into the water.

Left to himself, the doctor considered that his friends should by now have escaped from the flooded galleries. He himself, he judged, had arrived too late. The water was still rising; he quickly abandoned the idea of diving through, and even tried to retrace his steps to where the tunnel was a little wider and the roof a little higher. It seemed a suitable spot in which to await the subsidence of the flood. The current, however, was too strong, and he was obliged to halt in a tunnel scarcely three feet wide. It was then about six o'clock in the evening.

Towards midnight another group of spelaeologists, who had been exploring a neighbouring cave, returned to the farm where they were staying and expected to find their friends back from the Trou de la Creuze. They found only Fréminet who was growing anxious. Equally alarmed, they hurried to the mouth of the cave, and were horrified to see that the river was in flood and that it was impossible to enter. A crowd of villagers had assembled and police were rushed to the scene. Searchlights were played on the entrance and it was only too clear that rescue work was, for the time being, out of the question.

At 2 a.m. the torrent threw out two bodies, those of Antonio Salvador and Jacques Durupt, both members of the Belfort party and both twenty-five years of age. Telephone calls were made to the prefectures, and the Air Minister placed aircraft at the disposal of the Paris fire-brigade and a number of spelaeological societies. Fire-brigades from Valentigney and Montbéliard, as well as local spelaeologists, were already standing by; but there was nothing they could do. At daybreak various articles appeared: a scarf, a couple of helmets, a damaged rubber boat. The bystanders hoped against hope that these were signs of life.

There seemed to be only one means of lowering the water level, and that was to enlarge the opening of the cave. Accordingly they set to work with pneumatic drills and explosives. Eager rescuers, friends and colleagues of those trapped in the cave, fought their way in against the swirling mass of water for about twenty yards. They recovered the body of a third victim wedged in a narrow passage; it was that of Raoul Simonin from Lure, aged twenty-one.

Some time later, after tiring and heroic efforts, three more bodies were brought out: Maurice Roth and Claude Vien, both aged twenty-eight, and Michel Mozer, aged eighteen. All three were from Belfort. The ill-omened cave had immolated half a dozen victims. Dr. Mairey was still to be accounted for, and there was little hope of finding him alive. Towards evening, however, one of the Paris firemen, who had forced his way into the flooded tunnel through which the water was still roaring, came out with news that he thought his calls had been answered. At about 9 p.m. Sergeant-Major Bédué, one of a group of military spelaeologists who had come by air from Toulouse, entered the cave and, by a combination of bold resolution and good luck, succeeded in bringing the doctor out, utterly exhausted but alive.

What had happened from the time when Dr. Mairey saw the last of his companions, Claude Vien, dive into the siphon?

The six unfortunate entomologists had been demoralized by the sudden rise of water. Who would have reacted otherwise in so appalling a situation? In headlong retreat, caught in the raging flood, swept along by that irresistible current, they had dashed for the entrance. Some of them, like Claude Vien, must have dived deliberately, others must have been engulfed, knocked over, and swept away by the tremendous weight of water. The very roofs were awash for too long a time to allow a chance of escape; the great gallery itself was like a huge pipe fully charged with water at high pressure, and all six were drowned.

Only Dr. Mairey maintained his self-control; he saw that to dive was sheer madness since it meant certain death. With a presence of mind that cannot be too highly commended, he decided to wait. The flood might subside, in which case there was a faint possibility of rescue; or it might rise still higher and he would drown.

Pressing against the wall of rock in order to withstand the powerful current, with his head braced against the low roof and his body shoulder-deep in water, he spent the night of 11th–12th November in total darkness, noting with agonized intensity the varying depth of icy water as it surged around him. Rock is a good conductor of sound, and he distinctly heard the pneumatic drills; but the roar of the torrent prevented him from identifying the noise, and he believed that he was suffering from hallucinations.

He waited and waited until at last he heard what seemed to be shouts, and his straining eyes caught the faint glimmer of a torch. He had been fighting for his life in ice-cold water for twenty-seven hours, under the constant menace of physical and mental collapse.

The tragedy of 11th–12th November remains an unsolved mystery. Some natural dam, maybe a barrier of rock, must have given way. It was, I repeat, no more than bad luck that such an incident occurred while there were men inside the cave. If they had reached the opening a few hours later, the flood of water would have made it impossible for them to enter; if they had come out a few hours earlier, they would never even have suspected the peril to which they had been exposed. Some journalists gave an impression that these young men had acted with senseless folly, since they must have known the great danger of entering a subterranean waterway in a period of heavy rain. True, it had been raining for several days; but it was precisely because the continuous rain had not so far caused the stream to rise that the poor fellows had entered the cave without the least shadow of misgiving. The spring at La Creuze had never in living memory flowed abnormally, nor had the villagers of Blamont the least mistrust of this little brook which leaves its rocky conduit to provide water for the communal wash-house.

13 'Sixteen Days of Supreme Strife'

SIR ERNEST SHACKLETON

In his 'Imperial Trans-Antarctic Expedition', Shackleton planned to cross the entire continent of Antarctica from the Weddell Sea, by way of the South Pole, to McMurdo Sound – the object, incidentally, of Sir Vivian Fuchs's expedition in 1956–58. But in 1915 Shackleton suffered a disastrous blow when, after being trapped for nine months in the ice, his ship the Endurance *was finally crushed by it. It became essential to fetch help for the main expedition, so in the* James Caird, *an ordinary twenty-foot ship's whaler (which can be seen in the Maritime Museum at Greenwich), Shackleton set out with five men from Elephant Island to South Georgia, an eight hundred mile voyage across some of the worst seas in the world. The present extract shows no more than part of the hardships involved – hardships made endurable only by the leadership of Shackleton himself. Subsequently it took four desperate attempts before the remainder of the expedition were rescued from Elephant Island.*

The tale of the next sixteen days is one of supreme strife amid heaving waters. The sub-Antarctic Ocean lived up to its evil winter reputation. I decided to run north for at least two days while the wind held and so get into warmer weather before turning to the east and laying a course for South Georgia. We took two-hourly spells at the tiller. The men who were not on watch crawled into the sodden sleeping-bags and tried to forget their troubles for a period; but there was no comfort in the boat. The bags and cases seemed to be alive in the unfailing knack of presenting their most uncomfortable angles to our rest-seeking bodies. A man might imagine for a moment that he had found a position of ease, but always discovered quickly that some unyielding point was impinging on muscle or bone. The first night aboard the boat was one of acute discomfort for us all, and we were heartily glad when the dawn came and we could set about the preparation of a hot breakfast.

This record of the voyage to South Georgia is based upon scanty notes made day by day. The notes dealt usually with the bare facts of distances, positions, and weather, but our memories retained the incidents of the passing days in a period never to be forgotten. By running north for the first two days I hoped to get warmer weather and also to avoid lines of pack-ice that might be extending beyond the main body. We needed all the advantage that we could obtain from the higher latitude for sailing on the great circle, but we had to be cautious regarding possible ice-streams. Cramped in our narrow quarters and continually wet by the spray, we suffered severely from cold throughout the journey. We fought the seas and winds and at the same time had a daily struggle to keep ourselves alive. At times we were in dire peril. Generally we were upheld by the knowledge that we were making progress towards the land where we would be, but there were days and nights when we lay hove to, drifting across the storm-whitened seas and watching, with eyes interested rather than apprehensive, the uprearing masses of water, flung to and fro by Nature in the pride of her strength. Deep seemed the valleys when we lay between the reeling seas. High were the hills when we perched momentarily on the tops of giant combers. Nearly always there were gales. So small was our boat and so great were the seas that often our sail flapped idly in the calm between the crests of two waves. Then we would climb the next slope and catch the full fury of the gale where the wool-like whiteness of the breaking water surged around us. We had our moments of laughter – rare, it is true, but hearty enough. Even when cracked lips and swollen mouths checked the outward and visible signs of amusement we could see a joke of the primitive kind. Man's sense of humour is always most easily stirred by the petty misfortunes of his neighbours, and I shall never forget Worsley's efforts on one occasion to place the hot aluminium stand on top of the Primus stove after it had fallen off in an extra heavy roll. With his frost-bitten fingers he picked it up, dropped it, picked it up again, and toyed with it gingerly as though it were some fragile article of lady's wear. We laughed, or rather gurgled with laughter.

The wind came up strong and worked into a gale from the north-west on the third day out. We stood away to the east. The increasing seas discovered the weaknesses of our decking. The continuous blows shifted the box-lids and sledge-runners so that the canvas sagged down and accumulated water. Then icy trickles, distinct from the driving sprays, poured fore and aft into the boat. The nails that the carpenter had extracted from cases at Elephant Island and used to fasten down the battens were too short to make firm the decking. We did what we could to secure it, but our means were very limited, and the water continued to enter the boat at a dozen points. Much baling was necessary, and nothing that we could do prevented our gear from becoming sodden. The searching runnels from the canvas were really more unpleasant than the sudden definite douches of the sprays. Lying under the thwarts during watches below, we tried vainly to avoid them. There were no dry places in the boat, and at last we simply covered our heads with our Burberrys and endured the all-prevailing water. The baling was work for the watch. Real rest we had none. The perpetual motion of the boat made repose impossible; we were cold, sore and anxious. We moved on hands and knees in the semi-darkness of the day under the decking. The darkness was complete by six p.m., and not until 7 a.m. of the following day could we see one another under the thwarts. We had a few scraps of candle, and they were preserved carefully in order that we might have light at meal-times. There was one fairly dry spot in the boat, under the solid original decking at the bows, and we managed to protect some of our biscuits from the salt water; but I do not think any of us got the taste of salt out of our mouths during the voyage.

The difficulty of movement in the boat would have had its humorous side if it had not involved us in so many aches and pains. We had to crawl under the thwarts in order to move along the boat, and our knees suffered considerably. When a watch turned out it was necessary for me to direct each man by name when and where to move, since if all hands had crawled about at the same time the result would have been dire confusion and many bruises. Then there was the trim of the boat to be considered. The order of the watch was four hours on and four hours off, three men to the watch. One man had the tiller-ropes, the second man attended to the sail, and the third baled for all he was worth. Sometimes when the water in the boat had been reduced to reasonable proportions, our pump could be used. This pump, which Hurley had made from the Flinders bar case of our ship's standard compass, was quite effective, though its capacity was not large. The man who was attending the sail could pump into the big outer cooker, which was lifted and emptied overboard when filled. We had a device by which the water could go direct from the pump into the sea through a hole in the gunwale, but this hole had to be blocked at an early stage of the voyage, since we found that it admitted water when the boat rolled.

While a new watch was shivering in the wind and spray, the men who had been relieved groped hurriedly among the soaked sleeping-bags and tried to steal a little of the warmth created by the last occupants; but it was not always possible for us to find even this comfort when we went off watch. The boulders that we had taken aboard for ballast had to be shifted continually in order to trim the boat and give access to the pump, which became choked with hairs from the moulting sleeping-bags and finneskoe. The four reindeer-skin sleeping-bags shed their hair freely owing to the continuous wetting, and soon became quite bald in appearance. The moving of the boulders was weary and painful work. We came to know every one of the stones by sight and touch, and I have vivid memories of their angular peculiarities even today. They might have been of consider-able interest as geological specimens to a scientific man under happier conditions. As ballast they were useful. As weights to be moved about in cramped quarters they were simply appalling. They spared no portion of our poor bodies. Another of our troubles, worth mention here, was the chafing of our legs by our wet clothes, which had not been changed now for seven months. The insides of our thighs were rubbed raw, and the one tube of Hazeline cream in our medicine-chest did not go far in alleviating our pain, which was increased by the bite of the salt water. We thought at the time that we never slept. The fact was that we would doze off uncomfortably, to be aroused quickly by some new ache or another call to effort. My own share of the general unpleasantness was accentuated by a finely developed bout of sciatica. I had become possessor of this originally on the floe several months earlier.

Our meals were regular in spite of the gales. Attention to this point was essential, since the conditions of the voyage made increasing calls upon our vitality. Breakfast, at 8 a.m., consisted of a pannikin of hot hoosh made from Bovril sledging ration, two biscuits, and some lumps of sugar. Lunch came at 1 p.m., and comprised Bovril sledging ration, eaten raw, and a pannikin of hot milk for each man. Tea, at 5 p.m., had the same menu. Then during the night we had a hot drink, generally of milk. The meals were the bright beacons in those cold and stormy days. The glow of warmth and comfort produced by the food and drink made optimists of us all. We had two tins of Virol, which we were keeping for an emergency; but, finding ourselves in need of an oil-lamp to eke out our supply of candles, we emptied one of the tins in the manner that most appealed to us, and fitted it with a wick made by shredding a bit of canvas. When this lamp was filled with oil it gave a certain amount of light, though it was easily blown out, and was of great assistance to us at night. We were fairly well off as regarded fuel, since we had 6½ gallons of petroleum.

A severe south-westerly gale on the fourth day out forced us to heave to. I would have liked to have run before the wind, but the sea was very high and the *James Caird* was in danger of broaching to and swamping. The delay was vexatious, since up to that time we had been making sixty or seventy miles a day; good going with our limited sail area. We hove to under double-reefed mainsail and our little jigger, and waited for the gale to blow itself out. During that afternoon we saw bits of wreckage, the remains probably of some unfortunate vessel that had failed to weather the strong gales south of Cape Horn. The weather conditions did not improve, and on the fifth day out the gale was so fierce that we were compelled to take in the double-reefed mainsail and hoist our small jib instead. We put out a sea-anchor to keep the *James Caird's* head up to the sea. This anchor consisted of a triangular canvas bag fastened to the end of the painter and allowed to stream out from the bows. The boat was high enough to catch the wind, and, as she drifted to leeward, the drag of the anchor kept her head to windward. Thus our boat took most of the seas more or less end on. Even then the crests of the waves often would curl right over us and we shipped a great deal of water, which necessitated unceasing baling and pumping. Looking out abeam, we would see a hollow like a tunnel formed as the crest of a big wave toppled over on to the swelling body of water. A thousand times it appeared as though the *James Caird* must be engulfed; but the boat lived. The south-westerly gale had its birthplace above the Antarctic Continent, and its freezing breath lowered the temperature far towards zero. The sprays froze upon the boat and gave bows, sides and decking a heavy coat of mail. This accumulation of ice reduced the buoyancy of the boat, and to that extent was an added peril; but it possessed a notable advantage from one point of view. The water ceased to drop and trickle from the canvas, and the spray came in solely at the well in the after part of the boat. We could not allow the load of ice to grow beyond a certain point, and in turns we crawled about the decking forward, chipping and picking at it with the available tools.

When the daylight came on the morning of the sixth day out we saw and felt that the *James Caird* had lost her resiliency. She was not rising to the oncoming seas. The weight of the ice that had formed in her and upon her during the night was having its effect, and she was becoming more like a log than a boat. The situation called for immediate action. We first broke away the spare oars, which were encased in ice and frozen to the sides of the boat, and threw them overboard. We retained two oars for use when we got inshore. Two of the fur sleeping-bags went over the side; they were thoroughly wet, weighing probably 40 lb. each, and they had frozen stiff during the night. Three men constituted the watch below, and when a man went down it was better to turn into the wet bag just vacated by another man than to thaw out a frozen bag with the heat of his unfortunate body. We now had four bags, three in use and one for emergency use in case a member of the party should break down permanently. The reduction of weight relieved the boat to some extent, and vigorous chipping and scraping did more. We had to be very careful not to put axe or knife through the frozen canvas of the decking as we crawled over it, but gradually we got rid of a lot of ice. The *James Caird* lifted to the endless waves as though she lived again.

About 11 a.m. the boat suddenly fell off into the trough of the sea. The painter had parted and the sea-anchor had gone. This was serious. The *James Caird* went away to leeward, and we had no chance at all of recovering the anchor and our valuable rope, which had been our only means of keeping the boat's head up to the seas without the risk of hoisting sail in a gale. Now we had to set the sail and trust to its holding. While the *James Caird* rolled heavily in the trough, we beat the frozen canvas until the bulk of the ice had cracked off it and then hoisted it. The frozen gear worked protestingly, but after a struggle our little craft came up to the wind again, and we breathed more freely. Skin frost-bites were troubling us, and we had developed large blisters on our fingers and hands. I shall always carry the scar of one of these frost-bites on my left hand, which became badly inflamed after the skin had burst and the cold bitten deeply.

We held the boat up to the gale during the day, enduring as best we could discomforts that amounted to pain. The boat tossed interminably on the big waves under grey, threatening skies. Our thoughts did not embrace much more than the necessities of the hour. Every surge of the sea was an enemy to be watched and circumvented. We ate our scanty meals, treated our frost-bites and hoped for the improved conditions that the morrow might bring. Night fell early, and in the lagging hours of darkness we were cheered by a change for the better in the weather. The wind dropped, the snow-squalls became less frequent, and the sea moderated. When the morning of the seventh day dawned there was not much wind. We shook the reef out of the sail and laid our course once more for South Georgia. The sun came out bright and clear, and presently Worsley got a snap for longitude. We hoped that the sky would remain clear until noon, so that we could get the latitude. We had been six days out without an observation, and our dead reckoning naturally was uncertain. The boat must have presented a strange appearance that morning. All hands basked in the sun. We hung our sleeping-bags to the mast and spread our socks and other gear all over the deck. Some of the ice had melted off the *James Caird* in the early morning after the gale began to slacken, and dry patches were appearing in the decking. Porpoises came blowing round the boat, and Cape pigeons wheeled and swooped within a few feet of us. These little black-and-white birds have an air of friendliness that is not possessed by the great circling albatross. They had looked grey against the swaying sea during the storm as they darted about over our heads and uttered their plaintive cries. The albatrosses, of the black or sooty variety, had watched with hard, bright eyes, and seemed to have a quite impersonal interest in our struggle to keep afloat amid the battering seas. In addition to the Cape pigeons an occasional stormy petrel flashed overhead. Then there was a small bird, unknown to me, that appeared always to be in a fussy, bustling state, quite out of keeping with the surroundings. It irritated me. It had practically no tail, and it flitted about vaguely as though in search of the lost member. I used to find myself wishing it would find its tail and have done with the silly fluttering.

We revelled in the warmth of the sun that day. Life was not so bad, after all. We felt we were well on our way. Our gear was drying, and we could have a hot meal in comparative comfort. The swell was still heavy, but it was not breaking and the boat rode easily. At noon Worsley balanced himself on the gunwale and clung with one hand to the stay of the mainmast while he got a snap of the sun. The result was more than encouraging. We had done over 380 miles and were getting on for half-way to South Georgia. It looked as though we were going to get through.

The wind freshened to a good stiff breeze during the afternoon, and the *James Caird* made satisfactory progress. I had not realized until the sunlight came how small our boat really was. There was some influence in the light and warmth, some hint of happier days, that made us revive memories of other voyages, when we had stout decks beneath our feet, unlimited food at our command, and pleasant cabins for our ease. Now we clung to a battered little boat, 'alone, alone, all, all alone, alone on a wide, wide sea'. So low in the water were we that each succeeding swell cut off our view of the sky-line. We were a tiny speck in the vast vista of the sea – the ocean that is open to all and merciful to none, that threatens even when it seems to yield, and that is pitiless always to weakness. For a moment the consciousness of the forces arrayed against us would be almost overwhelming. Then hope and confidence would rise again as our boat rose to a wave and tossed aside the crest in a sparkling shower like the play of prismatic colours at the foot of a waterfall. My double-barrelled gun and some cartridges had been stowed aboard the boat as an emergency precaution against a shortage of food, but we were not disposed to destroy our little neighbours, the Cape pigeons, even for the sake of fresh meat. We might have shot an albatross, but the wandering king of the ocean aroused in us something of the feeling that inspired, too late, the Ancient Mariner. So the gun remained among the stores and sleeping-bags in the narrow quarters beneath our leaking deck, and the birds followed us unmolested.

The eighth, ninth and tenth days of the voyage had few features worthy of special note. The wind blew hard during those days, and the strain of navigating the boat was unceasing, but always we made some advance towards our goal. No bergs showed on our horizon, and we knew that we were clear of the ice-fields. Each day brought its little round of troubles, but also compensation in the form of food and growing hope. We felt that we were going to succeed. The odds against us had been great, but we were winning through. We still suffered severely from the cold, for, though the temperature was rising, our vitality was declining owing to shortage of food, exposure, and the necessity of maintaining our cramped position day and night. I found that it was now absolutely necessary to prepare hot milk for all hands during the night, in order to sustain life till dawn. This meant lighting the Primus lamp in the darkness and involved an increased drain on our small store of matches. It was the rule that one match must serve when the Primus was being lit. We had no lamp for the compass and during the early days of the voyage we would strike a match when the steersman wanted to see the course at night; but later the necessity for strict economy impressed itself upon us, and the practice of striking matches at night was stopped. We had one water-tight tin of matches. I had stowed away in a pocket, in readiness for a sunny day, a lens from one of the telescopes, but this was of no use during the voyage. The sun seldom shone upon us. The glass of the compass got broken one night, and we contrived to mend it with adhesive tape from the medicine-chest. One of the memories that comes to me from those days is of Crean singing at the tiller. He always sang while he was steering, and nobody ever discovered what the song was. It was devoid of tune and as monotonous as the chanting of a Buddhist monk at his prayers; yet somehow it was cheerful. In moments of inspiration Crean would attempt 'The Wearing of the Green'.

On the tenth night Worsley could not straighten his body after his spell at the tiller. He was thoroughly cramped, and we had to drag him beneath the decking and massage him before he could unbend himself and get into a sleeping bag. A hard north-westerly gale came up on the eleventh day (May 5) and shifted to the south-west in the late afternoon. The sky was overcast and occasional snow-squalls added to the discomfort produced by a tremendous cross-sea – the worst, I thought, that we had experienced. At midnight I was at the tiller and suddenly noticed a line of clear sky between the south and south-west. I called to the other men that the sky was clearing, and then a moment later I realized that what I had seen was not a rift in the clouds but the white crest of an enormous wave. During the twenty-six years' experience of the ocean in all its moods

I had not encountered a wave so gigantic. It was a mighty upheaval of the ocean, a thing quite apart from the big white-capped seas that had been our tireless enemies for many days. I shouted, 'For God's sake, hold on! It's got us!' Then came a moment of suspense that seemed drawn out into hours. White surged the foam of the breaking sea around us. We felt our boat lifted and flung forward like a cork in breaking surf. We were in a seething chaos of tortured water; but somehow the boat lived through it, half-full of water, sagging to the dead weight and shuddering under the blow. We baled with the energy of men fighting for life, flinging the water over the sides with every receptacle that came to our hands and after ten minutes of uncertainty we felt the boat renew her life beneath us. She floated again and ceased to lurch drunkenly as though dazed by the attack of the sea. Earnestly we hoped that never again would we encounter such a wave.

The conditions in the boat, uncomfortable before, had been made worse by the deluge of water. All our gear was thoroughly wet again. Our cooking-stove had been floating about in the bottom of the boat, and portions of our last hoosh seemed to have permeated everything. Not until 3 a.m., when we were all chilled almost to the limit of endurance, did we manage to get the stove alight and make ourselves hot drinks. The carpenter was suffering particularly, but he showed grit and spirit. Vincent had for the past week ceased to be an active member of the crew, and I could not easily account for his collapse. Physically he was one of the strongest men in the boat. He was a young man, he had served on North Sea trawlers, and he should have been able to bear hardships better than McCarthy, who, not so strong, was always happy.

The weather was better on the following day (May 6),

and we got a glimpse of the sun. Worsley's observation showed that we were not more than a hundred miles from the north-west corner of South Georgia. Two more days with a favourable wind and we should sight the promised land. I hoped that there would be no delay, for our supply of water was running very low. The hot drink at night was essential, but I decided that the daily allowance of water must be cut down to half a pint per man. The lumps of ice we had taken aboard had gone long ago. We were dependent upon the water we had brought from Elephant Island, and our thirst was increased by the fact that we were now using the brackish water in the breaker that had been slightly stove in in the surf when the boat was being loaded. Some sea-water had entered at that time.

Thirst took possession of us. I dared not permit the allowance of water to be increased since an unfavourable wind might drive us away from the island and lengthen our voyage by many days. Lack of water is always the most severe privation that men can be condemned to endure, and we found, as during our earlier boat voyage, that the salt water in our clothing and the salt spray that lashed our faces made our thirst grow quickly to a burning pain. I had to be very firm in refusing to allow any one to antici-pate the morrow's allowance, which I was sometimes begged to do. We did the necessary work dully and hoped for land. I had altered the course to the east so as to make sure of our striking the island, which would have been impossible to regain if we had run past the northern end. The course was laid on our scrap of chart for a point some thirty miles down the coast. That day and the following day passed for us in a sort of nightmare. Our mouths were dry and our tongues were swollen. The wind was still strong and the heavy sea forced us to navigate carefully, but any thought of our peril from the waves was buried beneath the consciousness of our raging thirst. The bright moments were those when we each received our one mug of hot milk during the long, bitter watches of the night. Things were bad for us in those days, but the end was coming. The morning of May 8 broke thick and stormy, with squalls from the north-west. We searched the waters ahead for a sign of land, and though we could see nothing more than had met our eyes for many days, we were cheered by a sense that the goal was near at hand. About ten o'clock that morning we passed a little bit of kelp, a glad signal of the proximity of land. An hour later we saw two shags sitting on a big mass of kelp, and knew then that we must be within ten or fifteen miles of the shore. These birds are as sure an indication of the proximity of land as a lighthouse is, for they never venture far to sea. We gazed ahead with increasing eagerness, and at 12.30 p.m., through a rift in the clouds, McCarthy caught a glimpse of the black cliffs of South Georgia, just fourteen days after our departure from Elephant Island. It was a glad moment. Thirst-ridden, chilled and weak as we were, happiness irradiated us. The job was nearly done.

We stood in towards the shore to look for a landing-place, and presently we could see the green tussock-grass on the ledges above the surf-beaten rocks. Ahead of us and to the south, blind rollers showed the presence of uncharted reefs along the coast. Here and there the hungry rocks were close to the surface, and over them the great waves broke, swirling viciously and spouting thirty and forty feet into the air. The rocky coast appeared to descend sheer to the sea. Our need of water and rest was wellnigh desperate, but to have attempted a landing at that time would have been suicidal. Night was drawing near, and the weather indications were not favourable. There was nothing for it but to haul off till the following morning, so we stood away on the starboard tack until we had made what appeared to be a safe offing. Then we hove to in the high westerly swell. The hours passed slowly as we waited the dawn, which would herald, we fondly hoped, the last stage of our journey. Our thirst was a torment and we could scarcely touch our food; the cold seemed to strike right through our weakened bodies. At 5 a.m. the wind shifted to the north-west and quickly increased to one of the worst hurricanes any of us had ever experienced. A great cross-sea was running, and the wind simply shrieked as it tore the tops off the waves and converted the whole seascape into a haze of driving spray. Down into the valleys, up to tossing heights, straining until her seams opened, swung our little boat, brave still but labouring heavily. We knew that the wind and set of the sea was driving us ashore, but we could do nothing. The dawn showed us a storm-torn ocean, and the morning passed without bringing us a sight of the land; but at 1 p.m., through a rift in the flying mists, we got a glimpse of the huge crags of the island and realized that our position had become desperate. We were on a dead lee shore, and we could gauge our approach to the unseen cliffs by the roar of the breakers against the sheer walls of rock. I ordered the double-reefed mainsail to be set in the hope that we might claw off, and this attempt increased the strain upon the boat. The *James Caird* was bumping heavily, and the water was pouring in everywhere. Our thirst forgotten in the realization of our imminent danger, as we baled unceasingly, and adjusted our weights from time to time; occasional glimpses showed that the shore was nearer. I knew that Annewkow Island lay to the south of us, but our small and badly marked chart showed uncertain reefs in the passage between the island and the mainland, and I dared not trust it, though as a last resort we could try to lie under the lee of the island. The afternoon wore away as we edged down the coast, with the thunder of the breakers in our ears. The approach of evening found us still some distance from Annewkow Island, and, dimly in the twilight, we could see a snow-capped mountain looming above us. The chance of surviving the night, with the driving gale and the implacable sea forcing us on to the lee shore, seemed small. I think most of us had a feeling that the end was very near. Just after 6 p.m., in the dark, as the boat was in the yeasty backwash from the seas flung from this iron-bound coast, then, just when things looked their worst, they changed for the best. I have marvelled often at the thin line that divides success from failure and the sudden turn that leads from apparently certain disaster to comparative safety. The wind suddenly shifted and we were free once more to make an offing. Almost as soon as the gale eased, the pin that locked the mast to the thwart fell out. It must have been on the point of doing this throughout the hurricane, and if it had gone nothing could have saved us; the mast would have snapped like a carrot. Our backstays had carried away once before when iced up and were not too strongly fastened now. We were thankful indeed for the mercy that had held that pin in its place throughout the hurricane.

We stood off shore again, tired almost to the point of apathy. Our water had long been finished. The last was about a pint of hairy liquid, which we strained through a bit of gauze from the medicine-chest. The pangs of thirst attacked us with redoubled intensity, and I felt that we must make a landing on the following day at almost any hazard. The night wore on. We were very tired. We longed for day. When at last the dawn came on the morning of May 10 there was practically no wind, but a high cross-sea was running. We made slow progress towards the shore. About 8 a.m. the wind backed to the north-west and threatened another blow. We had sighted in the meantime a big indentation which I thought must be King Haakon Bay, and I decided that we must land there. We set the bows of the boat towards the bay and ran before the freshening gale. Soon we had angry reefs on either side. Great glaciers came down to the sea and offered no landing-place. The sea spouted on the reefs and thundered against the shore. About noon we sighted a line of jagged reef, like blackened teeth, that seemed to bar the entrance to the bay. Inside, comparatively smooth water stretched eight or nine miles to the head of the bay. A gap in the reef appeared, and we made for it. But the fates had another rebuff for us. The wind shifted and blew from the east right out of the bay. We could see the way through the reef, but we could not approach it directly. That afternoon we bore up, tacking five times in the strong wind. The last tack enabled us to get through, and at last we were in the wide mouth of the bay. Dusk was approaching. A small cove, with a boulder-strewn beach guarded by a reef, made a break in the cliffs on the south side of the bay, and we turned in that direction. I stood in the bows directing the steering as we ran through the kelp and made the passage of the reef. The entrance was so narrow that we had to take in the oars, and the swell was piling itself right over the reef into the cove; but in a minute or two we were inside, and in the gathering darkness the *James Caird* ran in on a swell and touched the beach. I sprang ashore with the short painter and held on when the boat went out with the backward surge. When the *James Caird* came in again three of the men got ashore, and they held the painter while I climbed some rocks with another line. A slip on the wet rocks twenty feet up nearly closed my part of the story just at the moment when we were achieving safety. A jagged piece of rock held me and at the same time bruised me sorely. However, I made fast the line, and in a few minutes we were all safe on the beach, with the boat floating in the surging water just off the shore. We heard a gurgling sound that was sweet music in our ears, and, peering around, found a stream of fresh water almost at our feet. A moment later we were down on our knees drinking the pure, ice-cold water in long draughts that put new life into us. It was a splendid moment.

14 A Queer Craft

THOR HEYERDAHL

The Incas of Peru declared that their forefathers had expelled the white chief-god Sun-Tiki, forcing him to escape across the Pacific. Heyerdahl came to the conclusion that this god was identical with the white chief-god Tiki, son of the Sun, whom the inhabitants of the eastern Pacific islands regarded as the founder of their race. He was convinced that in the distant past, tribes from Peru had migrated across that vast ocean. But – it was known that they had no boats, only rafts. In the true spirit of the explorer-scientist, Heyerdahl built a special raft, using only materials that would have been available to the ancient peoples in question, and, with five other Scandinavians, modern Vikings indeed, set out on a fantastic voyage of more than four thousand miles to try to prove his theory. His Kon-Tiki *expedition was one of the most famous 20th century adventure-stories.*

When the sea was not too rough we were often out in the little rubber dinghy taking photographs. I shall not forget the first time the sea was so calm that two men felt like putting the balloon-like little thing into the water and going for a row. They had hardly got clear of the raft when they dropped the little oars and sat roaring with laughter. And as the swell lifted them away and they disappeared and reappeared among the seas, they laughed so loud every time they caught a glimpse of us that their voices rang out over the desolate Pacific. We looked round us with mixed feelings and saw nothing comic but our own hirsute bearded faces; but as the two in the dinghy should be accustomed to those by now, we began to have a lurking suspicion that they had suddenly gone mad. Sunstroke, perhaps. The two fellows could hardly scramble back on board the *Kon-Tiki* for sheer laughter, and gasping, with tears in their eyes, beg us just to go and see for ourselves.

Two of us jumped down into the dancing rubber dinghy, and were caught by a sea which lifted us clear. Immediately we sat down with a bump and roared with laughter. We had to scramble back on to the raft as quickly as possible and calm the two last who had not been out yet, for they thought we had all gone stark staring mad.

It was ourselves and our proud vessel which made such a completely hopeless, lunatic impression on us the first time we saw the whole thing at a distance. We had never before had an outside view of ourselves in the open sea. The logs of timber disappeared behind the smallest waves, and when we saw anything at all it was the low cabin with the wide doorway and the bristly roof of leaves that bobbed up from among the seas. The raft looked exactly like an old Norwegian hay-loft lying helpless, drifting about in the open sea, a warped hay-loft full of sunburnt bearded ruffians. If anyone had come paddling after us at sea in a bath we should have felt the same spontaneous urge to laughter. Even an ordinary swell rolled halfway up the cabin wall and looked as if it must pour in unhindered through the wide open door in which the bearded fellows lay gaping. But then the crazy craft came up on the surface again and the vagabonds lay there as dry, shaggy and intact as before. If a higher sea came racing by, cabin and sail and the whole mast might disappear behind the mountain of water, but just as certainly the cabin with its vagabonds would be there again next moment.

It looked bad, and we could not realize that things had gone so well on board the peculiar craft.

Next time we rowed out to have a good laugh at ourselves, we nearly had a disaster. The wind and sea were higher than we supposed, and the *Kon-Tiki* was cleaving a path for herself over the swell much more quickly than we realized. We in the dinghy had to row for our lives out in the open sea, in an attempt to regain the unmanageable raft which could not stop and wait, and could not possibly turn round and come back. Even when the boys on board the *Kon-Tiki* got the sail down, the wind got such a grip of the bamboo cabin that the balsa raft drifted away to westward as fast as we could splash after her in the dancing round rubber dinghy with its tiny toy oars. There was only one thought in the head of every man – we must not be separated. Those were horrible minutes we spent out on the sea before we got hold of the runaway raft and crawled on board to the others, home again.

From that day it was strictly forbidden to go out in the rubber dinghy without having a long line made fast to the bows, so that those who remained on board could haul the dinghy in if necessary. We never went far away from the raft, therefore, except when the wind was light and the Pacific curving itself in a gentle swell. But we had these conditions when the raft was halfway to Polynesia and the ocean, all-dominating, arched itself round the globe towards every point of the compass. Then we could safely leave the *Kon-Tiki* and row away into the blue space between sky and sea. When we saw the silhouette of our craft grow smaller and smaller in the distance, and the big sail at last shrunken to a vague black square on the horizon, a sensation of loneliness sometimes crept over us. The sea curved away under us as blue upon blue as the sky above, and where they met all the blue flowed together and became one. We could almost feel as if we were suspended in space; all our world was empty and blue; there was no fixed point in it but the tropical sun which burned our necks, golden and warm. Then the distant sail of the lonely raft drew us to it like a magnetic point on the horizon. We rowed back and crept on board and felt that we had come home again to our own world, on board and yet on firm, safe ground. And inside the bamboo cabin we found shade, and the scent of bamboos and withered palm leaves. The sunny blue purity outside was now served to us in a suitably large dose through the open cabin wall. So we were accustomed to it, and so it was good, for a time, till the great clean blue tempted us out again.

It was most remarkable what a psychological effect the shaky bamboo cabin had on our minds. It measured eight by fourteen feet, and to diminish the pressure of wind and sea it was built so low that we could not stand upright under the ridge of the roof. Walls and roof were made of strong bamboo canes lashed together and guyed, and covered with a tough wickerwork of split bamboos. The green and yellow bars, with fringes of foliage hanging down from the roof, were restful to the eye as a white cabin wall never could have been, and despite the fact that the bamboo wall on the starboard side was open for one third of its length, and roof and walls let in sun and moon, this primitive lair gave a greater feeling of security than white-painted bulkheads and closed portholes would have given in the same circumstances. We tried to find an explanation for this curious fact, and came to the following result. Our own consciousness was totally unaccustomed to associate a palm-covered bamboo dwelling with sea travel. There was no natural harmony between the great rolling ocean and the draughty palm hut which was floating about among the seas. Therefore, either the hut would seem entirely out of place in among the waves, or the waves would seem entirely out of place round the hut wall. So long as we only kept on board, the bamboo hut and its jungle scent were plain reality and the tossing seas seemed rather visionary. But from the rubber boat, waves and hut exchanged roles. The fact that the balsa logs always rode the seas like a gull, and let the water right through aft if a wave broke on board, gave us an unshakeable confidence in the dry part in the middle of the raft where the cabin was. The longer the voyage lasted the safer we felt in our cosy lair, and we looked at the white-crested waves that danced past outside our doorway as if they were an impressive cinema show conveying no menace to us at all. Even though the gaping wall was only five feet from the unprotected edge of the raft and only a foot and a half above the waterline, yet we felt as if we had travelled many miles away from the sea and occupied a jungle dwelling remote from the sea's perils, once we had crawled inside the door. There we could lie on our backs and look up at the curious roof which twisted about like boughs in the wind, and enjoy the jungle smell of raw wood, bamboos and withered palm leaves.

Sometimes, too, we went out in the rubber boat to look at ourselves by night. Coal-black seas towered up on all sides, and a glittering myriad of tropical stars drew a faint reflection from plankton in the water. The world was simple, stars in the darkness. Whether it was 1947 B.C. or A.D. suddenly became of no significance. We lived, and that we felt with alert intensity. We realized that life had been full for men before the technical age also – indeed, fuller and richer in many ways than the life of modern man. Time and evolution somehow ceased to exist; all that was real and all that mattered were the same today as they had always been and would always be; we were swallowed up in the absolute common measure of history, endless unbroken darkness under a swarm of stars. Before us in the night the *Kon-Tiki* rose out of the seas to sink down again behind black masses of water that towered between her and us. In the moonlight there was a singular atmosphere about the raft. Stout shining wooden logs fringed with seaweed, the square pitch-black outline of a Viking sail, a bristly bamboo hut with the yellow light of a paraffin lamp aft – the whole suggested a picture from a fairy tale rather than the actual reality. Now and then the raft disappeared completely behind the black seas; then she rose again and stood out sharp in silhouette against the stars, while glittering water poured from the logs.

When we saw the atmosphere about the solitary raft, we could well see in our mind's eye the whole flotilla of such vessels, spread in fan formation beyond the horizon to increase the chances of finding land, when the first men made their way across this sea. The Inca Tupak Yupanqui, who had brought under his rule both Peru and Ecuador, sailed across the sea with an armada of many thousand men on balsa rafts, just before the Spaniards came, to search for islands which rumour had told of out in the Pacific. He found two islands, which some think were the Galapagos, and after eight months' absence he and his numerous paddlers succeeded in toiling their way back to Ecuador. Kon-Tiki and his followers had certainly sailed in a similar formation several hundred years before, but having discovered the Polynesian islands, they had no reason for trying to struggle back.

*   *   *

Our green parrot, alas, did not share our good luck in the narrow escape we had had when the rubber dinghy nearly drifted away from the raft.

It had been a farewell present from a friendly soul in Lima and was a colourful character who could swear fluently in Spanish. It was always quite thrilled when we had a shark on deck. It came scurrying out of the bamboo cabin and climbed up the wall at frantic speed till it found itself a good safe look-out post on the palm-leaf roof, and there it sat shaking its head, or fluttered to and fro along the ridge, shrieking with excitement. It had at an early date become an excellent sailor, and was always bubbling over with humour and laughter. We reckoned ourselves as seven on board, us six and the green parrot. The crab Johannes had after all to reconcile himself to being regarded as a cold-blooded appendage. At night the parrot crept into its cage under the roof of the bamboo cabin, but in the day-time it strutted about the deck, or hung on to guy-ropes and stays and did the most fascinating acrobatic exercises. To begin with we had turnbuckles on the stays of the mast, but they wore the ropes, so we replaced them by ordinary running knots. When the stays stretched and grew slack from sun and wind, all hands had to turn to and brace up the mast, so that the mangrove-wood masts, as heavy as iron, should not bump against and cut into the ropes till they fell down. And while we were hauling and pulling, at the most critical moment, the parrot began to call out with his cracked voice: 'Haul! Haul! ho, ho, ho, ho, ha, ha, ha!' And if it made us laugh, it laughed till it shook at its own amusingness and swung round and round on the stays.

To begin with the parrot was inimical to our wireless operators. They might be sitting happily absorbed in the wireless corner with their magic earphones on, and perhaps in contact with a wireless fan in Oklahoma. Then their earphones would suddenly go dead, and they could not get a sound however much they coaxed the wires and turned the knobs. The parrot had been busy and bitten off the wire of the aerial. This was specially popular in the early days, when the wire of the aerial stretched upwards attached to a balloon. But one day the parrot became seriously ill. It sat in its cage and moped, and touched no food for two days, while its droppings glittered with golden scraps of aerial. Then the wireless operators repented of their angry words and the parrot its misdeeds, and from that day Torstein and Knut were its chosen friends, and the parrot would never sleep anywhere but in the wireless corner. The parrot's mother tongue was Spanish when it first came on board, and Bengt declared that it took to talking Spanish with a Norwegian accent, long before it began to imitate Torstein's favourite ejaculations in full-blooded Norwegian.

We enjoyed the parrot's humour and brilliant colours for two months, until a big sea came on board from astern while it was on its way down the stay from the masthead. When we discovered that the parrot had gone overboard, it was too late. We did not see it. And the *Kon-Tiki* could not be turned or stopped; if anything went overboard from the raft we had no chance of turning back for it – numerous experiences had shown that.

The loss of the parrot had a depressing effect on our spirits the first evening; we knew that exactly the same thing would happen to ourselves if we fell overboard on a solitary night watch.

We tightened up all the safety regulations, brought into use new life-lines for the night watch, and frightened one another out of believing that we were safe because things had gone well in the first two months. One careless step, one thoughtless movement, could send us where the green parrot had gone, even in broad daylight.

Some time later, Herman was a good deal luckier than the parrot. He was at work on 'deck' one day with his anemometer, which was already measuring fifty feet and more per second, when suddenly Torstein's sleeping bag went overboard. And what happened in the next few seconds took a much shorter time than it takes to tell it.

Herman tried to catch the bag as it went, took a rash step and fell overboard. We heard a faint cry for help amid the noise of the waves, and saw Herman's head and a waving arm, as well as some vague green object twirling about in the water near him. He was struggling for life to get back to the raft through the high seas which had lifted him out from the port side. Torstein, who was at the steering oar aft, and I myself, up in the bows, were the first to perceive him, and we went cold with fear. We bellowed 'man overboard!' at the pitch of our lungs as we rushed to the nearest life-saving gear. The others had not heard Herman's cry at all because of the noise of the sea, but in a trice there was life and bustle on deck. Herman was an excellent swimmer, and though we realized at once that his life was at stake, we had a fair hope that he would manage to crawl back to the edge of the raft before it was too late.

Torstein, who was nearest, seized the bamboo drum round which was the line we used for the lifeboat, for this was within his reach. It was the only time on the whole voyage that this line got caught up. The whole thing happened in a few seconds. Herman was now on a level with the stern of the raft, but a few yards away, and his last hope was to crawl to the blade of the steering oar and hang on to it. As he missed the end of the logs, he reached out for the oar-blade, but it slipped away from him. And there he lay, just where experience had shown we could get nothing back. While Bengt and I launched the dinghy, Knut and Erik threw out the lifebelt. Carrying a long line, it hung ready for use on the corner of the cabin roof, but today the wind was so strong that when they threw the lifebelt it was simply blown back to the raft. After a few unsuccessful throws Herman was already far astern of the steering oar, swimming desperately to keep up with the raft, while the distance increased with each gust of wind. He realized that henceforth the gap would simply go on increasing, but he set a faint hope on the dinghy, which we had now got into the water. Without the line which acted as a brake, it would perhaps have been practicable to drive the rubber raft to meet the swimming man, but whether the rubber raft would ever get back to the *Kon-Tiki* was another matter. Nevertheless, three men in a rubber dinghy had some chance, one man in the sea had none.

Then we suddenly saw Knut take off and plunge head first into the sea. He had the lifebelt in one hand and was heaving himself along. Every time Herman's head appeared on a wave-back Knut was gone, and every time Knut came up Herman was not there. But then we saw both heads at once; they had swum to meet each other and both were hanging on to the lifebelt. Knut waved his arm, and as the rubber raft had meanwhile been hauled on board, all four of us took hold of the line of the lifebelt and hauled for dear life, with our eyes fixed on the great dark object which was visible just behind the two men. This same mysterious beast in the water was pushing a big greenish-black triangle up above the wave-crests; it almost gave Knut a shock when he was on his way over to Herman. Only Herman knew then that the triangle did not belong to a shark or any other sea monster. It was an inflated corner of Torstein's water-tight sleeping bag. But the sleeping bag did not remain floating for long after we had hauled the two men safe and sound on board. Whatever dragged the sleeping bag down into the depths had just missed a better prey.

'Glad I wasn't in it,' said Torstein, and took hold of the steering oar where he had let it go.

But otherwise there were not many cheery cracks that evening. We all felt a chill running through nerve and bone for a long time afterwards. But the cold shivers were mingled with a warm thankfulness that there were still six of us on board.

We had a lot of nice things to say to Knut that day, Herman and the rest of us too.

15 With the Prince's caravan

PETER FLEMING

The author of News from Tartary, *the book from which this sketch is taken, would almost certainly discount the suggestion that his had been a journey into danger. But dangers – and great difficulties and frustrations – there undoubtedly were in the seven-month, 3,500-mile trek on foot, horse and camel, that he and Ella Maillart made from Peking to Kashmir in 1935. Sinkiang or Chinese Turkestan was scantily known, except by previous explorers such as Sir Aurel Stein and Sven Hedin. Civil war raged in China. The Japanese were in occupation of Manchuria. The Russians were probing the frontiers of the region. Altogether Sinkiang in those days was as hazardous and difficult an objective as, shall we say, Mount Everest.*

One night our stuff was still being unloaded from the camels when we received a summons from the Prince of Dzun who was travelling in the same direction. The Prince ought, I am conscious, to be a romantic figure, a true-blue, boot-and-saddle, hawk-on-wrist scion of the house of Chinghis Khan, with flashing eyes and a proud, distant manner and a habit of getting silhouetted on sky-lines. But God, not Metro-Goldwyn-Mayer, made the Prince, and I must tell you what I saw, not what you will be able to see for yourself when Hollywood gets loose in Tartary.

The Prince's tent, by virtue of a blue design worked on it, stood out a little from the rest; but inside magnificence was neither achieved nor attempted. Dirty felts covered the floor; bundles and boxes were stacked round the perimeter of the tent. Half a dozen men were squatting round a fire of dried dung. They made room for us in the place of honour, which is at the left of the back of the tent as you go in.

The Prince greeted us non-committally; it would have been beneath his dignity to show surprise or curiosity. He reminded me of a cat. At first it was something about the way his eyes moved in his head, about the way he sat and watched you; then later, when I saw him walk, there was something cat-like in his gait as well. He was a young man, probably in his early thirties, though with those people it is hard to judge. He wore a cap lined with squirrel fur, and a voluminous scarlet robe, also fur-lined. He was a man of little ceremony, but, although he received from his followers few outward signs of respect, his writ appeared to run effectively and all the time we travelled with him we were conscious that his will directed the caravan. Exactly what he was prince of – how many people, how much land – we never rightly discovered. The Tsaidam, has been studied less, has in fact been visited less, by foreigners than (I should think) any inhabited area of comparable size in Asia. All I know about the tribal organization of the Mongols who live there is that they are divided into four *hoshuns*: Dzun and Barun in the east, Teijinar in the south and west, and Korugu, reputedly the largest, in the north.

Li, our general helpmeet, who had travelled the Tsaidam, on and off, for ten years, spoke Mongol well, and through him we conveyed fumbling courtesies. When the Prince asked where we were going I said 'To Teijinar' (which was the next place of importance after the Prince's own head-quarters at Dzunchia); after that, I said, we didn't know – for it would have been indiscreet to talk about getting through to Sinkiang. We had given him our cards, and presently we showed him our various Chinese passports, which neither he nor Li could read but which looked good and had our photographs on them. We were very much on our best behaviour.

At last the time came to produce our gift. It was a small second-hand telescope. I handed it across the fire with a low bow, holding it on the unturned palms of both hands in the approved style. With it went a *katag*, the flimsy light blue ceremonial scarf which must accompany all presents. The Prince had never seen a telescope before (which was just as well, for this one was a gimcrack affair). He and his staff spent some time peering through it, with faces contorted in the effort to keep one eye shut; and at first it appeared that visibility was poor. We were a prey to those misgivings which assail you when you give a child a toy and the toy, in spite of all they told you at the shop, declines to work. But at last somebody got the focus right, and there were grunts of amazement and delight as a distant camel was brought magically nearer. We withdrew from the audience feeling that we had been accepted at court.

That first day, and for several days thereafter, life in the camp was made irksome by sightseers. There was a crowd perpetually round the tent; all our actions, all our belongings, were closely scrutinized – by the Mongols with vacant gravity, by the Chinese with ill-concealed amusement and a magpie curiosity. 'How much did this cost, Mr. Fu? (As they called me). How much this cost?' It was laughable to recall that we had brought with us a tiny portable gramophone (and three records) because it would be *so* useful to attract the natives; there were times, at this period, when we would gladly have exchanged the gramophone for its weight in tear-gas bombs.

With the Prince's caravan

After our call on the Prince I left Kini to play the two-headed calf alone and went out with the ·22 rifle. I had seen a couple of mandarin duck go down behind a little hill opposite the camp, and I followed them up and had a splendid afternoon, crawling about a soggy little valley through which a stream ran. There were a lot of bar-headed geese there; they had never been under fire before and they usually let me get within a hundred yards, crawling in full view. I shot very moderately, but came back to camp with three. I wanted to present one to the Prince, for this, I thought, would be taken as an appropriate and charming gesture; Li only stopped me in the nick of time. Buddhism, as interpreted in these parts, forbids the Mongols the meat of geese, ducks and hares, but allows them antelope and pheasants. To give the goose would have been a frightful solecism.

The Chinese in the party were less scrupulous. They happened to be Moslems, and as such they should have touched no meat which had not died by the knife; but there is a proverb about Chinese Moslems which gives a good idea of their attitude to Koranic law. 'Three Moslems are one Moslem; two Moslems are half a Moslem; one Moslem is no Moslem.' In other words, the eyes of a man matter more than the eyes of God. So our fellow-travellers contented themselves with cutting the throats of the two dead birds we gave them and began plucking them without a qualm of conscience. We boiled ours – or as much of it as we could get into the pot – and ate it with rice. It was delicious. We felt very Swiss Family Robinson.

We travelled for seventeen days with the Prince of Dzun. Every morning there it wound, stately, methodical, through the bleak and empty land, 250 camels pacing in single file.

At the head of it, leading the first string, usually rode an old woman on a white pony, a gnarled and withered crone whose conical fur-brimmed hat enhanced her resemblance to a witch. Scattered along the flanks, outriders to the main column, went forty or fifty horsemen. Both Chinese and Mongols wore Tibetan dress, which the Mongols, I suppose, originally adopted as a kind of protective disguise, for they are milder, less formidable people than the warlike Tibetans. The little ponies were dwarfed by the bulging sheepskins which encased their masters. Everyone carried, slung across his back, an ancient musket or a matchlock with a forked rest, and a few of the Chinese had repeating carbines, mostly from the arsenal at Taiyuanfu and all of an extremely unreliable appearance. Some people wore broadswords as well.

Thus we marched. For the first two or three hours it was always cold, and we would walk to restore the circulation in our feet. Sooner or later, every day, the wind got up. It came tearing out of the west and scourged us without mercy. It was enough to drive you mad. You could not smoke, you could not speak (for nobody heard you anyway), and after a time you could not think consecutively. The wind was the curse of our life; ubiquitous and inescapable, it played the same part on the Tibetan plateau as insects do in the tropical jungle. It did us no harm (except to chap our faces), but it plagued us and got on our nerves.

However, the wind never blew all day, and there were times when the sun shone and the march was a joy. Men climbed on lightly loaded camels and went to sleep in perilous positions. The Mongols and the Chinese ragged each other and played – with, I always thought, an under-lying hint of fierce and ancient hatreds – a primitive game which consisted of lashing your opponent and his horse with your whip until you or he were put to flight; the whips were light and the sheepskins gave plenty of protection, but it was a tough game for all that. Sometimes a hare was sighted and pursued. Sometimes a few of us would ride on and sit down in the shelter of a hollow to smoke; the long-stemmed, small-bowled pipes would be passed from hand to hand, and mine with them if it was asked for, for I saw no reason to be haughty and exclusive in this matter! When people know no customs but their own, and when their own customs are few because of the extreme simplicity of their life, it is only courteous to respect those customs when you can. Besides, my pipe was a great marvel to them. They had little acquaintance with wood (many of them would not see a tree again until they went back to the markets on the edge of the plateau) and they were used to pipes with metal bowls; they could not conceive how I could smoke mine without setting fire to it. Mongols, though hopelessly uncommercial, know a good thing when they see it, and they appreciated the pipe in the same way that they appreciated my ·22 rifle or my field-glasses.

The hours passed at varying speeds. If it was warm and windless you fell sometimes into a meditation which blotted out a segment of the march, so that when you returned from the far-off things and places that had filled your mind you remembered the country you had passed through hazily, as you remember country in a dream. But if the wind blew no anaesthetic availed; for every yard of every mile you had your wits too much about you, and progress was a slow and wearisome routine.

Towards the end of the seventh hour you began, like everybody else, to watch the Prince, riding his pale horse near the head of the column with three or four followers about him. The moment he wheeled off the trail and dismounted everyone who had a horse put it into a gallop. From all down the mile-long column ponies scurried out across the steppe, their manes and tails streaming, their riders whooping in the headlong race for tent-sites. We always chose one – at his invitation – near the Prince. While we waited for the camels to come up we unsaddled the horses (by no means everyone did this) and hobbled them. Even Greys, my horse, submitted meekly to the hobble, which fastened both hind legs and one foreleg; I never saw a Tibetan pony object to having its legs handled.

Soon the camels arrived, string after string; were claimed and separated; knelt, roaring, to be unloaded. It was a scene of great confusion, yet it resolved itself astonishingly quickly into a neat, placid cluster of tents. All the tents except ours were circular; they were pitched with their backs to the wind, and the loads were stacked in a low rampart under their flaps. Men scattered to collect dung in the wide skirts of their sheepskins; others brought water in big kettles from the stream; and presently the smoke of cooking fires, flattened by the wind, was streaming from the door of every tent. But the Prince, who was a pious man, prayed before he cooked; a low, rhythmic mutter came from inside his tent, and one of his staff walked round and round it, his lips moving mechanically, sprinkling drops of water from a wooden bowl upon the ground.

It was always one of the best moments of the day when we had got our tent pitched and the things stowed inside it, and could plunge in and lie luxuriously on our sleeping bags, out of the wind. Out of the wind; it made such a difference. The air still roared outside and the thin walls bulged in upon us; but we could talk and smoke and rub butter on our chapped and burning faces and feel at peace. Presently there would be tea with red pepper in it and tsamba to abate the gnawing in our bellies. Tsamba is parched barley meal, and can be mistaken, even in a good light, for fine sawdust. You eat it in tea, with butter if you have got butter, or with melted mutton fat if you haven't got butter, or with neither if you have got neither. You fill your shallow wooden bowls with tea, then you let the butter melt in the tea (the butter is usually rancid and has a good cheesy flavour); then you put a handful of tsamba in. At first it floats; then, like a child's castle of sand, its foundations begin to be eaten by the liquid. You coax it with your fingers until it is more or less saturated and has become a paste; this you knead until you have a kind of doughy cake in your hand and the wooden bowl is empty and clean. Your meal is ready.

Tsamba has much to recommend it, and if I were a poet I would write an ode to it. For three months we lived on a diet of tsamba.

We marched usually from 6 a.m. to about 2 p.m., so we had several hours of daylight still before us. After lunch I always went out with the ·22, to wander happily along the lake or, when we left the lake, among the hills, recalling with an exile's pleasure many evenings similarly spent elsewhere, and coming back to camp with a goose or a duck or a hare, even the odd antelope, or with nothing at all. But Kini never took the afternoon off, except to photograph, for there was nothing for her to do out of camp. She read or wrote or darned or slept; and whichever she did she was sooner or later interrupted by somebody who wanted medicine. The Mongols seldom bothered us, but any of the Chinese who were ill, or who had once been ill, or thought they might be going to be ill, came regularly. They fell into three classes: those who had nothing the matter with them at all, those who had had something the matter with them for years and years, and those whom we were able to help. The third class was the smallest.

What with my wretched Chinese and their determination to pile on the agony, it took a long time to discover even approximately the nature of their various afflictions. We were at our best with cuts and sores, which Kini disinfected and bandaged with skill and care (she had once done some Red Cross training with a view to becoming a professional ski teacher). Internal complaints were not so easy, but when in doubt we gave castor oil, a policy which scored several medical triumphs and once won us the gratitude of the most important Chinese by curing him of a fearful belly-ache. One nice and unusually intelligent boy had an old abscess in his thigh and wanted us to cut it open; this we declined to do, but Kini worked on it so successfully with fomentations that in the end it was giving him hardly any trouble. At the close of a long day one of the last things you want to do is to attend to stinking sores on unwashed anatomies, but Kini did it cheerfully and took immense trouble over it; all along the road it was she, not I, who did the dirty work.

It was she, for instance, who went out into the cold and saw to the cooking of the evening meal, while I squatted in the warm tent, cleaning the rifle or writing my diary or playing patience on a suitcase, and asking at frequent intervals how soon the food would be ready. When it was, we put the great black pot just inside the tent and Li brought his bowl and we got out our enamel plates and dinner was served: rice or mien or a kind of noodles which we called by its Russian name of *lapsha*, and whatever meat we had in hand. How we ate! We did not speak. We shovelled the food down until the pot was empty and we were distended. It was my misfortune that I had only a teaspoon to shovel with, for three or four larger spoons which we bought in Sining had broken almost on sight; but it is wonderful what you can do with a teaspoon when you are in the mood, and it equalled things up with Kini, who was a slow eater but had the only larger spoon. They were delicious meals.

As soon as we had finished eating we felt sleepy. Washing up was not a very arduous business, for we had only one plate and one mug each; all the same, it was usually omitted. We pulled off the soft sheepskin boots which I had had made at Tangar for use in camp, wriggled into our flea-bags, and covered ourselves with our overcoats. We made pillows of rolled up sweaters on a foundation of boots and field-glasses; Kini's was always very neat, mine was always a lumpy scrabble. Just outside, our horses munched their barley, making a sound as charming and as soporific as the sound of running water or of waves upon a beach. The tiny tent looked very warm and cheerful in the candle-light, and one of us would perhaps grow suddenly talkative, theorizing about the future or reminiscing about the past. But conversation became increasingly one-sided; mono-syllables were succeeded by grunts, and grunts by a profound indifferent silence. Whichever of us was talking abandoned soliloquy and blew out the candle.

The wind dropped at night. Outside the iron land froze in silence under the moon. The silver tents were quiet. The watchman moved among them squatly (it was bandit country), like a goblin – thinking what thoughts, suppressing what fears?). A wolf barked. A star fell down the tremendous sky. The camp slept.

16 Death on the Mountain

F. S. SMYTHE

Not all international expeditions – or national, for that matter – succeed in maintaining amicable relations among their members. But Smythe, one of the best known mountaineers between the wars, was happier in his experiences. In 1930 he was among a party composed of climbers from four nations – Germany, Austria, Switzerland and Britain. They were successful in the case of the near-25,000 feet Jonsong and other great peaks of the eastern Himalayas, but the notoriously difficult 28,000 feet Kanchenjunga, the 'Five Treasures of the Snow', defeated them. Danger is always close at hand on the mountainside and in this instance Smythe was the helpless witness of the tragedy he describes.

I lay long in my tent that evening writing, and it was nearly midnight before I blew out the candle, and composed myself to sleep. But sleep would not come. I was quite comfortable, my digestive organs were in good order, and acclimatization had reduced my pulse-rate to nearly normal. The night was curiously warm, in fact, the warmest night we had had since we arrived at the Base Camp. Now and again came the long-drawn-out thunder of avalanches.

Perhaps it was the atmosphere, or maybe some trick of the imagination, but the sound of the avalanches seemed dull and muffled. It was as though Kangchenjunga was choking with suppressed wrath. My body was ready for sleep, but my mind was not. It was troubled and restless, groping in a catacomb of doubt and fear. I have known fear before on a mountain, but that was fear of a different nature, sharp and sudden in the face of an immediate danger, but I have never known what it was to lie awake before a climb, tortured by devils of misgiving.

Some people may call this a premonition, but I do not think it can be so defined. Premonition of danger is, after all, an anticipation of danger, where, theoretically, danger ought not to exist. That danger existed in this case cannot be denied. The mind had brooded over it consciously and subconsciously to the detriment of the nerves, and these had become temporarily unstrung. That is a more logical explanation than the acceptance of the premonition theory, which is more dependent upon a belief in psychical phenomena.

When, at last, I fell asleep, I was troubled with terrible dreams. These dreams were not dreams of personal danger, but of danger to the porters. They were always getting into an impossible position, and would turn to me appealingly for help. But I was unable to help. Afterwards, Wood Johnson told me he used frequently to dream this too. Possibly it was due to an innate sense of responsibility. Others on Himalayan expeditions have probably experienced the same sort of dream.

It was a bad night.

I crawled out of my tent the next morning, dull, heavy, and unrefreshed. I looked at the ice wall of the mountain, and the weary track leading up through the snow to it, with loathing. Neither mentally nor physically did I feel fit to start.

The morning was ominously warm and a steamy heat beat down through sluggish mists. The sun was obscured, but for the first time on the mountain we were able to sit outside and keep reasonably warm without its rays on us.

It was decided that the scheme arranged the previous day should be adhered to: all except the cook and myself were to leave and try to establish Camp Three on the terrace.

Schneider with his usual boundless energy was the first to leave. He was accompanied by his servant, 'Satan' Chettan, who was carrying a considerable load.

There was no porter in the expedition of a finer physique than 'Satan', and I remember watching him swing on his load with effortless ease, and start off in the wake of his master, his legs propelling him uphill in shambling powerful strides, the gait of a born hillman and mountaineer.

Duvanel and three porters carrying cinematograph apparatus came next, as the former wished to obtain 'shots' of the last party, which consisted of Hoerlin, Wieland and eight porters carrying heavy loads. For a while I sat on a packing case, watching them as they slowly plodded up the slopes of soft snow, then I adjourned to my tent in order to write some letters.

Perhaps half an hour later I was startled by a tremendous roar. Two thoughts flashed through my mind. Firstly, that only an exceptionally large ice avalanche falling close at hand could make such a din, and secondly, with a sudden clutch of horror at my heart, that the noise came, not from the usual direction of Kangchenjunga's face, but from the ice wall!

I dashed outside. What I saw is indelibly engraved on my memory.

An enormous portion of the ice wall had collapsed. Huge masses of ice as high as cathedrals, were still toppling to destruction; billowing clouds of snow spray were rushing upwards and outwards in the van of a huge avalanche. On the slope below was the party, mere black dots, strung out in a straggling line. They were not moving. For an instant, during which I suppose my brain must have been stunned, the scene was stamped on my mind like a still photograph, or perhaps a more apt comparison would be a ciné film that has jammed for a fraction of a second. Then everything jerked on again. I remember feeling no surprise, it was almost like a fantastic solution to something that had been puzzling me.

Now the dots were moving, moving to the left; they were running, but how slowly, how uselessly before the reeling clouds of death that had already far outflanked them. The next moment the avalanche had swept down upon them; they were engulfed and blotted out like insects beneath a tidal wave.

In the tent I had been conscious of noise, but now I was no longer aware of it. The clouds of snow swept nearer. At first they had seemed to move slowly, but now they were shooting forwards with incredible velocity. Vicious tongues of ice licked out under them. Here and there solitary blocks broke free from the pall; behind them I caught a glimpse of a confused jumble of ice blocks, grinding together like the boulders in a stream bed caught up by the flood waters of a cloudburst.

The thought of personal danger had not occurred to me at first, but now, suddenly, came the realization that the avalanche might sweep the camp away. I glanced round for the cook – he was standing outside the cooking tent – and yelled at him to run for it.

I had stood and watched the avalanche like one rooted to the spot in a nightmare. Running was nightmarish too. The feet sank deeply into the snow; at the height (20,000 feet) every step was an effort. We floundered along for perhaps twenty yards, then heart and lungs gave out, and neither of us could continue. We looked round; the avalanche was stopping two hundred yards away. Though I had not been conscious of any noise after the initial roar, I was paradoxically conscious of it ceasing.

The avalanche stopped, only the clouds of snow, driven by the wind displaced by the falling masses, writhed far into the air. There was no sign of my companions. I turned to the cook: 'They are all killed, but we must do what we can.' We retraced our steps to the camp, seized ice-axes, and set out for the scene of the disaster. We tried to move quickly, but it was impossible at that altitude, it was better to go slowly and steadily, and how slow this was.

The clouds of snow began to settle, the veil thinned. It was a terrible moment. I expected to see no sign of the party. Then, to my immense relief, I saw dimly a figure away to the left, and then some more figures. We toiled upwards, skirting the edge of the avalanche; it was sharply defined, and the ice blocks were piled several feet high. Beyond it the snow was untouched, save where it had been scored by solitary blocks flung forwards from the main mass of ice.

Two hundred yards from the camp the track vanished beneath the debris of the avalanche. We reached a little group of porters. They were standing stupidly, without moving or speaking, on the edge of the debris, all save one, who was probing energetically with an ice-axe between the ice blocks. It was Nemu. I asked him what he was doing, whether there was a man buried there, and he replied, 'Load, sahib, I look for load.' In order to run and escape from the avalanche he had dropped his load, and this was seriously worrying him. Who were alive and who were dead did not concern him, he had dropped his load, the load entrusted to him by the sahibs.

I counted the party, two were missing. Hoerlin, Wieland

and Duvanel I could see above me. The missing ones were Schneider and Chettan. Two hundred feet higher I saw Wieland approaching something sticking out between the ice blocks. It was Chettan's hand. By the time I had climbed up he had been dug out. He was dead, having been carried down at least three hundred feet, and crushed in the torrent of ice blocks. His head had been severely injured, but as a forlorn hope we administered artificial respiration for over an hour.

In the middle of it Schneider reappeared. He had had a marvellous escape. He had actually been under the ice wall when it came down. He said: 'I heard a crack; then down it came, huge masses of ice from hundreds of feet above. I thought I was dead, but I ran to the left, and the avalanche missed me by five metres.'

Chettan had been too far behind Schneider to save himself.

The remainder of the party had amazing luck. They had been on the track where it ran farthest to the left. Had they been ten minutes earlier or later, nothing could have saved them. Even so, they had had to run for their lives, and the track was swept almost from end to end. Duvanel told me that when he saw it coming, the thought of being able to escape never even occurred to him. But, like the others, he had run to the left, as it seemed better to be killed *doing something* than waiting for apparently certain death. So narrow had been the escape of the main body of the porters that some of them had actually been bruised by blocks of ice on the edge of the avalanche.

The escape of the party can only be called a miracle of the mountains.

The portion of the wall that had fallen had been that outlined by a crack noted by Hoerlin and Schneider the previous day. In falling it swept the route on the ice wall diagonally, completely obliterating the lower part of the route that Wieland and I had made, destroying the snow bridge over a crevasse we had reconnoitred, and the ice hump under which we had sat. In fact, the topography of the route we had made at the expense of so much labour had been altered completely. The area of snow slopes covered by the debris must have been nearly a mile square, and the avalanche can scarcely have weighed less than a million tons.

We returned to camp, two of the porters taking turns at carrying Chettan. According to those who had been highest, another crack had opened up above the ice wall, and there was a strong possibility of another avalanche, possibly greater even than the first, which might conceivably sweep away the camp. It was advisable to retire to Camp One with all speed.

But before doing so we buried Chettan.

It was a simple, yet impressive ceremony. A hole was dug in the snow, and the body, dressed as it was in climbing clothes, laid within with folded arms. A handful of rice was roasted by the porters, and this was scattered over the body to the accompaniment of muttered prayers. We stood round with bared heads. Then someone gave an order, and snow was quickly shovelled into the grave. As this was done the mists dispersed, and the sun shone through for a few instants. Almost one could see the brave soul winging its way over the mountains. We drove in an ice-axe to mark the spot, and silently turned away. We had lost not a porter, but a valued friend. We left him buried amid one of the grandest mountain cirques in the world.

So died a genuine lover of the mountains, a real adventurer at heart, and one whom members of several Himalayan expeditions will mourn. Of all Himalayan porters Chettan was the most experienced in mountaineering, for he had accompanied all three Everest expeditions and performed miracles of endurance on Kangchenjunga the previous year.

We descended to Camp One in a wet and soaking snowstorm, that later developed into a blizzard. Wind was howling, and snow lashing the tents, as we ate supper and crept miserably into our sleeping bags.

17 The Other Battle of the Nile

JOHN HANNING SPEKE

An almost mystical reverence surrounded the Nile which had been the cradle of so much civilization – the literal cradle of Moses – the sacred river of the Pharaohs – the river Homer called 'Heaven-fed'. For long centuries its source had remained a mystery; many attempts had been made to trace it upriver from the north. At last in 1862 Speke, in company with James Grant, came to the conclusion that lake Victoria in Uganda must be the source of this, the world's longest river, which stretches four thousand one hundred and sixty miles to the sea. Richard Burton, with whom Speke had quarrelled on a previous expedition, bitterly disputed his findings, and some people criticized him in not following the entire course of the river, but later explorers confirmed Speke's discovery. Here we find Speke making his first 'voyage' on the Nile – and encountering what might be called a little local difficulty.

When at last I stood on the brink of the Nile, most beautiful was the scene, nothing could surpass it! It was the very perfection of the kind of effect aimed at in a highly kept park; with a magnificent stream from 600 to 700 yards wide, dotted with islets and rocks, the former occupied by fishermen's huts, the latter by sterns and crocodiles basking in the sun – flowing between fine high grassy banks, with rich trees and plantains in the background, where herds of nsunnu and hartebeest could be seen grazing, while the hippopotami were snorting in the water, and florikan and guinea-fowl rising at our feet. Unfortunately, the chief 'district officer', Mlondo, was from home, but we took possession of his huts – clean, extensive and tidily kept – facing the river, and felt as if a residence here would do one good. Delays and subterfuges, however, soon came to damp our spirits. Mlondo's deputy was sent for, and asked for the boats; they were all scattered, and could not be collected for a day or two; but, even if they were at hand, no boat ever went up or down the river. The chief was away and would be sent for, as the king often changed his orders, and, after all, might not mean what had been said in respect of providing us with boats. The district belonged to the Sakibobo, and no representative of his had come here. These excuses, of course, would not satisfy us. The boats must be collected, seven, if there were not ten, for we must try them, and come to some understanding about them, before we march up stream, when, if the deputy values his life, he will let us have them, otherwise a complaint will be sent to the king.

We were now approaching Usoga, a country which may be said to be the very counterpart of Uganda in its richness and beauty. Here the people use such huge iron-headed spears with short handles, that, on seeing one, my people remarked that they were better fitted for digging potatoes than piercing men. Elephants, as we had seen by their devastations during the last two marches, were very numerous in this neighbourhood. Till lately, a party from Unyoro, ivory-hunting, had driven them away. Lions were also described as very numerous and destructive to human life. Antelopes were common in the jungle, and the hippopotami, though frequenters of the plantain-garden and constantly heard, were seldom seen on land in consequence of their unsteady habits.

The king's page again came, begging I would not forget

the gun and stimulants I had promised, and bringing with him the things I asked for – two spears, one shield, one dirk, two leopard-cat skins and two sheets of small antelope skins. I told my men they ought to shave their heads and bathe in the holy river, the cradle of Moses – the waters of which, sweetened with sugar, men carry all the way from Egypt to Mecca, and sell to the pilgrims. But 'Bombay' (my chief factotum), who is a philosopher of the Epicurean school, said, 'We don't look on those things in the same fanciful manner that you do; we are contented with all the common-places of life, and look for nothing beyond the present. If things don't go well, it is God's will; and if they do go well, that is His will also.'

Meanwhile, to mollify me, the acting chief brought a present of one cow, one goat and pombe for drink, with a mob of his courtiers to pay his respects. He promised that the seven boats would be ready the next day, and while he was there he asked to be shown my books of birds and animals, and no sooner saw some specimens of Wolf's handi-work, than, in utter surprise he exclaimed: 'I know how these are done; a bird is caught and stamped upon the paper,' using action to his words, and showing what he meant.

We slaughtered and cooked two cows for the journey and gave the women of the place beads in return for their hospitality. They are nearly all Wanyoro, having been cap-tured in that country by king Mtesa and given to Mlondo. They said their teeth were extracted, four to six lower incisors, when they were young, because no Myoro would allow a person to drink from his cup unless he conformed to that custom.

In the end we got just five boats: and in those five boats of five planks each, tied together and caulked with mbugu rags, I started with twelve Wanguana, Kasoro and his page-followers, and a small crew, to reach Kamrasi's palace in Unyoro – goats, dogs and kit, besides grain and dried meat, filling up the complement – but how many days it would take nobody knew. However, at least it was our first voyage on the Nile.

Paddles propelled these vessels, but the lazy crew were slow in the use of them, indulging sometimes in racing spurts, then composedly resting on their paddles whilst the gentle current drifted us along. The river, very unlike what it was from Ripon Falls (as I had named them) downward, bore at once the character of river and lake – clear in the centre, but fringed in most places with tall rush, above which the green banks sloped back like park lands. It was all very pretty and very interesting, and would have continued so, had not Kasoro disgraced the Union Jack, turning it to piratical purposes in less than one hour.

A party of Wanyoro, in twelve or fifteen canoes, made of single tree trunks, had come up the river to trade with the Wasoga, and having stored their vessels with mbugu, dried fish, plantains cooked and raw, pombe and other things, were taking their last meal on shore before they returned to their homes. Kasoro seeing this, and bent on a boyish spree, quite forgetting we were bound for the very places they were bound for, ordered our 'sailors' to drive in amongst them, landed himself, and sent the Wanyoro flying before I knew what game was up, and then set to pillaging and feasting on the property of those very men whom it was our interest to propitiate, as we expected them shortly to be our hosts.

The ground we were on belonged to king Mtesa, being a dependency of Uganda, and it struck me as singular that Wanyoro should be found there; but I no sooner discovered the truth than I made our boatmen disgorge everything they had taken, called back the Wanyoro to take care of their things, and extracted a promise from Kasoro that he would not practise such wicked tricks again, otherwise we could not travel together. Getting to boat again, after a very little paddling we pulled in to shore, on the Uganda side, to stop for the night, and thus allowed the injured Wanyoro to go down the river before us.

I was much annoyed by this interruption, but no argument would prevail on Kasoro to go on. This was the last village on the Uganda frontier, and before we could go any farther in boats it would be necessary to ask leave of Kamrasi's frontier officer, N'yamyonjo, to enter Unyoro. The Wanguana demanded ammunition in the most imperious manner, whilst I, in the same tone, refused to issue any lest a row should take place and they would desert, alluding to their dastardly desertion in Msalala, when Grant was attacked. If a fight should take place, I said they must flock to me at once, and ammunition, which was always ready, would be served out to them. They laughed at this, and asked, Who would stop with me when the fight began? This was making a jest of what I was most afraid of – that they would all run away.

I held a levee to decide on the best manner of proceeding. The Waganda wanted us to stop for the day and feel the way gently, arguing that etiquette demands it. Then, trying to terrify me, they said N'yamyonjo had a hundred boats, and would drive us back to a certainty if we tried to force past them, if he were not first spoken with, as the Waganda had often tried the passage and been repulsed. On the other hand, I argued that Grant must have arrived long ago at Kamrasi's, and removed all these difficulties for us; but, I said, if they would send men, let Bombay start at once by land, and we will follow in boats, after giving him time to say we are coming. This point gained after a hot debate, Bombay started at 10 a.m., and we not till 5 p.m., it being but one hour's journey by boat. The frontier line was soon crossed; and then both sides of the river, Usoga as well as Unyoro, belong to Kamrasi.

I flattered myself all my walking this journey was over, and there was nothing left but to float quietly down the Nile, for Kidgwiga had promised boats, on Kamrasi's account, from Unyoro to Gani, where Petherick's* vessels were said to be stationed; but this hope shared the fate of so many others in Africa. In a while an enormous canoe, full of well-dressed and well-armed men, was seen approaching us. We worked on, and found they turned, as if afraid. Our men paddled faster, they did the same, the pages keeping time playfully by beat of drum, until at last it became an exciting chase, won by the Wanyoro, by their superior numbers. The sun was now setting as we approached N'yamyonjo's. On a rock by the river stood a number of armed men, jumping, jabbering and thrusting with their spears, just as the Waganda do. I thought, indeed, they were Waganda doing this to welcome us; but a glance at Kasoro's glassy eyes told me such was not the case, but, on the contrary, their language and gestures were threats, defying us to land.

The bank of the river, as we advanced, then rose higher, and was crowned with huts and plantations, before which stood groups and lines of men, all fully armed. Further, at this juncture, the canoe we had chased turned broadside on us, and joined in the threatening demonstrations of the people on shore. I could not believe them to be serious – thought they had mistaken us – and stood up in the boat to

* Petherick was a friendly ivory trader who helped Speke.

show myself, hat in hand. I said I was an Englishman going to Kamrasi's, and did all I could, but without creating the slightest impression.

They had heard a drum beat, they said, and that was a signal of war, so war it should be; and Kamrasi's drums rattled up both sides of the river, preparing everybody to arm. This was serious. Further, a second canoe full of armed men issued out from the rushes behind us, as if with a view to cut off our retreat, and the one in front advanced upon us, hemming us in. To retreat together seemed our only chance, but it was getting dark, and my boats were badly manned. I gave the order to close together and retire, offering ammunition as an incentive, and all came to me but one boat, which seemed to be paralysed with fright, it kept spinning round and round like a crippled duck.

The Wanyoro, as they saw us retreating, were now heard to say: 'They are women, they are running, let us at them;' whilst I kept roaring to my men: 'Keep together – come for powder;' and myself loaded with small shot, which even made Kasoro laugh and inquire if it was intended for the Wanyoro. 'Yes, to shoot them like guinea-fowl;' and he laughed again.

But confound my men! they would not keep together, and retreat with me. One of those served with ammunition went as hard as he could go up stream to be out of harm's way, and another preferred hugging the dark shade of the rushes to keeping the clear open, which I desired for the benefit of our guns. It was now getting painfully dark, and the Wanyoro were stealing on us, as we could hear, though nothing could be seen. Presently the shade-seeking boat was attacked, spears were thrown, fortunately into the river instead of into our men, and grappling-hooks were used to link the boats together.

My men cried: 'Help, Bana! (Master) They are killing us;' whilst I roared to my crew: 'Go in, go in, and the victory will be ours;' but not a soul would – they were spellbound to the place; we might have been cut up in detail, it was all the same to those cowardly Waganda, whose only action consisted in crying: 'N'yawo! N'yawo!' – Mother, mother, help us!

Three shots from the hooked boat now finished the action. The Wanyoro had caught a Tartar. Two of their men fell – one killed, one wounded. They were heard saying their opponents were not Waganda, it were better to leave them alone; and retreated, leaving us, totally uninjured, a clear passage up the river. But where was 'Bombay' all this while! He did not return till after us, and then, in considerable excitement, he told his tale. He reached N'yamyonjo's village before noon, asked for the chief, but was desired to wait in a hut until the chief should arrive, as he had gone out on business; the villagers inquired, however, why we had robbed the Wanyoro yesterday, for they had laid a complaint against us. Bombay replied that it was no fault of Bana's (myself), he did everything he could to prevent it, and returned all that the boatmen took.

These men then departed, and did not return until evening, when they asked Bombay, impudently, why he was sitting there, as he had received no invitation to spend the night; and unless he walked off soon they would set fire to his hut. Bombay, without the smallest intention of moving, said that he had orders to see N'yamyonjo, and until he did so he would not budge.

'Well,' said the people, 'you have got your warning, now look out for yourselves;' and Bombay, with his Waganda escort, was left again. Drums then began to beat, and men to hurry to and fro with spears and shields, until at last our guns were heard, and, guessing the cause, Bombay with his Waganda escort rushed out of the hut into the jungle, and, without daring to venture on the beaten track, through thorns and thicket worked his way back to me, lame, and scratched all over with thorns.

Crowds of Waganda, all armed as if for war, came to congratulate us in the morning, jumping, jabbering and shaking their spears at us, denoting a victory gained – for we had shot Wanyoro and no harm had befallen us. 'But the road,' I cried, 'has that been gained – the way forward, that is? I am not going to show my back. We must go again, for there is some mistake; Grant is with Kamrasi, and N'yamyonjo cannot stop us. If you won't go in boats, let us go by land to N'yamyonjo's, and the boats will follow after.'

Not a soul, however, would stir. N'yamyonjo was described as an independent chief, who listened to Kamrasi only when he liked. He did not like strange eyes to see his secret lodges on the N'yanza; and if he did not wish us to go down the river, Kamrasi's orders for us to be helped would go for nothing. His men had now been shot; to go within his reach would be certain death. Argument was useless, boating slow, to send messages worse; so I gave in, turned my back on the Nile, and some days later rejoined Grant who informed me that two great objections had been raised against us by Kamrasi; one was that we were reported to be cannibals, and the other that our advancing by two roads – that is to say, Grant and I having separated for the time being – at once was suspicious . . .

It appeared evident to me that the great king Unyoro, 'the father of all kings', was merely a nervous, fidgety creature, half afraid of us because we were attempting his country by the unusual mode of taking two routes at once, but wholly so of our friends the Waganda, who had never ceased plundering his country for years.

A further parley was absolutely necessary.

18 The Heretic

DR. ALAIN BOMBARD

Distressed by the number of deaths through thirst, starvation and general demoralization that occur among the victims of shipwreck, Bombard aimed to demonstrate that it was possible for survivors to exist on the natural resources of the sea – for instance, to obtain water by squeezing the juices from the fish they could catch – to feed on plankton – even to drink sea-water provided this was taken in small quantities from the beginning. To try to prove his theories, he used himself as a human guinea-pig, built a special makeshift craft with double floats, and after first crossing the Mediterranean sailed from Casablanca on the Moroccan coast, across the Atlantic to Barbados, an immensely courageous voyage in which he endured great hardship. People had scoffed at his ideas, so, appropriately, he named his craft L'Hérétique. *In this extract from* The Bombard Story, *we catch him up in mid-passage.*

'Land! Land!' is the cry of the castaway when he sights the first coast. My cry on the 11th November was 'Rain! Rain!'

I had noticed for some time that the surface of the sea had become strangely calm, exactly as if it were sleeked down with oil, and suddenly I realized why: 'Rain! Here comes the rain,' I cried aloud.

I stripped ready for it, so that I could wash all the salt off my body, and then sat down on one of the floats. I stretched out the tent on my knees, and held between my legs an inflatable rubber mattress, capable of holding some fifteen gallons of water. I waited. Like the sound of a soda syphon, monstrously magnified, I heard advancing from far away the noise of water beating on water. I must have waited nearly twenty minutes, watching the slow approach of this manna from heaven. The waves were flattened under the weight of the rain and the wind buffeted me as the squall hit the boat. The cloud passed over slowly, writhing with the vertical turbulence of a small cyclone. I was drenched in a tropical downpour, which rapidly filled the tent sheet and made it sag with the weight between my knees. I plunged my head in it and as quickly spat the water out again. It was impregnated with salt from the tent and I let it all spill overboard. At the second fill, although the water tasted strongly of rubber, it was like nectar. I washed myself voluptuously. The squall did not last long, but the rainfall was tremendous. Not only did I drink my fill that day, but I was able to store three or four gallons in my rubber mattress. I was going to have a gurgling pillow, but each night my reserve of water was going to renew my hopes for the next day. Even if I had nothing to eat, even if I caught no fish, I at least had something to drink.

For three weeks I had not a drop of fresh water, only the liquid I pressed from my fish, but my reactions were perfectly normal, just the marvellous sensation of swallowing a real drink at last. My skin was still in good order, although much affected by the salt, my mucous membranes had not dried, and my urine had remained normal in quantity, smell and colour. I had proved conclusively that a castaway could live for three weeks (even longer, because I could have continued perfectly well) without fresh water. It is true that Providence was to spare me the ordeal of having to rely again on the flat, insipid fish juice. From that day on I always had enough rainwater to slake my thirst. It sometimes seemed as if my stock was about to run out, but a shower always came in time.

I found that it was impossible to wash the salt out of my clothes and bedding, and I had to remain until the end 'a man of salt water' (as the Polynesians say of people who live off the sea) completely encrusted with it until the day of my arrival.

The day of the rain brought me both pleasure and perturbation. The pleasure consisted in a new sort of bird, an attractive creature called, in English, I believe, a white-tailed tropic bird, and which the French call a *paille-cul*. It looks like a white dove with a black beak and has a long quill in its tail, which, with an impertinent air, it uses as an elevator. I rummaged quickly for my raft book, written for the use of castaways, and read that the appearance of this bird did not necessarily mean that one was near land. But as it could only come from the American continent, being completely unknown in the Old World, it was a good sign. For the first time, I had met a bird which came, without a shadow of doubt, from my destination.

This pleasant interlude was succeeded at about two o'clock in the afternoon by twelve hours of terror, which lasted until two the next morning. Just as I was peacefully reading a little Æschylus, there was a violent blow on the rudder: 'That's another shark,' I thought, and looked up. What I saw was a large swordfish of undeniably menacing aspect. He was following the dinghy at a distance of about twenty feet, seemingly in a rage, his dorsal fin raised like hackles. In one of his feints round the boat, he had collided with my rudder oar. I found I had a determined enemy. If I only succeeded in wounding him, he would surely attack again, and that would be the end of *L'Hérétique*. What was worse, as I was hurriedly getting my harpoon ready, a clumsy movement knocked it into the sea. It was my last one. Now I was disarmed. I fixed my pocket knife on to my underwater gun as a makeshift bayonet, determined to sell my life if he attacked in earnest.

This intolerable anxiety lasted twelve long hours. As night fell I could follow the swordfish's movements by his luminous wake and the noise his dorsal fin made cutting the water. Several times his back bumped the underside of the dinghy, but he still seemed a little afraid of me. He never approached from ahead, and every time he came at me he changed course at the last moment before striking the floats. I came to believe that he was frightened, probably as frightened as I was. Every living creature possesses some means of defence, but it must perturb an attacker not to know what it is. In the early hours of the morning his wake disappeared, but I spent a sleepless night.

One of the lulls in this encounter brought a minor relief, which I interpreted as a message from the land. It was one of those little glass floats used on fishing nets, encrusted with little shell-fish, cirripedia and other sorts of barnacle. It had clearly been in the water a long time, but it was a sign of human life.

It was an exhausting day, and by the time it was over I was utterly miserable. It rained so hard during the night that I thought I was going to have too much fresh water, after having gone without it for so long. I wrote: 'It would really be too much if I drowned in fresh water, but that is what is going to happen if this downpour goes on. I have enough for a month. My God, what a cloudburst! What is more, the sea is rising. A pale sun poked through this morning, but it is still raining.'

Another excitement was what I took to be my first clump of Sargasso seaweed. In fact, it was a magnificent jellyfish, the float blue and violet, of the type known as a Portuguese man-of-war. Its long treacherous filaments, hanging to a considerable depth, can cause dangerous stings, which often develop into ulcers.

I realized after one or two wakeful nights, how essential it was to get a good sleep: 'Forty-eight hours without sleep, and I am utterly depressed; the ordeal is really beginning to get me down. Moreover, the sea is infested with tunny and swordfish. I can see them leaping all round me. I do not mind the tunny and the birds so much, but the sword-fish are a real menace. Am making good speed, but would willingly add another five or six days to the voyage if I could rest up in comparative calm. This dark, forbidding sea has a depressing effect.' It really seemed as if the sea was in mourning. It was as black as ink, flecked from time to time by a white crest, which the plankton made luminous by night. It looked like an evening dress with occasional white flowers, or a Japanese mourning robe. Not a star to be seen and the low sky seemed about to crush me. I realized the full meaning of the term 'heavy weather'; it felt like a physical weight on my shoulders.

At five o'clock on 12th November I noted: 'Rain and yet more rain, this is more than I can stand. But I wonder if I am not nearer the coast than I think, as there are several more birds. There are ten round me at the same time, and my bird book says that more than six mean that one is not more than a hundred or two hundred miles from the coast.' Little did I think that I was only just over a hundred miles away from the Cape Verde Islands.

During the night of the 12th and 13th November, I had another visit from a shark, or at least so I hoped. There was no way of telling whether it was a shark or a swordfish.

Every time a shark appeared during the day, I felt perfectly safe. I gave it the ritual clout on the nose and off it went. But during the night, fearing that one of those devilish creatures might spear me with his sword, I was no longer able to be so bold. I had to remain watchfully awake, trying to identify the intruder, and waiting wide-eyed for it to make off. Sleep was effectively banished. And often it seemed that sharks or other creatures were playing some sort of ball-game during the night with my dinghy, without my daring to interfere.

It was still raining in torrents. Under such a deluge I was obliged to stretch the tent over my head, but it formed great pockets of water which trickled down through the gaps. After a certain time, the weight threatened to break the guy ropes, and I had to push from underneath to spill the water overboard. It must be difficult to realize the sacrifice involved for a castaway in thus jettisoning his reserve of fresh water. Even without sharks and swordfish, sleep had become practically impossible. The rain thundered down and every quarter of an hour or so I had to heave it overboard. An unbelievable quantity of water fell on the tent and trickled through every crevice.

I began to believe, in a confused sort of way, in the active hostility of certain inanimate objects. I might decide to write up the log or work out some calculation. I would sit down, with a pencil ready at hand. I only needed to turn round for ten seconds, and it found some means of disappearing. It was like a mild form of persecution mania, although up till then I had always been able to meet such annoyances with good humour, thinking of the similar misfortunes suffered by the *Three Men in a Boat*.

'*Friday, 14th November*. The last forty-eight hours have been the worst of the voyage. I am covered with little spots and my tongue is coated. I do not like the look of things at all. The storm has been short and violent. Was obliged to put out the sea anchor for several hours, but hoisted sail again at about 9.30. Raining in sheets and everything soaked through. Morale still fairly good, but I am starting to get physically tired of the perpetual wetness, which there is no sun to dry. I do not think I have lost a great deal of time, but it is impossible to determine my latitude as I can see neither sun nor stars, and another of these confounded rain-storms is blowing up from the horizon. The sea is calmer, but yesterday I shipped plenty. They say, "fine weather follows rain". I can hardly wait for it.'

During the night a tremendous wave, catching me by the stern, carried me along at great speed and then flooded *L'Hérétique*, at the same time breaking my rudder oar. The dinghy immediately turned broadside on and my sail started to flap in a sinister manner, straining at my rough stitches. I plunged forward to gather it in, but stumbled against the tent and tore a great rent near the top of one of the poles. There would be no way of mending it properly and it happened just as I had to battle for life with the waves. I threw out both my sea anchors. Docilely *L'Hérétique* turned her stern to my normal course and faced up to her assailants. By this time I was at the end of my strength and, accepting all the risks, I decided that sleep was the first necessity. I fastened up the tent as close as I could and made up my mind to sleep for twenty-four hours, whatever the weather did and whatever happened.

The squalls continued for another ten hours, during which my eggshell craft behaved admirably. But the danger was not yet passed. The worst moments came after the wind had dropped, while the sea continued to rage. The wind seemed to enforce a sort of discipline on the sea,

propelling the waves without giving them time to break:
left to themselves, they were much less disciplined. They
broke with all their force in every direction, overwhelming
everything in their path.

'*Saturday, 15th November, 1330.* Taking advantage of
the rain to do a little writing. Have only two rudder oars
left. Hope they will hold out. Rain has been coming down
in torrents since ten o'clock yesterday evening, no sign of
the sun; am wet through. Everything is soaked and I have
no means of drying a thing, my sleeping bag looks like
a wet sack. No hope of taking my position. The weather
was so bad during the night that I wondered for a time if
I had not drifted into the Doldrums. Fortunately there is
no doubt that the trade wind is still with me. Making good
time, almost too fast for comfort. Still worried about the
sail. When will the weather clear up? There was one patch
of blue sky in the west, but the wind is from the east.
Perhaps tomorrow will be better, but I am going to have
another thick night. About seven o'clock this morning an
aircraft flew over me, quite low. Tried to signal it, but my
torch would not work. First sign of human life since 3rd
November, hope there will be more. Sky to the west now
clearing rapidly, difficult to understand why.'

There was a sort of battle in the sky the whole day
between the two fronts of good and bad weather. I called
it the fight between the blue and the black. It started with
the appearance in the west of a little patch of blue, no
bigger than a gendarme's cap, as the French song has it,
and there seemed little hope of it growing. The black
clouds, impenetrable as ink, seemed fully conscious of their
power, and marched in serried ranks to attack the tiny blue
intruder, but the blue patch seemed to call up reinforce-
ments on its wings, and in a few hours to the south and

north, that is to say to my left and right, several more
blue patches had appeared, all seemingly about to be engulfed in the great black flood advancing towards them. But
where the clouds concentrated on frontal attacks, the blue
of the sky used infiltration tactics, breaking up the mass
of black until the good weather predominated. By four
o'clock in the afternoon its victory was clear. 'Thank God
for the sun! I am covered with little spots, but the sun is
back.' Little did I know that the most troublesome part of
my voyage was about to begin.

I had not the faintest idea where I was. With no sun
for three days I was in a state of complete ignorance, and
on Sunday the 16th when I got my sextant ready, I was in
a fever of apprehension. By a miracle I had not drifted
much to the south. I was still on latitude 16° 59', which
passes to the north of Guadeloupe. That vital point was
settled, but my boat looked like a battlefield. My hat had
blown off in the storm and all I now had as protection for
my head was a little white floppy thing, made out of water-
proofed linen, quite inadequate in such a climate. The tent
was torn in two places and although the dinghy seemed to
have suffered no damage, everything in it was drenched.
Even after the long sunny days which were now to come,
the night dew continued to re-impregnate my warm clothes
and sleeping bag, so I was never again to know a dry night
until I touched land.

A disturbing incident then showed that I could not
afford to relax my vigilance for one moment. During the
storm, I had tried to protect the after part of *L'Hérétique*
from the breaking waves by trailing a large piece of rubberized cloth fixed firmly to the ends of my two floats. This
seemed to divert the force of the waves as they broke behind
me. Even though the storm had died down, I saw no point

in removing this protection. But the following night, a frightful noise brought me out of my sleeping bag at one bound. My protective tail was no longer there. The piece of cloth had been torn away. I checked anxiously that the floats had not been damaged and that they were still firmly inflated. Some creature which I never saw, probably attracted by the vivid yellow colour of the cloth which hung down between the floats, had torn it off by jumping out of the water. This it had done with such precision that there was no other visible sign of its attack.

Like the boat, I too had taken a buffeting. I was much weakened and every movement made me terribly tired, rather like the period after my long fast in the Mediterranean. I was much thinner, but was more worried about the state of my skin. My whole body was covered with tiny red spots. At first they were little more than surface discolorations, not perceptible to the touch, but in a day or two they became hard lumps that finally developed into pustules. I was mortally afraid of a bad attack of boils, which, in the condition I was in, would have had serious consequences. The pain alone would have proved unbearable and I would no longer have been able to sit or lie down.

The only medicament I had to treat such an outbreak was mercurochrome, which made me look as if I was covered in blood. During the night the pain became bad and I could not bear anything in contact with my skin. The least little abrasion seemed to turn septic and I had to disinfect them all very carefully. The skin under my nails was all inflamed, and small pockets of pus, very painful, formed under half of them. I had to lance them without an anaesthetic. I could probably have used some of the penicillin I had on board, but I wanted to keep up my medical observations with a minimum of treatment for as long as I could stand it. My feet were peeling in great strips and in three days I lost the nails from four toes.

I would never have been able to hold out if the deck had not been made of wood, which I regard as an essential piece of equipment in a liferaft. Without it I would have developed gangrene or, at the very least, serious arterial trouble.

For the time being my ailments were still localized. My blood pressure remained good and I was still perspiring normally. In spite of that, I greeted with relief the victorious sun which appeared on the 16th, expecting it to cure the effects of the constant humidity which I had endured. I did not know that the sun was to cause even worse ordeals during the cruel twenty-seven days which were to follow.

The castaway must never give way to despair, and should always remember, when things seem at their worst, that 'something will turn up' and his situation may be changed. But neither should he let himself become too hopeful; it never does to forget that however unbearable an ordeal may seem, there may be another to come which will efface the memory of the first. If a toothache becomes intolerable, it might almost seem a relief to exchange it for an earache. With a really bad pain in the ear, the memory of the toothache becomes a distinctly lesser evil. The best advice that I can give is that whether things go well or ill, the castaway must try to maintain a measure of detachment. The days of rain had been bad enough, but what followed, in spite of the rosy future the sun at first seemed to promise, was to seem much worse.

The 16th November was my twenty-ninth day at sea, and I had every reason for optimism. There had been a decline in my health, but at least the worst part of the journey was now behind me. Up till then I had had to maintain a course across the wind, but now I was sailing directly before it. I had collected enough fresh water for about a month, and the fish which had accompanied me from the start still surrounded the boat. The old hands, those that I had succeeded in wounding during the first few days, had not forgotten their experience and remained out of reach. Every morning I saw them rise from the depths, give me a suspicious look, and then take up their position on a parallel course. Their company became increasingly welcome, partly because they were old friends, and even more because they encouraged other fish to join them. The newcomers arrived in shoals, duped by their more cunning relations, and sported all around me, providing an endless supply of innocent victims.

Certain 'specialists' had advised me to install a small tank in the bottom of the boat in which to keep the fish I caught. The reader will by now appreciate how superfluous was such advice. My larder followed me wherever I went. Not only that, but my faithful dolphins chased unlimited flying fish in my direction. They scared them into flight so that they crashed into my sail, and I picked up five or ten every morning. They never landed in the dinghy during the day, presumably because they saw me and could avoid the obstacle, but I could watch them all the time, as there was never an interval of more than five minutes before a squadron or two took the air. The ingenuity and skill with which the dolphins chased them, after flushing a covey, was a spectacle of which I never got tired. With wide-open mouths they usually managed to be at the exact spot where the flying fish hit the water again. A few of the intended victims, probably taught by experience, changed direction in mid-air, and by bouncing from one wave crest to another managed to elude their pursuers.

Once the storm was over, I carried out an under-water inspection of the dinghy, with a secure lifeline around my waist. Almost all the repairs effected at Las Palmas had succumbed to the battering of the sea. The glue had not held, and strips of rubberized fabric fluttered down lamentably. A whole colony of cirripedia, a type of barnacle, had affixed themselves along the seams. Of all the experts familiar with my type of boat, only M. Debroutelle, the manufacturer of the dinghy, and a real specialist in everything that concerned it, had warned me: 'You cannot expect to avoid barnacles.'

The one detail of construction of L'Hérétique which I considered a potential weakness was the seams which connected the sections of fabric. There was little likelihood of the floats bursting from internal pressure. Every seam had been covered with a safety band, but it was still possible for these tiny shell-fish to penetrate underneath it, tearing it loose as they grew. I had already noticed at Tangier that even when the dinghy was moored to a deep bay, a dense submarine growth attached itself to the bottom, particularly along the seams. The main seams held the sternboard in position between the rubber bottom and the floats, and secured the floats to the rubber bottom.

From Casablanca to the Canaries, the depth of the water and the speed at which I travelled arrested the growth of these marine parasites, but during the time I spent at Las Palmas, the bottom of the dinghy became covered with an absolute forest of sea-weed and barnacles. After I had scraped them off, I noticed with foreboding the little bumps under my safety bands where some of the organisms had penetrated, and I therefore stuck on a double layer. These were precisely the points where the fabric had given way from the effect of the storm. I could carry out no further repairs under water, and had no option but to trust in the confidence which M. Debroutelle had in his boat, and climbed back inboard without much difficulty.

19 Search for the City of Gold

HEDLEY A. CHILVERS

According to popular tradition there were seven lost treasure trails in Africa. If only they could be found they would lead to immense riches that would make Croesus look like a candidate for supplementary benefits. One, for example, was a Rhodesian cache in which Lobengula, King of the Matabele, was supposed to have salted away a hoard worth two millions; another led to the old silver mines on the Zambesi, from which it was believed that the ancient kingdoms of the oriental world had been supplied. The lure of great wealth has always led men into perilous adventures; what is even more astonishing than the dangers they have been prepared to face in order to seek that wealth is the readiness to snatch at the flimsiest rumour of its existence.

According to a distinguished American engineer, an ancient, alien people mined and removed gold to the value of £150,000,000 from Southern Rhodesia. During what period they came and went, leaving their forts and ruins behind them, none can say. Some authorities believe them to have been Babylonians or possibly Indians of Solomon's time; others hold that they were a race of Africans of much later date.

But where has this vast treasure gone? Was it, indeed, convoyed in its entirety across Africa and shipped to the courts of King Solomon? Or was it mined for a mediaeval India or Arabia? None at the moment can say. Those who have stood near the Zimbabwe ruins in Southern Rhodesia, the centre of the activity of these miners, and have asked themselves those questions, will have entered a domain of impenetrable shadow. But, as the sun sinks over that temple of dead things, thought will always leap to some answer; will always silhouette, there on the skyline, the little black shapes of camels and caravans crawling coastwards, the dark, bearded guards ever watchful lest they fall into ambush and lose their gold.

Gold! Gold! Along the uneven highways of human effort lie the remains of peoples and men sacrificed to the service of the metal; their lives snuffed out when scarce begun, a solemn testimony to human folly. And here as we soliloquize in the dreamy valley, little lizards dart around the stones and the drowsing insects hum in the sun. Here and there the blue lotus flashes from the pools, the tree-trunks glow with orchids, the pink-blossomed Zimbabwe Creeper, the yellow blooms, the red sealing-wax flower, the mimosa, acacias, wistarias, palms and tree-ferns all mock the dreamer with an exquisite indifference.

Rumour has it that after Frobenius* and his associates examined the ruins closely, and afterwards in 1929 visited India to forge the last links in the chain of evidence, they found themselves able to present an irrefutable case for a minefield that had been worked in Rhodesia long before the days of Christ. They will seek to prove that while Solomon was dispensing wisdom from his throne of white ivory inlaid with peacocks' feathers and gold, drinking from vessels made from the same metal, and boasting of his three

* Professor Leo Frobenius was granted £5,000 in 1929 by the South African Government to enable him to investigate in India ancient workings with towers and walls similar to those of Mashonaland, Southern Rhodesia.

hundred great shields of beaten gold, that at that time a dark-skinned race of engineers, worshipping strange gods, mined Rhodesia for gold. Their caravans trailed eastward from Zimbabwe to the port of Sofala. Ships took the gold thence – towards Palestine, India and China. But, as the trans-African journey was made in constant fear of death and ambush, they built their relay forts by way of sanctuary.

Whether the views of Frobenius will win acceptance or not, it is obvious that one hundred and fifty million pounds' worth of gold was not mined in a day. With the rough extraction processes then available, mining must have gone on over a long period. During that period it is, as indicated, not unreasonable to assume that the convoys were often overpowered and plundered.

Some goodly proportion of that vast amount of gold, therefore, of which today there is no trace in Africa, might conceivably have been diverted to the 'great palaces' of the robber chiefs. Is there then any tradition among the natives of Rhodesia, or any experience within the memory of white men, which might support such a belief?

The following remarkable experience is given for what it is worth.

There died in St. John's Wood, London, in 1908, one Francis Ryskes-Chandler at the age of 45. His life ended prematurely as the result mainly of fever, but also partly because of certain experiences which affected his nervous health, and of which in after years he was reluctant to speak. Nevertheless, as they involved the possession of knowledge which might perhaps hold a clue to great treasure, he resolved to give a complete account of them to a bank official who had joined the service of the African

Banking Corporation, and who sailed for Cape Town by the *Dunvegan Castle* in August 1901. This official had been in the service previously of the London and Brazilian Bank, but after a severe attack of yellow fever had transferred to the African institution. Ryskes-Chandler felt that if this official were dispatched in the course of his duty to Beira, he might perhaps seize an early opportunity to make his way inland and to bid for success where he himself had failed. The bank official, however, died two years after reaching Cape Town, and his opportunity thus failed to develop.

The story refers to an extensive city hidden somewhere to the north of the route between Zimbabwe and Sofala. Its whereabouts are known only to the witch-doctors and local chiefs (and nowadays to a few white men), and it is said to lie in a remote part of the Amatonga Forest. Tradition has it that long ago whenever the chiefs in that part died, their gold was buried with them. Ryskes-Chandler heard the story in Beira; and it impressed him so much that he decided to combine with his hunting – he had planned a hunting-tour – a search for the forgotten city. Accordingly, he made his way inland with a number of bearers, inquiring of chiefs and witch-doctors as he went. At first his inquiries proved abortive; moreover, the quest made his porters reluctant to proceed; for they conceived these ruins to be bewitched, the sanctuary inviolate of the dead.

One day, however, he found himself in the vicinity of a witch-doctor's hut. The old savage, with his high, brown hat and girdles of snake, leopard and monkey skins, glared at him truculently.

Ryskes-Chandler boldly asked him, through one of his porters, if he knew of 'the great ruin in the forest'.

To his astonishment the old man answered readily:

'Well O hunter do I know it . . . In the forest over the mountain with the dog's head. But woe to the white man who goes there!'

'Why?'

'He would die. It is guarded by the spirit of the forest.'

Ryskes-Chandler handed the old wizard some coins.

'Yes,' he went on a little more amicably, 'it is the city of the chiefs. They are buried there.'

'And what else is there in this city?'

'Tombs and high places . . . and all that the chiefs had of gold and money . . . It was all buried with them.'

'Gold? Whence came the gold?'

'From the older people who worked in the mines.'

'Will you lead me there?'

The witch-doctor frowned. 'I have already spoken,' he said. Nor would he utter another word, realizing apparently that he had said too much.

So the explorer went away with his porters and pitched his camp.

That night these porters deserted him. He sought vainly in the morning to replace them from the adjoining village, for word had evidently gone forth that this white man had come to intrude into sacred places. So, realizing the futility of argument he shouldered his gun, and made his way alone towards the mountain with the dog's head, which he estimated to be ten miles distant.

Some hours later he entered a gloomy gorge and was amused to see a little blue duiker (a small antelope standing about thirteen inches at the shoulder) watching his approach from a rock, until presently it entered the defile before him as if leading the way. It evinced no sign of fear.

The cliffs soon ceased to loom vertically and began to shelve at a less aggressive angle, while the slopes became covered with forest. The duiker bounded on, and the white man, excited and yet apprehensive of the risk of pushing on alone, plunged deeper into the forest. Even the flashing parakeets, the hornbills and monkeys seemed to have made a compact of silence, so that the hunter's footfalls echoed around with curious intensity. The great 'dog's head' was now towering above, a grim monument of glaring rock; and although the sun indicated late afternoon, and he knew that he would have to spend the night in the forest, yet something impelled him on, something sinister, unaccountable and irresistible. The path had been made by game. In the deepening gloom he had no difficulty in following it. Then suddenly a strange thing happened.

Something whizzed past his head. He heard the clangour of metal on rock. It was an assegai! Instantly he turned and pointed his gun in the direction of the unseen enemy, but nothing moved in the thicket; nor could he hear aught save the dying echoes of the spear impacting on the rock.

'Show yourself, you devil!' he muttered, facing the woods with his weapon upraised; but only after a while did he hear the far-off sound, as it seemed, of strange, inhuman laughter. Then he continued his journey:

> Like one that on a lonesome road,
>   Doth walk in fear and dread,
> And, having once turned round, walks on,
>   And turns no more his head;
> Because he knows a frightful fiend
>   Doth close behind him tread.

Ryskes-Chandler was no poltroon. He braced his shoulders, threw off the trepidation which was now assailing him, and resolved that not all the witch-doctors, javelin-men and jungle sprites of Africa should deter him from prosecuting his quest. He was tempted to light his pipe, but reasoned that the glow of it might expose him to the attacks of the javelin-thrower.

It was not yet quite dark when the white man was startled to observe a long lateral ray of sunlight through a rift in the thick foliage, and there, in the full radiance of the beam, on a lofty wall of stone, stood the little duiker, like a statuette. As he looked it vanished. Then with a cry of exultation he stumbled forward, and realized that this wilderness of high walls, breached here and there and overgrown with bush, was the City of the Forest.

Entering through a breach in the stone-work, the explorer found himself in an extensive region of altars and towers, and great slabs of fallen masonry. It all spread away as far as he could see, white and mysterious.

He realized that he must spend the night in the ruins, and determined to make the best of things. He wondered, withal, if the mysterious assegai-thrower had tracked him there, and whether he might venture to light his pipe. He decided to take no risks. Sitting there, then, on a rough slab of stone and moving his heels idly on the flagging underfoot he presently dislodged a heavy piece of metal. He rubbed it on the stone and although he could not see it clearly, felt certain from its weight that it was of gold. He put it in his pocket and discovered afterwards that it was a small golden phallus.

However, as the darkness deepened over that city of sepulchres, the eeriness of it all began to oppress him, and throwing discretion aside he lit his pipe, and then his lantern, noting with misgiving that there was very little oil in it. Indeed, it presently flickered out. Ryskes-

Chandler, nevertheless, determined to keep awake. He occasionally left his bench and walked sharply to the nearest conical tower and back, a track defined by the whiteness of the stone. As the hours wore on the night became bitterly cold.

He judged it to be well past midnight when the intense quiet was sharply broken by a peal of hideous laughter. It died away, then burst forth again, louder and, as it seemed, close at hand. The white man recognized it as the same diabolical laughter that had followed the throwing of the assegai, and he seized his gun and made ready to fire at the first threatening object that presented itself.

'It might have been a hyena!' he muttered, as if to still his doubts. 'I'm jumpy tonight.'

He was. And the leaden hours brought no relief; indeed, he found he could no longer essay his walk to the conical tower but remained motionless on his bench. At last through a thin patch in the trees he descried a greenish glitter as of a thousand emeralds, and he knew that the moon was rising. While watching it listlessly he heard once again the demoniacal laughter. This time it was just behind him. He whipped round, gun in hand; and, at a distance of a few yards, saw an immensely tall figure, with a grotesque face, so distorted as to resemble a mask.

Taking quick aim, he fired, and as he fired heard a prolonged yell, saw the tall figure swaying and receding; then giddiness overcame him, and a stunning blow on the back of the head was followed by unconsciousness.

When he recovered, it was day. He felt ill and dizzy; there was blood on the back of his head. Clearly as he could now see the full extent of the city – which was a vast labyrinth overgrown with trees and thorn – his only desire was to leave it. He accordingly picked himself up, grasped his rifle, and stumbled forth through the breach in the wall, presently striking the trail outside which led to the defile. Some hours later he staggered through the native village of the witch-doctor and got back to his lonely tent. Then he became seriously ill. He would probably have died had his bearers not returned and explained shamefacedly that they had deserted him under threats from the wizard.

'Where then is the witch-doctor?' the sick man demanded. 'Go and tell him to come to me.'

'Master,' explained one of the boys, 'he went away into the forest and has not yet returned.'

Ryskes-Chandler smiled.

'Had he been a better man with the assegai he might have come back,' he told himself. 'And I might have stayed behind.'

While, of course, there is a distinct element of fraud in African black magic, the fact is not entirely surprising that some missionaries and officials long resident in native territories have a certain respect for it. For occasionally the wizards of the tribes seem to make contact with the supernatural. In 1930, for example, two witch-doctors were arguing heatedly at Teyateyaneng in North Basutoland as to their respective powers and knowledge of medicine. They had a crowd of natives for audience. The elder constantly referred to the younger as a 'boy', and even claimed that he had only to will the other's death and he would die. The younger defied him, whereupon the elder, pointing his stick at him, cried: 'Then, die!'

To the utter amazement of all present, the other staggered and fell – dead. The European authorities arrested the older man, but had to release him as the post-mortem revealed the cause of death as heart-failure. The natives remained awestruck, and even the Europeans were mystified by this uncanny exhibition of power.

In September 1923 a *Cape Times* correspondent drew attention to the exploits of the witch-doctor Njenjalwa, near King William's Town in the Cape Province. He twice informed white folk who went to him of the whereabouts of missing money. His revelations were punctuated by a chorus of five young natives who clapped their hands whenever the oracle prophesied, crying '*siyavuma*' ('we agree'), as is the witch-doctor custom. Sometimes, however, black magic takes fantastic form, as in the case of Nozinqundula, the witch of Maritzburg, who in 1927 held public conversation with 'Abalozi', the man of the air, 'who can be heard and not seen'. She quite overawed the natives by talking with the mysterious unseen, who would whistle to her shrilly from above. The leper witch-doctor of Livingstone, Chakopo Kawindi, claims to be able to make silver and gold come out of the ground, but he is a recognized artist in legerdemain.

The most sinister form of wizardry is the practice of killing 'human meat' for burial in the fields to promote crops or bring rain. The end of this is inevitably murder, of course, as in the case of the woman in the Spelonken district who was seized by seven witch-doctors in 1925, kept in durance for a fortnight, and then clubbed to death, her baby being cut up to make ground 'medicine'. Perhaps the wisest of black tyrants was the bloodthirsty Tshaka, who on one occasion secretly slaughtered an ox and spread the blood outside his kraal. He then summoned the witch-doctors and invited them to discover the author of the outrage. They announced that someone was seeking to bewitch the king; whereupon Tshaka ordered them all to be executed, for, he said, their magic had departed. Next, Tshaka sent for an *isangoma* or wise-woman, and invited her to smell out the author of the blood-spilling. The old woman threw the bones, then leered at him.

'Thou hast done it, O King!' she said.

Tshaka was thunderstruck.

' Take her away,' he cried; 'and burn her. She knows too much.' Thus the black art of Africa mystifies us still. In spite of fraud, it rises sometimes to strange heights; and who can say what the witch-doctor knew of the city in the forest, or of its reputed treasure of ancient gold?

That this city exists, and that it is the repository of treasure, is the firm belief of certain hunter-prospectors who have had no opportunity of hearing Ryskes-Chandler's specific story. I myself have now heard circumstantial references to the forgotten city from three independent sources. One hunter, named Webb, who actually visited it, succumbed to blackwater fever before he could return.

Towards the end of 1930 a well-equipped expedition will leave Johannesburg in search of this city of gold. Its leader claims to know its site to within twenty miles – this having been ascertained by the skilful questioning of reluctant natives.

As long as man remains he will no doubt be prepared to journey to the ends of the earth in search of gold!

20 A Camp in the Dark

ROBERT LOUIS STEVENSON

The only opportunity for 'exploration' most of us can enjoy is during our holidays when many thousands of young people go hiking and camping through the length and breadth of Europe. We take it all very much for granted, yet a century ago this kind of adventure was a romantic novelty. After buying a donkey to carry his gear, Stevenson set off through the rugged mountains of the Cévennes – not, one would think, particularly a journey into danger. But the people of the region thought it hazardous enough, for they still talked with awe of the Beast of Gévaudan, a wolf which had claimed many victims; some of the peasants would not even venture out of doors at night, as Stevenson found. In his Travels with a Donkey, *Stevenson left us not only one of the most enjoyable travel books, but he started a new line in holiday-adventures which have brought pleasure to successive generations.*

The next day (Tuesday, September 24th, 1878) it was two o'clock in the afternoon before I got my journal written up and my knapsack repaired, for I was determined to carry my knapsack in the future and have no more ado with baskets; and half an hour afterwards I set out for Le Cheylard l'Évêque, a place on the borders of the forest of Mercoire. A man, I was told, should walk there in an hour and a half; and I thought it scarce too ambitious to suppose that a man encumbered with a donkey might cover the same distance in four hours.

All the way up the long hill from Langogne it rained and

hailed alternately; the wind kept freshening steadily, although slowly; plentiful hurrying clouds – some dragging veils of straight rain-shower, others massed and luminous as though promising snow – careered out of the north and followed me along my way. I was soon out of the cultivated basin of the Allier, and away from the ploughing oxen, and such-like sights of the country. Moor, heathery marsh, tracts of rock and pines, woods of birch all jewelled with the autumn yellow, here and there a few naked cottages and bleak fields – these were the characters of the country. Hill and valley followed valley and hill; the little green and stony cattle-tracks wandered in and out of one another, split into three or four, died away in marshy hollows, and began again sporadically on hillside or at the borders of a wood.

There was no direct road to Cheylard, and it was no easy affair to make a passage in this uneven country and through this intermittent labyrinth of tracks. It must have been about four when I struck Sagnerousse, and went on my way rejoicing in a sure point of departure. Two hours afterwards, the dusk rapidly falling, in a lull of the wind, I issued from a fir-wood where I had long been wandering, and found, not the looked-for village, but another marish bottom among rough-and-tumble hills. For some time past I had heard the ringing of cattle-bells ahead; and now, as I came out of the skirts of the wood, I saw near upon a dozen cows and perhaps as many more black figures, which I conjectured to be children, although the mist had almost unrecognizably exaggerated their forms. These were all silently following each other round and round in a circle, now taking hands, now breaking up with chains and reverences. A dance of children appeals to very innocent and lively thoughts; but, at nightfall on the marshes, the thing was eerie and fantastic to behold. Even I, who am well enough read in Herbert Spencer, felt a sort of silence fall for an instant on my mind. The next I was pricking Modestine forward, and guiding her like an unruly ship through the open. In a path, she went doggedly ahead of her own accord, as before a fair wind; but once on the turf or among heather, and the brute became demented. The tendency of lost travellers to go round in a circle was developed in her to the degree of passion, and it took all the steering I had in me to keep even a decently straight course through a single field.

While I was thus desperately tacking through the bog, children and cattle began to disperse, until only a pair of girls remained behind. From these I sought direction on my path. The peasantry in general were but little disposed to counsel a wayfarer. One old devil simply retired into his house, and barricaded the door on my approach; and I might beat and shout myself hoarse, he turned a deaf ear. Another, having given me a direction which, as I found afterwards, I had misunderstood, complacently watched me going wrong without adding a sign. He did not care a stalk of parsley if I wandered all night upon the hills! As for these two girls, they were a pair of impudent sly sluts, with not a thought but mischief. One put out her tongue at me, the other bade me follow the cows, and they both giggled and jogged each other's elbows. The Beast of Gévaudan ate about a hundred children in this district; I began to think of him with sympathy.

Leaving the girls, I pushed on through the bog, and got into another wood and upon a well-marked road. It grew darker and darker. Modestine, suddenly beginning to smell mischief, bettered the pace of her own accord, and from that time forward gave me no trouble. It was the first sign of intelligence I had occasion to remark in her. At the same time, the wind freshened into half a gale, and another heavy discharge of rain came flying up out of the north. At the other side of the wood I sighted some red windows in the dusk. This was the hamlet of Fouzilhic; three houses on a hillside, near a wood of birches. Here I found a delightful old man, who came a little way with me in the rain to put me safely on the road for Cheylard. He would hear of no reward, but shook his hands above his head almost as if in menace, and refused volubly and shrilly, in unmitigated *patois*.

All seemed right at last. My thoughts began to turn upon dinner and a fireside, and my heart was agreeably softened in my bosom. Alas, and I was on the brink of new and greater miseries! Suddenly, at a single swoop, the night fell. I had been abroad in many a black night, but never in a blacker. A glimmer of rocks, a glimmer of the track where it was well beaten, a certain fleecy density, or night within night, or a tree – this was all that I could discriminate. The sky was simply darkness overhead; even the flying clouds pursued their way invisibly to human eyesight. I could not distinguish my hand at arm's length from the track, nor my goad, at the same distance, from the meadows or the sky.

Soon the road that I was following split, after the fashion of the country, into three or four in a piece of rocky meadow. Since Modestine had shown such a fancy for beaten roads, I tried her instinct in this predicament. But the instinct of an ass is what might be expected from the name; in half a minute she was clambering round and round among some boulders, as lost a donkey as you would wish to see. I should have camped long before had I been properly provided; but as this was to be so short a stage, I had brought no wine, no bread for myself, and little over a pound for my lady friend. Add to this, that I and Modestine were both handsomely wetted by the showers. But now, if I could have found some water, I should have camped at once in spite of all. Water, however, being entirely absent, except in the form of rain, I determined to return to Fouzilhic, and ask a guide a little farther on my way – 'a little farther lend they guiding hand'.

The thing was easy to decide, hard to accomplish. In this sensible roaring blackness I was sure of nothing but the direction of the wind. To this I set my face. The road had disappeared, and I went across country, now in marshy opens, now baffled by walls unscalable to Modestine, until I came once more in sight of some red windows. This time they were differently disposed. It was not Fouzilhic, but Fouzilhac, a hamlet little distant from the other in space, but worlds away in the spirit of its inhabitants. I tied Modestine to a gate, and groped forward, stumbling among rocks, plunging mid-leg in bog, until I gained the entrance of the village. In the first lighted house there was a woman who would not open to me. She could do nothing, she cried to me through the door, being alone and lame; but if I would apply at the next house, there was a man who could help me if he had a mind.

They came to the next door in force, a man, two women, and a girl and brought a pair of lanterns to examine the wayfarer. The man was not ill-looking, but had a shifty smile. He leaned against the doorpost, and heard me state my case. All I asked was a guide as far as Cheylard.

'*C'est que, voyez-vous, il fait noir*,' said he.

I told him that was just my reason for requiring help.

'I understand that,' said he, looking uncomfortable; '*mais – c'est – de la peine.*'

I was willing to pay, I said. He shook his head. I rose as high as ten francs; but he continued to shake his head.

'Name your own price, then,' said I.

'*Ce n'est pas ça*,' he said at length, and with evident difficulty; 'but I am not going to cross the door – *mais je ne sortirai pas de la porte*.'

I grew a little warm, and asked him what he proposed that I should do.

'Where are you going beyond Cheylard?' he asked by way of answer.

'That is no affair of yours,' I returned, for I was not going to indulge his bestial curiosity; 'it changes nothing in my present predicament.'

'*C'est vrai, ça*,' he acknowledged, with a laugh; '*oui, c'est vrai. Et d'où venez-vous?*'

A better man than I might have felt nettled.

'Oh,' said I, 'I am not going to answer any of your questions, so you may spare yourself the trouble of putting them. I am late enough already; I want help. If you will not guide me yourself, at least help me to find someone else who will.'

'Hold on,' he cried suddenly. 'Was it not you who passed in the meadow while it was still day?'

'Yes, yes,' said the girl, whom I had not hitherto recognized; 'it was monsieur; I told him to follow the cows.'

'As for you, mademoiselle,' said I, 'you are a *farceuse*.'

'And,' added the man, 'what the devil have you done to be still here?'

What the devil, indeed! But there I was.

'The great thing,' said I, 'is to make an end of it;' and once more proposed that he should help me find a guide.

'*C'est que*,' he said again, '*c'est que – il fait noir*.'

'Very well,' said I; 'Take one of your lanterns.'

'No,' he cried, drawing a thought backward, and again intrenching himself behind one of his former phrases; 'I will not cross the door.'

I looked at him. I saw the unaffected terror struggling on his face with unaffected shame; he was smiling pitifully and wetting his lip with his tongue, like a detected schoolboy. I drew a brief picture of my state, and asked him what I was to do.

'I don't know,' he said; 'I will not cross the door.'

Here was the Beast of Gévaudan, and no mistake.

'Sir,' said I with my most commanding manners, 'you are a coward.'

And with that I turned by back upon the family party, who hastened to retire within their fortifications; and the famous door was closed again, but not till I had overheard the sound of laughter. *Filia barbara pater barbarior.* Let me say it in the plural: the Beasts of Gévaudan.

The lanterns had somewhat dazzled me, and I ploughed distressfully among stones and rubbish-heaps. All the other houses in the village were both dark and silent; and though I knocked here and there a door, my knocking was unanswered. It was a bad business; I gave up Fouzilhac with my curses. The rain had stopped, and the wind, which still kept rising, began to dry my coat and trousers. 'Very well,' thought I, 'water or no water, I must camp.' But the first thing was to return to Modestine. I am pretty sure I was twenty minutes groping for my lady in the dark; and if it had not been for the unkindly services of the bog, into which I once more stumbled, I might have still been groping for her at dawn. My next business was to gain the shelter of a wood, for the wind was cold as well as boisterous. How, in this well-wooded district, I should have been so long in finding one, is another of the insoluble mysteries of this day's adventures; but I will take my oath that I put near an hour to the discovery.

At last black trees began to show upon my left, and, suddenly crossing the road, made a cave of unmitigated blackness right in front. I call it a cave without exaggeration; to pass below that arch of leaves was like entering a dungeon. I felt about until my hand encountered a stout branch, and to this I tied Modestine, a haggard, drenched, desponding donkey. Then I lowered my pack, laid it along the wall on the margin of the road, and unbuckled my straps. I knew well enough where the lantern was; but where were the candles? I groped and groped among the tumbled articles, and, while I was thus groping, suddenly I touched the spirit-lamp. Salvation! This would serve my turn as well. The wind roared unwearyingly among the trees; I could hear the boughs tossing and the leaves churning through half a mile of forest; yet the scene of my encampment was not only as black as the pit, but admirably sheltered. At the second match the wick caught flame. The light was both vivid and shifting; but it cut me off from the universe, and doubled the darkness of the surrounding night.

I tied Modestine more conveniently for herself, and broke up half the black bread for her supper, reserving the other half against the morning. Then I gathered what I should want within reach, took off my wet boots and gaiters, which I wrapped in my waterproof, arranged my knapsack for a pillow under the flap of my sleeping-bag, insinuated my limbs into the interior, and buckled myself in like a *bambino*. I opened a tin of Bologna sausage and broke a cake of chocolate, and that was all I had to eat. It may sound offensive, but I ate them together, bite by bite, by way of bread and meat. All I had to wash down this revolting mixture was neat brandy; a revolting beverage in itself. But I was rare and hungry; ate well, and smoked one of the best cigarettes in my experience. Then I put a stone in my straw hat, pulled the flap of my fur cap over my neck and eyes, put my revolver ready to my hand, and snuggled well down among the sheepskins.

I questioned at first if I were sleepy, for I felt my heart beating faster than usual, as if with an agreeable excitement to which my mind remained a stranger. But as soon as my eyelids touched, that subtle glue leaped between them, and they would no more come separate. The wind among the trees was my lullaby. Sometimes it sounded for minutes together with a steady, even rush, not rising nor abating; and again it would swell and burst like a great crashing breaker, and the trees would patter me all over with big drops from the rain of the afternoon. Night after night, in my own bedroom in the country, I have given ear to this perturbing concert of the wind among the woods; but whether it was a difference in the trees, or the lie of the ground, or because I was myself outside and in the midst of it, the fact remains that the wind sang to a different tune among these woods of Gévaudan. I hearkened and hearkened; and meanwhile sleep took gradual possession of my body and subdued my thoughts and senses; but still my last waking effort was to listen and distinguish, and my last conscious state was one of wonder at the foreign clamour in my ears.

Twice in the course of the dark hours – once when a stone galled me underneath the sack, and again when the poor patient Modestine, growing angry, pawed and stamped upon the road – I was recalled for a brief while to consciousness, and saw a star or two overhead, and the lace-like edge of the foliage against the sky. When I awoke for the third time (Wednesday, September 25th), the world was flooded with a blue light, the mother of the dawn. I saw the leaves labouring in the wind and the ribbon of the road; and, on turning my head, there was Modestine tied to a beech, and standing half across the path in an attitude of inimitable patience. I closed my eyes again, and set to thinking over the experience of the night. I was surprised to find how easy and pleasant it had been, even in this tempestuous weather. The stone which annoyed me would not have been there, had I not been forced to camp blindfold in the opaque night; and I had felt no other inconvenience, except when my feet encountered the lantern or the second colume of Peyrat's *Pastors of the Desert* among the mixed contents of my sleeping-bag; nay, more, I had felt not a touch of cold, and awakened with unusually lightsome and clear sensations.

With that, I shook myself, got once more into my boots and gaiters, and, breaking up the rest of the bread for Modestine, strolled about to see in what part of the world I had awakened. Ulysses, left on Ithaca, and with a mind unsettled by the goddess, was not more pleasantly astray. I have been after an adventure all my life, a pure dispassionate adventure, such as befell early and heroic voyagers; and thus to be found by morning in a random woodside nook in Gévaudan – not knowing north from south, as strange to my surroundings as the first man upon the earth, an inland castaway – was to find a fraction of my day-dreams realized. I was on the skirt of a little wood of birch, sprinkled with a few beeches; behind, it adjoined another wood of fir; and in front, it broke up and went down in open order into a shallow and meadowy dale. All around there were bare hilltops, some near, some far away, as the perspective closed or opened, but none apparently much higher than the rest. The wind huddled the trees. The golden specks of autumn in the birches tossed shiveringly. Over head the sky was full of strings and shreds of vapour, flying, vanishing, reappearing and turning about an axis like tumblers, as the wind hounded them through heaven. It was wild weather and famishing cold. I ate some chocolate, swallowed a mouthful of brandy, and smoked a cigarette before the cold should have time to disable my fingers. And by the time I had got all this done, and had made my pack and bound it on the pack-saddle, the day was tiptoe on the threshold of the east. We had not gone many steps along the lane before the sun, still invisible to me, sent a glow of gold over some cloud mountains that lay ranged along the eastern sky.

The wind has us on the stern, and hurried us bitingly forward. I buttoned myself into my coat, and walked on in a pleasant frame of mind with all men, when suddenly, at a corner, there was Fouzilhic once more in front of me. Not only that, but there was the old gentleman who had escorted me so far the night before, running out of his house at sight of me, with hands upraised in horror.

'My poor boy!' he cried. 'What does this mean?'

I told him what had happened. He beat his old hands like clappers in a mill, to think how lightly he had let me go; but when he heard of the man of Fouzilhac, anger and depression seized upon his mind.

'This time, at least,' said he, 'there shall be no mistake.'

And he limped along, for he was very rheumatic, for about half a mile, and until I was almost within sight of Cheylard, the destination I had hunted for so long.

21 The Treacherous Desert

HENRY BARTH

*The exploits of this young German explorer have never
fully received the recognition they deserve. In 1849, with a
compatriot, Dr. Overweg, he went on a British Government expedition to North Africa to negotiate commercial
treaties with the chiefs of the interior. By arrangement,
midway across the Sahara, Dr. Barth parted from James
Richardson, the leader, and continued his perilous journey
to Kano, which he reached so destitute that he had to
borrow sufficient cowrie shells, local currency, to proceed
with his explorations which took him in search of the
Benue, the Niger's greatest tributary, and then to Lake
Chad. In this extract we find him and his companions at
the mercy of the hostile Touareg, though subsequently
Barth faced even greater danger in Timbuktu.*

After a march of twelve and a half hours, which I would
have gladly doubled, provided our steps had been directed
in a straight line towards the longed-for regions of Negro-
land, we arrived at the half-way stage between Ghat and
Air, a place regarded with a kind of religious awe by the
natives, who in passing it place each a stone upon the
mighty granite blocks which mark the spot.

At twenty minutes past six o'clock we at length encamped, but were again in the saddle at eleven o'clock at
night, and in pale moonlight, sleepy and worn out as we
were, began a dreadful night's march. But altogether it
proved to be a wise measure taken by our companions of the
Kel-owi tribe, who had reason to be afraid lest the Hogar,

of whom they appeared to have trustworthy news might overtake us before we reached the wells of Asiu, and then treat us as they pleased. Our companions, who were of course themselves not quite insensible to fatigue, as night advanced, became very uncertain in their direction, and kept much too far to the south.

When day dawned our road lay over a flat, rocky, sandstone surface, while we passed on our left a locality remarkable for nothing but its name, Efinagha. We then descended from the rocky ground into the extremely shallow valley of Asiu, overgrown with scanty herbage of a kind not much liked by camels. Here we encamped, near a group of four wells, which still belong to the Azkar tribe, while a little further on there are others which the Kel-owi regard as their own property. How it was that we did not encamp near the latter I cannot say. But the people were glad to have got so far. The wells, or at least two of them, afforded an abundant supply of water; but it was not of a good quality, and had a peculiar taste, I think on account of the iron ore with which it was impregnated.

This then was Asiu, a place important for the caravan trade at all times, on account of the routes from Ghadames and from Tawat joining here, and which did so even as far back as the time when the famous traveller Ibn Batuta returned from his enterprising journey to Sudan homewards by way of Tawat (in the year 1353-4). Desolate and melancholy as it appeared, it was also an important station to us, as we thought that we had now left the most difficult part of the journey behind us. For though I myself had some forebodings of a danger threatening us, we had no idea that the difficulties which we should have to encounter were incomparably greater than those which we had passed through. Mr. Richardson supposed that because we had reached the imaginary frontier of the territories of the Azkar and Kel-owi, we were beyond the reach of any attack from the north. With the utmost obstinacy he reprobated as absurd any supposition that such a frontier might be easily crossed by nomadic roving tribes, asserting that these frontiers in the desert were respected much more scrupulously than any frontier of Austria, notwithstanding the innumerable host of its land-waiters. But he was soon to be undeceived on all the points of his desert diplomacy – at his own expense and that of us all.

There was little attraction for roving about in this broad gravelly plain. Now and then a group of granite blocks interrupted the monotonous level, bordered on the north by a gradually ascending rocky ground, while the southern border rose to a somewhat higher elevation. Desolate as the spot was, and gloomy as were our prospects, the arrival of our friends of the Tinylkum (after our temporary separation) in the course of the afternoon afforded a very cheerful sight, and inspired some confidence, as we felt that our little party had once more resumed its strength. All the people, however, displayed an outward show of tranquillity and security, with the exception of Serki-n-turawa, who was bustling about in a state of the utmost excitement. Watering the camels and filling the water-skins employed the whole day.

After a two hours' march next day we began to ascend, first gradually, then more steeply, all the rocks hereabouts, consisting of slate, being greatly split and rent, and covered with sand. In twenty-five minutes we reached the higher level, which consisted of pebbly ground, with a ridge running, at the distance of about four miles, to the west.

While we were quietly pursuing our road, with the

Kel-owi in the van, the Tinylkum marching in the rear, suddenly Mohammed the Sfaksi came running behind us, swinging his musket over his head, and crying lustily, '*He awelad, awelad bu, aduna ja!*' (Lads, lads, our enemy has come!'), and spreading the utmost alarm through the whole of the caravan. Everybody seized his arms, whether musket, spear, sword, or bow, and whosoever was riding jumped down from his camel. Some time elapsed before it was possible, amid the noise and uproar, to learn the cause of the alarm. At length it transpired. A man named Mohammed, belonging to the caravan, having remained a little behind at the well, had observed three Touareg, mounted on swift camels, approaching at a rapid rate; and while he himself followed the caravan, he left his slave behind to see whether others were in the rear. The slave, after a while, overtook him, with the news that several more camels had become visible in the distance; and then Mohammed and his slave hurried on to bring us the intelligence. Even Mr. Richardson, who, being rather hard of hearing, judged of our situation only from the alarm, descended from his slender little she-camel and cocked his pistols. A warlike spirit seemed to have taken possession of the whole caravan, and I am persuaded that had we been attacked at this moment, all would have fought valiantly. But such is not the habit of freebooting parties: they will cling artfully to a caravan, and first introduce themselves in a tranquil and peaceable way, till they have succeeded in disturbing the little unity which exists in such a troop, composed as it is of the most different elements; they then gradually throw off the mask, and in general attain their object.

When at length a little tranquillity had been restored, and plenty of powder and shot had been distributed among those armed with firelocks, the opinion began to prevail that, even if the whole of the report should be true, it was not probable that we should be attacked by daylight. We therefore continued our march with a greater feeling of security, while a body of archers were despatched to learn the news of a small caravan which was coming from Sudan, and marching at some distance from us, behind a low ridge of rocks. They were a few Tebu, with ten camels and between thirty and forty slaves, unconsciously going to meet a terrible fate; for we afterwards learned that the Imghad of the Hogar tribes, disappointed at our having passed through their country without their getting anything from us, had attacked this little troop, murdering the Tebu, and carrying off their camels and slaves.

While the caravan was going slowly on, I was enabled to allow my camel a little feeding on the nesi plant, much liked by camels, in a spot called Tahasasa. At noon we began to ascend on rocky ground, and, after a very gradual ascent of three miles, reached the higher level, strewn with pebbles, but exhibiting further on a rugged slaty soil, till we reached the valley Fenorang. This valley, which is a little less than a mile in breadth and two in length, is famous for its rich supply of herbage, principally of the kind called *bu rekkebah*, and the far-famed *el had* (the camel's dainty), and is on this account an important halting-place for the caravans coming from the north, after having traversed that naked part of the desert, which produces scarcely any food for the camel. Notwithstanding, therefore, the danger which threatened us, it was determined to remain here not only this, but also the following day.

As soon as the loads were taken off their backs, the half-starved camels fell to devouring eagerly the fine herbage offered them. Meanwhile we encamped as close together as possible, preparing ourselves for the worst, and looking anxiously around in every direction. But nobody was to be seen till the evening, when the three men on their swift camels made their appearance, and, being allowed to approach the caravan, made no secret of the fact that a greater number were behind them.

Aware of what might happen, our small troop had all their arms ready, in order to repulse any attack; but the Kel-owi and the few Azkar who were in our caravan kept us back, and, after a little talk, allowed the visitors to lie down for the night near our encampment, and even solicited our hospitality in their behalf. Nevertheless, all of them well knew that the strangers were freebooters, who could not but have bad designs against us; and the experienced old Awed el Kher, the sheikh of the Kafila, came expressly to us, warning and begging us to be on our guard, while Boro Serki-n-turawa began to play a conspicuous part, addressing the Kel-owi and Tinylkum in a formal speech, and exhorting them to stand by us. Everybody was crying for powder, and nobody could get enough. Our clever but occasionally very troublesome servant Mohammed conceived a strategical plan, placing on the north side of the two tents the four pieces of the 'boat' we were carrying, behind each of which one of us had to take his station in case of an attack.

Having had some experience of freebooters' practices in my former wanderings, I knew that all this was mere farce and mockery, and that the only way of ensuring our safety would have been to prevent these scouts from approaching us at all. We kept watch the whole night; and of course the strangers, seeing us well on our guard, and the whole caravan still in high spirits and in unity, ventured upon nothing.

In the morning (August 19) our three 'guests' (who, as I made out, did not belong to the Azkar, but were Kel-fade from the northern districts of Air) went slowly away, but only to join their companions, who had kept at some distance beyond the rocky ridge which bordered, or rather interrupted, the valley to the westward. There some individuals of the caravan, who went to cut herbage, found the fresh traces of nine camels. In spite of outward tranquillity, there was much matter for anxiety and much restlessness in the caravan, and suddenly an alarm was given that the camels had been stolen, but fortunately it proved to be unfounded. Abd el Kader, a Tawati, trying to take advantage of this state of things, came to Mr. Overweg, and urgently pressed him to deposit everything of value with Awed el Kher, the Kel-owi, and something 'of course' with him also. This was truly very disinterested advice; for if anything had happened to us, they would of course have become our heirs! In the evening we again had three guests – not, however, the same as before, but some of their companions, who belonged to the Hadanara, one of the divisions of the Azkar.

The following day we started at an early hour, with an uneasy feeling. With the first dawn the true believers had been called together to prayer, and the bond which united the Mohammedan members of the caravan with the Christian travellers had been loosened in a very conspicuous manner. Then the encampment broke up, and we set out – not, however, as we had been accustomed to go latterly, every little party starting off as soon as they were ready, but all waiting till the whole caravan had loaded their camels, when we began our march in close order, first along the valley, then entering upon higher ground, sometimes gravelly, at others rocky. The range to our right, here a little more than a mile distant, bears different names, corresponding to the more prominent parts into which it is separated by hollows or saddles, the last cone towards the south being called Timazkaren, a name most probably connected with that of the Azkar tribe, while another is named Tin-durdu-rang. The Tarki or Amoshagh is very expressive in names; and whenever the meaning of all these appellations shall be brought to light, I am sure we shall find some interesting significations. Though I paid a good deal of attention to their language, the Tarkiyeh or Temashight, I had leisure enough to become master of the more difficult and obsolete terms; and, of course, very few even among themselves can at present tell the exact meaning of a name derived from ancient times.

But in any case my ruminations were now interrupted: at length we had left behind us that remarkable ridge, and entering another shallow valley full of young herbage, followed its windings, the whole presenting a very irregular structure, when suddenly four men were seen ahead of us on an eminence, and instantly a troop of lightly armed people, amongst them three archers, were despatched, as it seemed, in order to reconnoitre, marching in regular order straight for the eminence.

Being in the first line of our caravan, and not feeling so sure on the camel as on foot, I dismounted, and marched forward, leading my animal by the nose-cord, and with my eyes fixed upon the scene before us. But how much was I surprised when I saw two of the four unknown individuals executing a wild sort of armed dance together with the Kel-owi, while the others were sitting quietly on the ground! Much perplexed, I continued to move slowly on, when two of the men who had danced suddenly rushed upon me, and grasping the rope of my camel, asked for tribute. Quite unprepared for such a scene under such circumstances, I grasped my pistol, when, just at the right time, I learnt the reason and character of this curious proceeding.

The little eminence on the top of which we had observed the people, and at the foot of which the armed dance was performed, is an important locality in the modern history of the country which we had reached. For here it was that when the Kel-owi (at that time an unmixed and pure Berber tribe, as it seems) took possession of the country of Old Gober, with its capital, Tinshaman, a compromise or covenant was entered into between the red conquerors and the black natives, that the latter should not be destroyed, and that the principal chief of the Kel-owi should only be allowed to marry a black woman. And as a memorial of this transaction, the custom has been preserved that when caravans pass the spot where the covenant was entered into, near the little rock Maket-n-ikelan, 'the slaves' shall be merry and be authorized to levy upon their masters a small tribute. The black man who stopped me was the 'serki-n-bai' (the principal or chief of the slaves).

These poor merry creatures, while the caravan was proceeding on its march, executed another dance; and the whole would have been an incident of the utmost interest, if our minds and those of all the well-disposed members of the caravan had not been greatly oppressed and vexed with sad forebodings of mishap. The fear was so great that the amiable and sociable Sliman (one of the Tinylkum, who at a later period manifested his sympathy with us in our misfortunes) begged me most urgently to keep more in the middle of the caravan, as he was afraid that one of those ruffians might suddenly rush upon me, and pierce me with his spear.

The soil hereabout consisted entirely of bare gravel; but farther on it became more uneven, and broken by granite rocks, in the cavities among which our people found some rain-water. The tract on our right was called Tisgawade, while the heights on our left bore the name Tin-ebbeke. I here rode awhile by the side of Emeli, a Tarki of the tribe of Azkar, a gentleman both in his dress and manners, who never descended from the back of his camel. Although he appeared not to be very hostile to the robbers on our track, and was certainly aware of their intentions, I liked him on account of his distinguished manners, and, under more favourable circumstances, should have been able to obtain a great deal of information from him. But there was with him a rather disagreeable and malicious fellow named Mohammed (or, as the Tuareg pronounce it, Mokhammed), from Yanet, who, in the course of the difficulties which befell us, did us a great deal of mischief, and was fully disposed to do us much more.

The country, which in the meantime had become more open, after a while became bordered ahead by elevations in the form of a semi-circle, while we began to ascend. The weather had been extremely sultry and close the whole day, and at last, about three o'clock in the afternoon, the storm broke out, but with less violence than on the day before our arrival at Asiu. We encamped at length on an open gravelly plain, surrounded by ridges of rocks, without pitching our tents; for our unwished-for guests had in the face of the Tinylkum openly declared that their design was to kill us, but that they wanted first to get more assistance. Notwithstanding this, Mr. Richardson even tonight was obliged to feed these ruffians; such is the weakness of a caravan – although in our case the difference or religion, and consequent want of unity, could not but greatly contribute to paralyze its strength. I here heard that some of the party were Imghad, from Tadomat. Under such circumstances, and in such a state of feeling, it was impossible to enjoy the sport and frolics of the slaves (that is, of the domestic slaves) of the Kel-owi, who with wild gestures and cries were running about the encampment to exact from all the free individuals of the caravan their little Maket-n-ikelan tribute, receiving from one a small quantity of dates, from another a piece of muslin or a knife, from another a shirt. Everybody was obliged to give something, however small. Notwithstanding our long day's march, Overweg and I found it necessary to be on watch the whole night.

Starting at an early hour on August 21, we ascended very rugged ground, the rocky ridges on both sides often meeting together and forming irregular defiles. After a march of five and a half miles, we reached the highest elevation, and obtained a view over the whole district in which ran several small valleys where the growth of trees was in places splendid and luxuriant. Some distance further on we found in this a very pretty and picturesque camping-ground. At the foot of our tents was a rocky bed of a deep and winding torrent, bordered by the most beautiful talha and aborak trees, and forming a small pond where the water, rushing down from the rocks behind, had collected; the fresh green of the trees, enlivened by recent rains, formed a beautiful contrast with the dark-yellowish colour of the rocks behind. Notwithstanding our perilous situation, I could not help straying about, and found, on the blocks over the tebki or pond, some coarse rock-sculptures representing oxen, asses, and a very tall animal which, according to the Kel-owi, was intended to represent the giraffe.

While I was enjoying the scenery of the place, one of the

men, named Didi, stepped suddenly behind me, and tried to throw me down, but not succeeding, laid his hands from behind upon the pistols which I wore in my belt, trying, by way of experiment, whether I was able to use them notwithstanding his grasp; but turning sharply round, I freed myself from his hold, and told him that no effeminate person like himself should take me. He was a cunning and insidious fellow, and I trusted him the least of our Kel-owi friends. Annur warned us that the freebooters intended to carry off the camels that we were ourselves riding, in the night; and it was fortunate that we had provided for the emergency, and were able to fasten them to strong iron rings.

While keeping the first watch during the night, I was enabled by the splendid moonlight to address a few lines in pencil to my friends at home.

Great though our anxieties were here, they increased considerably when, a day or two later, we entered the valley called Taghajit, important as being the first in the frontier region of Air or Asben where there is a fixed settlement – a small village of leathern tents, inhabited by people of the tribe of Fade-ang, who preserve a certain independence of the Kel-owi, while they acknowledge the supremacy of the Sultan of Agades.

The sensations of our guides and camel-drivers had been uneasy from the very moment of our encamping; and Mr. Richardson, at the suggestion of Annur, had on the preceding day sent Emeli and Mohammed in advance, in order to bring to us the chief of Fade-ang. This person was represented to us as a man of great authority in this lawless country, and able to protect us against freebooting parties, which our guests of the other day, who had gone on in advance, were sure to collect against us. But Mohammed, as I have observed, was a great rascal himself, who would do all in his power to increase our difficulties, in order to profit by the confusion. The chief was accordingly reported as being absent, and a man who was said to be his brother was to take his place. This person made his appearance, accompanied by some people from the village; but it became immediately apparent that he had no authority whatever, and one of the Imghad of Tadomat, who had stuck to us for the last two days, struck him repeatedly with his spear upon the shoulder – in order to show us what respect he had for this man. Among the companions of our new protector was a Taleb of the name of Buheda, distinguished by his talkativeness and a certain degree of arrogance, who made himself ridiculous by trying to convince us of his immense learning. What an enormous difference there was between these mean-looking and degraded half-castes and our martial pursuers, who stood close by! Though I knew the latter could and would do us much more harm than the former, I liked them much better.

Overweg and I had sat down in the shade of a talha-tree at a little distance from our tent, and had soon a circle of visitors around us, who in the beginning behaved with some modesty and discretion, but gradually became rather troublesome. I gave them some small presents, such as scissors, knives, mirrors and needles, with which they expressed themselves well pleased. But the whole character of these people appeared very degraded. They were totally devoid of the noble and manly appearance which the most careless observer cannot fail to admire even in a common Tarki freebooter, and the relations between the sexes appeared in a worse light than one would expect in such a situation as this. However, we have ample testimony in ancient Arabian writers that licentious manners have always prevailed among the Berber tribes on the frontier of the desert.

We were anxious to buy some of the famous Air cheese, for which we had been longing the whole way over the dreary desert, and had kept up our spirits with the prospect of soon indulging in this luxury; but we were not able to procure a single one, and our endeavours to buy a sheep or a goat were equally fruitless. Instead of the plenty which we had been led to expect in this country, we found nothing but misery. In spite of such drawbacks, we were tolerably composed, and reclining at our ease (though our weapons were always at hand), when we were a little alarmed by a demand of six 'riyals' payment for the use of the pond in Jinninau. Our amiable but unenergetic friend Annur seconded the demand, by way of satisfying in some way the intruders upon our caravan. These claims were scarcely settled when a dreadful alarm was raised, by the report that a body of from fifty to sixty raiders on swift Mehara camels were about to attack us. Though no good authority could be named for this intelligence, the whole caravan was carried away by excitement, and all called out for powder and shot. Boro Serki-n-turawa once more delivered eloquent speeches, and exhorted the people to be courageous; but many of the Tinylkum, very naturally, had a great objection to come to open hostilities with the Touareg, which might end in their being unable to travel any longer along this route.

In this moment of extreme excitement Khweldi arrived, the chief merchant of Murzuk, whom we had not expected to see, though we knew that he was on his way from Sudan to the north. We were in a situation wherein he was able to render us the most material service, both by his influence upon the individuals of whom our caravan was composed,

and by his knowledge of the country whose frontier territories we had just entered. But unfortunately, though a
very experienced merchant, he was not a practical, sharp-
sighted man; and instead of giving us clear information as
to the probable amount of truth in the reports, and what
sort of difficulties we might really have to encounter, and
how by paying a sort of passage-money to the chiefs we
might get over them, he denied in private the existence
of any danger at all, while openly he went round the whole
caravan extolling our importance as a mission sent by a
powerful government, and encouraging the people to
defend us if we should be in danger. In consequence of his
exhortations, the Tinylkum took courage, but had the im-
prudence and absurdity to supply also the three intruders
with powder and shot, who, though protesting to be now
our most sincere friends, of course made no other use of the
present than to supply their band with this material, which
alone gave us a degree of superiority and constituted our
security.

Any one accustomed to look closely at things could not
be at all satisfied with the spirit of our caravan, notwithstanding its noise and waste of powder, and with its entire
want of union; but the scene which followed in the bright
moonlight evening, and lasted throughout the night, was
animating and interesting in the extreme. The whole caravan was drawn up in line of battle, the left wing being
formed by ourselves and the detachment of the Kel-owi who
had left their own camping-ground and posted themselves
in front of our tent, while the Tinylkum and the Sfaksi
formed the centre, and the rest of the Kel-owi with Boro,
the right wing, leaning upon the cliffs, our exposed left
being defended by the four pieces of the boat. About ten
o'clock a small troop of Mehara riders appeared, when a

heavy fusillade was kept up over their heads, and firing and
shouting were continued the whole night.

Our situation remained the same the whole of the following day; another alarm having been raised in vain, the
leaders of the expedition which was collecting against us
came out with the promise that they would not further
molest the caravan if the Christians were given up to them.
This demand having been at once rejected, we were left
in tolerable tranquillity for a while, as the freebooters now
saw that in order to obtain their object, which was plunder,
they should be obliged to bring really into the field the whole
force they had so long boasted of. But before sunset our tranquillity was greatly disturbed by the appearance of five of
our well-known marauding companions, mounted on camels,
and leading six others. They dismounted within less than a
pistol-shot from our tents, and with wild ferocious laughter
were discussing their projects with the Azkar in our caravan.

I could scarcely suppress a laugh when several of the
Tinylkum came and brought us the ironical assurance that
there was now perfect security, and that we might indulge
in sound sleep. Others came with the less agreeable but
truer warning that we ought not to sleep that night. The
greatest alarm and excitement soon spread through the
caravan. Later in the evening, while our benevolent 'guests'
were devouring their supper, Mohammed el Tunsi called
me and Overweg aside, and informed us that we were
threatened with great danger indeed, these Hogar raiders,
as he called them, having brought a letter from Nakhnukhen, authorizing them to collect people in the territory
of the Kel-owi, and there to dispatch us in such a way that
not even a trace of us should be found, but not to touch us
so long as we were within the confines of the Azkar.

I was convinced that this account, so far as it regarded Nakhnukhen, was an absurd fiction of our persecutors; and I sent our servant to the caravan to this effect. A council of war was held and a resolution passed, that if a number of from twenty to thirty people came to attack us, the caravan would undertake to defend us, but if we should be threatened by a more numerous host they would try to make a compromise by yielding up a part of our goods. In consequence of this resolution, all possible warlike preparations were made once more, and Boro delivered another speech; but it seemed rather irreconcilable with such a state of things that while we, as well as the Tinylkum, brought all our camels close to our tents at an early hour, the Kel-owi left theirs out the whole night. Perhaps, being natives of the country, they did not expect that the freebooters would seize their animals.

Be this as it may, great anxiety arose when early in the morning it was found that the camels were gone; and when day broke our guests of last night, who had stolen away before midnight, were seen riding down from the rocky ridge on the south, and with a commanding air calling the principal men of the caravan to a council. Then followed the scenes which Mr Richardson has so graphically described elsewhere.

I will only mention that Boro Serki-n-turawa, sword in hand, led us on with great energy. He called me to keep close to him; and I think that now (when we had atoned for the neglect with which he had been treated by us, by assuring him that we were convinced of his high position and influence in the country) he had the honest intention to protect us. Of the Tinylkum only our faithful Musa and the amiable young Sliman adhered to us and of the other people, the Tawati and Mohammed e' Sfaksi, although the latter trembled with fear and was as pale as death, Yusuf Mukni remained behind. Farreji on this occasion behaved with great courage, and bravely challenged the enemy. What frightened the latter most were the bayonets on our guns, as they saw that, after having received our fire, they would not yet have done with us, but would still have a weapon to encounter at least as formidable as their own spears. As soon as the enemy had protested that he was only come against us as Christians, all sympathy for us ceased in the caravan. All expected that we would become Moslemin without great difficulty; and our servant Mohammed, when we rejected this condition as an impossibility, immediately relapsed into his ordinary impudence, laughing in our faces because, forsooth, we were so absurd as still to think of some other expedient. And this clever but spoiled young-ster was a protégé of the British consulate in Tunis.

At length all seemed to be settled. The whole host of the enemy, besides its rich booty, had been treated with an enormous quantity of mohamsa provisions, and we had repeatedly been assured that now we might be certain of reaching the chief Annur's residence without any further disturbance – when the little Annur, a man of honest but mild character, came to beg us most earnestly to be on our guard, lest behind the rocks and ridges there might still be some persons in ambush. At length we left this inhospitable place; but we were far from being at ease, for it was clear that there was still a cloud on the horizon, which might easily gather to another storm. In due course the storm broke.

By August 27 we were only about eight miles from Selufiet where we might expect to be tolerably safe; and we had not the least doubt that we were to sleep there, when suddenly, before noon, our old Azkar madogu Awed el Kker turned off the road to the right, and chose the camping-ground at the border of a broad valley richly overgrown with herbage. As if moved by supernatural agency, and in ominous silence, the whole caravan followed; not a word was spoken. It was then evident that we were to pass through another ordeal, which, according to all appearance, would be of a more serious kind than that we had already undergone. How this plot was laid is rather mysterious; and it can be explained only by supposing that a diabolical conspiracy was entered into by the various individuals of our caravan. Some certainly were in the secret; but Annur, not less certainly, was sincere in our interest, and wished us to get through safely. But the turbulent state of the country did not allow this weak, unenergetic man to attain his object. Blackmail had been levied upon us by the frontier tribes; here was another strong party to be satisfied, that of the Merabetin or Anislimen, who, enjoying great influence in the country, were in a certain degree opposed to the paramount authority of the old chief Annur in Tintellust; and this man, who alone had power to check the turbulent spirit of these wild and lawless tribes, was laid up with sickness. In Agades there was no Sultan, and several parties still stood in opposition to each other, while by the great expedition against the Welad Sliman all the warlike passions of the people had been awakened, and their cupidity and greediness for booty and rapine excited to the utmost pitch. All these circumstances must be borne in mind in order to form a right view of the manner in which we were sacrificed.

The whole affair had a very solemn appearance from the beginning, and it was apparent that this time there were really other motives in view besides that of robbing us.

Certainly our property, to say the least, was at stake. The amount of the spoil taken from us was regulated by the sum which we had paid to our Kel-owi escort, the party concerned presuming that they had just the same demands upon us as our companions. The principal, if not the only actors in this affair were the Merabetin; and Annur, the chief of Tintellust, afterwards stated to us that it was to them we had to attribute all our losses and mishaps. There was also at this period a young *sherif* from Medina at Tintagh-ode, with whom we afterwards came into intimate relations, and who confessed to us that he had contributed his part to excite the hatred of the people against the Christian intruders. Experienced travellers have very truly remarked that this sort of *sherifs* are at the bottom of every intrigue. To the honour of Boro Serki-n-turawa, I have to state that he was ashamed of the whole affair, and tried to protect us to the best of his power, although in the beginning he had certainly done all that he could to bring us into difficulties.

It was one of the defects of the expedition that our merchandize, instead of comprising a few valuable things, was for the most part composed of worthless bulky objects, and that it made the people believe that we were carrying with us enormous wealth, while the whole value of our things scarcely amounted to two hundred pounds. We had besides about ten large iron cases filled with dry biscuit, but which all the ignorant people believed to be crammed with money. The consequence was that when all the claims had at length been settled there was still great danger that the rabble, which had not yet dispersed, would fall upon the rest of our luggage; and we were greatly obliged to the Sfaksi, who not only passed some of our luggage as his own, but also dashed to pieces one of the iron cases, when, to the astonishment of the simple people, instead of heaps of dollars, a dry and tasteless sort of bread came forth from the strong enclosure.

Perhaps disappointed thus, a large mob of lawless people came to us in the course of the night, howling like hungry jackals, and we were obliged to assure them, by frequent firing, that we were on the watch. Nevertheless, all our camels were driven away and we never recovered more than a few of them.

So much for our property. Our lives were in dire peril at this time. Some of our companions evidently thought that here, at such a distance from our homes and our brethren in faith, we might yield to a more serious attack upon our religion, and so far were sincerely interested in the success of the proceeding; but whether they had any accurate idea of the fate that awaited us, whether we should be allowed to proceed, I cannot say. But it is probable that the fanatics thought little of our future destiny; and it is absurd to imagine, that if we had changed our religion as we would a suit of clothes, we should have thereby escaped absolute ruin. Our people, who well knew what was going on, desired us to pitch only a single tent for all three of us, and not to leave it, even though a great many people should collect about us. The excitement and anxiety of our friend Annur had reached the highest pitch, and Boro was writing letter after letter. Though a great number of Merabetin had collected at an early hour, and a host of other people arrived before sunset, the storm did not break out; but as soon as all the people of our caravan, arranged in a long line close to our tent, under the guidance of the most respected of the Merabetin as Imam, had finished their Mughreb prayers, the calm was at an end, and the scene which followed was awful.

Our own people were so firmly convinced that, as we stoutly refused to change our religion, though only for a day or two, we should immediately suffer death, that our servant Mohammed, as well as Mukni, requested us most urgently to testify, in writing, that they were innocent of our blood. Mr. Richardson himself was far from being sure that the sheikhs did not mean exactly what they said. Our servants, and the chiefs of the caravan, had left us with the plain declaration that nothing less than certain death awaited us; and we were sitting silently in the tent, with the inspiring consciousness of going to our fate in a manner worthy alike of our religion and of the nation in whose name we were travelling among these barbarous tribes, when Mr. Richardson interrupted the silence which prevailed, with these words: 'Let us talk a little. We must die; what is the use of sitting so mute?' For some minutes death seemed really to hover over our heads, but the awful moment passed by. We had been discussing Mr. Richardson's last propositions for an attempt to escape with our lives, when, as a forerunner of the official messenger, the benevolent and kind-hearted Sliman rushed into our tent, and with the most sincere sympathy stammered out the few words – 'You are not to die!'

22 Struggle for the North

THE SIEUR DE LA POTHERIE

From the days of Jacques Cartier who, in 1535, sailed up the St. Lawrence river, believing he had found the North-West Passage, France took a keen interest in Canada. Canadian history, especially in the 17th century, is studded with the names of French explorers – Etienne Brulé who lived among the Huron Indians – his great contemporary, Champlain, who sowed wheat and planted vines in Quebec – Pierre Radisson, the daring fur-trader – Father Hennepin who discovered the Niagara Falls – and many others. Fired by the reports of such explorers, Louis XIV coveted this marvellous land and in 1697 he sent a naval squadron to oust the British once and for all. Here is an extract from a letter written by his special commissioner which not only gives an account of an almost unique battle in the ice but exemplifies the 'journeys into danger' that were entailed in 'exploration earth'.

Although we were now at the entrance of Hudson's Bay, we could not get into it. All the ice in that vast body of water was passing out into this strait. The continual movements of the icebergs in the current forced us also to take a capricious course and the currents drove the *Pelican* back more than eight leagues into the strait. On August 25 we made all sail through the ice because we were quite a distance behind the other three ships which were by then at the end of the strait, and we were anxious to join them.

Now the *Profond* saw three vessels approaching. Dugue, who was in command of her, thought at first that they were the other three ships of our squadron. They came up to him gradually with the currents. Then he was surprised to see such a sudden change, for they were three English ships of fifty-six, thirty-six and thirty-two guns. He ungrappled from the ice immediately and ran at all hazards into a field of ice rather than surrender, for he had on board all our munitions and provisions for the Fort Nelson expedition. The English gave chase. Serigny and Chartrier in the *Weesph* and *Palmier* wanted to go to his assistance but they were fast in the ice. The *Profond* was now also fast and close to the English ships *Dering* and *Hudson's Bay*. Then on August 26, at about nine in the morning, the battle began. Dugue attacked them; the enemy riddled him with balls, cutting his rigging in pieces, because he could only fight with two cannon which had been placed in the rear of the gunroom.

The *Hampshire* of fifty-six guns was not able to join the other English ships till the evening. After ten hours of intermittent fighting all three fired broadsides at the *Profond* and left her, thinking she was certain to go down. Four men were killed on the *Profond*. The English must also have lost some, because several human arms were found on the ice. As to our own ship, we were not in this glorious battle, which may be said to have been the first sea fight ever waged amid the ice.

The currents now brought the *Pelican* out into Hudson's Bay, and our sailors had reason to be pleased at seeing themselves freed from the ice. A fresh breeze arose which helped us greatly as we sailed to the south-west.

On September 3, 1697, we in the *Pelican* arrived within sight of Fort Nelson, from which the English fired some cannon-shots, which were apparently signals for the ships they were expecting from England. We anchored three leagues and a half to the south-west of this fort, in the open sea. We were surprised not to find there the *Palmier*, the *Weesph*, and the *Profond*, which ought to have arrived before us, as they had been off Cape Digges while we were still detained in the ice.

At daybreak on the 5th we perceived three vessels to leeward that we took to be ours. After weighing anchor about seven in the morning, we sailed down on them and made signals to which they made no response. This made us think they were English and so they were, being the *Hampshire*, the *Dering* and the *Hudson's Bay*.

Every man was at his post. La Salle, the ship's ensign, and Grandville, a marine guard, commanded the lower battery; Bienville, the brother of M. d'Iberville, and the Chevalier de Ligondez, a marine guard, the upper battery. M. d'Iberville asked me to take command of the forecastle and, with a detachment of *Canadiens* that he gave me to meet the enemy as they tried to come on board.

The enemy drew up in line. The *Hampshire* was at the head, the *Dering* followed, and the *Hudson's Bay* came behind, all three close together. The fight began at half-past nine in the morning. We made straight for the *Hampshire*, which, thinking we were going to board her, let fall her mainsail and shook out her topsails. After this refusal, we went to the *Dering* and our fire cut the tackle of her mainsail, and then, the *Hudson's Bay* coming in front, we sent her the rest of our broadside. The *Hampshire*, putting about to windward, fired a volley of musketry on our forecastle and sent a broadside of grape which cut the halliards of our fore-topsail, a back stay of our top gallant mast, and our mizzen stay. The fight grew stubborn, the three vessels keeping up a continual fire on us, with the object of dismasting our ship.

Now the *Hampshire*, seeing that she could not engage us between a shoal and their own two vessels, and that all the efforts they had made during two hours and a half were useless, determined to run us down, and, for that purpose, tried to get to windward of us (which she was unable to do), but we ran alongside of her, yard-arm to yard-arm. As we were so close to each other, I ordered a volley of musketry to be fired at her forecastle where there were many sailors who called out for us to leap aboard. They immediately returned our volley with a discharge of grape which cut nearly all our rigging in pieces and wounded many of our men. As they ran along by our ship, we fired our batteries, which were so well aimed that they proved most effective, for we were no sooner separated from one another than the *Hampshire* immediately foundered. The *Dering*, which was close to us, sent us her broadside, but the encounter was a cruel catastrophe for the English, because the *Hudson's Bay* lowered her flag, and the *Dering* took to flight.

We had fourteen men wounded by two discharges of shot from the last broadside of the *Hampshire*, which fell in the lower battery. We had seven shots below the water-line and the water came pouring in, not to speak of several shots which passed through the *Pelican* from side to side. We had been so overwhelmed with their musketry fire and the discharge of grape-shot which they fired at us from pistol range, that our mizzen mast was filled with musket balls on all sides to the height of ten or twelve feet; and if I had not looked after my men we should not have had four people left on the forecastle. I got off very cheaply myself with having my coat all tattered, and my cap pierced by a ball. In fact I was in as good condition and with as much coolness after the battle as when M. d'Iberville bade us enter the

lists, except that one would have mistaken me for a veritable blackamoor, my face was so peppered with powder. I
think the English took me for some prince of Guinea,
for I heard someone crying out: 'Fire at that fine-looking
darkey from Guinea.'

We gave chase to the *Dering*, and we should have captured her if we had not, three days before, had our
mainyard broken in half by a squall. In any case our prize,
the *Hudson's Bay*, which was a league distant, might have
got away into the mouth of the river on which Fort Nelson
is situated, so we put about and, after having put a prize
crew on board, we went towards the *Hampshire* in order
to save her sailors. We found that she had stranded on the
shoal where the enemy had wished to engage us, and the
weather became so rough after the battle that it was impossible for us to lower a boat. We anchored close to the
Hampshire with the chagrin of being unable to aid her in
so dangerous and unfortunate a situation.

The east-north-east wind, which was then blowing, kept
getting stronger and stronger. A frightful sea arose, driving
us steadily towards the shore till next morning between
nine and ten o'clock, when our rudder struck bottom a
couple of times. We were obliged to cut our cable at midday so as to make sail, and drove before the wind till four
o'clock in the afternoon. The bitter cold, the snow, and the
ice which covered our rigging were cruel obstacles. As we
could not reach the shore, we anchored in nine fathoms of
water. Our anchors held till nine in the evening, when the
great anchor broke. I cannot express to you the sad state
of the crew. Some were suffering from disease. The very
strongest were in desperate straits. It was night, and the
horror of darkness was added to the fear of death. The tossing and the disorder reacted quickly upon people in so

downcast a state, and when the panic spread we could not reassure them.

The vessel was headed into the wind and anchored again, but the kedge anchor broke. As the small remaining anchor could not hold, we had to cut the cable and get under way again. A wave swept off our stern galley, and broke the table and benches which were in the main cabin. At ten o'clock in the evening our rudder was carried away and we thought ourselves utterly lost. As the tide rose, our ship, which was drawn along in the current, went aground. All these various movements made the hair of the most careless stand on end. Finally, about midnight, the ship split along the middle of the keel and filled with water above the between-decks. We spent the night in this wretched state and, at daybreak, we saw the land two leagues away.

In our cruel situation we did not lose hope of saving our lives. M. d'Iberville, who had all the forethought possible in such a catastrophe, was bent on saving his crew. He begged me to take the canoe and try where we could make a landing in some safety.

So, on September 8, the Nativity of the Virgin, I embarked in a canoe with some *Canadiens*,* and after we had leapt into the sea, which was up to our shoulders, with our muskets and powder-horns on our heads, and some balls, I sent the canoe back to the ship. Meanwhile, rafts and floats were being made to save the sick. We drew ourselves as well as we could out of the water, which was extremely cold.

For all my vigour and presence of mind, I felt myself suffering keenly and, as I was utterly exhausted, I wished to find somewhere to rest. I was suddenly overcome with hunger which forced me, in my despair, to eat the weeds floating on the sea.

* French fur-traders & trappers.

After having crossed more than a league of sea, we came to a snow bank more than two feet thick under which was mud. Our passage was very rough and cost the lives of eighteen soldiers who died of cold, and I myself should have succumbed but for the help of some *Canadiens* who found me lying on the snow.

The next day, we crossed over a marsh which would have been impassable for horses and then we made another camp at a place we called the 'Outpost'. I forgot to state that the *Hudson's Bay* had met the same fate as ourselves, having foundered eight leagues further south.

In the meantime, the *Palmier*, the *Weesph* and the *Profond* arrived at the mouth of the river. The first had lost her rudder forty leagues to the west of this, having been steered these forty leagues with oars and outriggers.

M. d'Iberville with some others went to reconnoitre Fort Nelson about eleven o'clock in the morning. We could not manage it without drawing the musket fire of the English, and they would have fired grape-shot at us if we had not defiled by narrow paths. We kept under cover till we were almost at the foot of the fort. Then M. d'Iberville sent for Martigny and ordered him to go and demand two Iroquois and two Frenchmen whom he knew to be in this place for they had not been able to get away last year before it had been recaptured by the English from the *Canadiens*.

When Martigny arrived with the white flag at the gates of the fort, the governor had his eyes bandaged and had him led into the place. He held a council of war. It was decided that the four men could not be given up under such circumstances. Some of the men from the *Hudson's Bay* had taken refuge in the fort after their shipwreck, and this had strengthened the garrison.

That afternoon we set up a mortar battery in the wood

two hundred paces from the fort, without letting the enemy become aware of what we were doing. When the platform was almost finished, they heard the noise of two or three blows of a sledge-hammer, which quickly brought upon us three cannon-shots, one of which came near killing M. d'Iberville.

On the night between the 11th and the 12th, we cut off some English who were going to and fro to fetch the sailors of the *Hudson's Bay*, who kept arriving every now and then. The clerk of the Hudson's Bay Company was killed in this encounter.

We began our bombardment of the fort at ten in the morning of the 12th. When we saw the third bombshell fall at the base of the fort, Serigny went to summon the governor to surrender. The latter declared that he did not wish to have his throat cut, and that he preferred to see the place burned rather than give it up. He admitted that there was no chance of his receiving any aid from England, and that, if he were forced to capitulate, it would be due to his bad luck.

We began to fire anew between one and two o'clock. They kept up a continual fire on us with cannon and with two mortars. They had very able cannoneers. They had nothing but the sound of our bombs to enable them to conjecture where we were, because the thick copse, in which our battery was, prevented them from getting an accurate knowledge of its position. This did not prevent two of their cannon-balls from hitting the parapet and another from covering us with earth.

Serigny summoned the English again at four o'clock and told the governor that it would be the last time he would do so. We had resolved to make a general assault and, if he should then make any proposals, they would not be received. We had surrounded their fort and with storming axes we would have cut down their palisades and bastions, and they might have expected that, had we stormed them sword in hand, they would have had no chance of escape. Serigny even assured the governor that, although the season would not allow our ships to remain more than ten or twelve days, forces would be left more than sufficient to capture the fort in the winter.

The English governor told Serigny that he was not wholly his own master and that he would give him an answer at sundown. We did not cease setting up a new battery on the south-south-west side, which would have thrown them into utter disorder, but at six o'clock, the governor sent a Protestant minister, Mr. Morrison, to bring a capitulation, in which he asked to keep all the beavers that belonged to the Hudson's Bay Company.

I was willing to act as interpreter, but I soon saw that I was wasting my Latin on this minister who could scarcely decline Musa. I was not surprised at it afterwards as there are very few Scottish ministers who know Latin.

This proposal of theirs was too advantageous for people who were at our mercy, and our gentle dealing with them was rather due to our natural French generosity. So we refused their demand.

They held a council of war, and at eight p.m. the governor sent Mr. Henry Kelsey, a King's Lieutenant, and the deputy governor with a letter in which he asked to be allowed to retain two mortars and four cannon (five-pounders), which they had brought last year from England. We would not let them have these. Finally, on the next day, the 13th, the governor sent us three hostages to tell us that he would surrender the place and to ask permission to evacuate it at an hour after midday.

The governor at the head of the garrison and part of the crew of the *Hudson's Bay* left the fort an hour after with drums beating, muskets loaded, matches lighted, banner waving (they had lowered it very quickly at the third bombshell we had fired at them, perceiving that we were using it as a target), and their arms and baggage.

I had the skins that were in the fort put on board the Hudson's Bay Company sloop *Albemarle*, which we had also captured. As our pilots were not well acquainted with the river, this vessel ran on a little rock which made a hole in her. There was a panic among our own people and the English who were on board. The barque filled with water. They tried to lighten her by jettisoning many cases and packages. It was a very dark night. Some threw themselves into the water, others, in trying to get safely to land, found themselves fast in the mud.

We left Fort Nelson on September 24, 1697, which is the date when the rivers and the sea begin to freeze over, or very fierce winds prevail.

We set sail with the wind south-south-west, at an hour after midday. The *Profond* – to which our crew had been transferred from the wreck of the *Pelican*, as well as a party from the *Hudson's Bay*, and from the garrison of the fort – went aground an hour later on the bank or shoal on the north side. However, as we still had an hour of flood tide, we got clear and continued our course. Otherwise, we should have been obliged to transfer some of our three hundred men to the *Weesph*, which had escaped our mischance, and to send back the rest to the fort. We should certainly in that event have suffered a famine there, and also on the *Weesph*, for the latter had only enough provisions for her own crew, and the fort no more than was necessary for the garrison we had left behind in it.

Next day the wind blew very hard. The cold increased because we were getting nearer the pole. The days became very short. The sun no longer was visible, so we could not get an altitude. A storm was indicated. We advanced without knowing where we were, and yet we had to get into Hudson's Strait. To enter it was a stumbling-block for us, as we were enclosed in a bay, the northern shore of which was quite unknown. We were wandering in a region full of dangers.

The constant working of our rigging exhausted our sailors. The wretched condition we were all in, owing to lack of linen and other clothes, due to our shipwreck, suddenly brought about an epidemic of scurvy; and I hardly venture to tell you, Sir, that we were all tormented with vermin to such an extent that some of our scurvy patients, who had become paralytics, actually died from this pest. When the sailors came down from the yards, they fell stiff with cold on the deck, and it required the use of fomentations to bring them round again.

We were running east when we found ourselves by good fortune in Hudson's Strait. We found no more ice-packs in the strait. There were still some icebergs of great height which had stranded a league or two from the land and had not been able to follow the current. The ice-packs in the bay and in the strait extend more than four hundred leagues. When they begin to break up, they pass out into the sea. These fragments are so large that five or six thousand men could be drawn up in order of battle upon them with ease. They usually break up in the month of July and they sometimes travel two hundred leagues in the open sea before being completely melted.

At this time the sea was clear, but the cold was so piercing that our crew could not endure it and nearly all the sailors took the scurvy. So few of us escaped that we were obliged to make use of our English prisoners in order to run the ship.

On October 5, at midday, we saw the Savage Isles to the north-east of us. They are on the north coast of the strait a mile or two distant from the mainland.

We began then to find ourselves out of danger, freed from those anxieties which had kept us in dread of perishing every moment.

As the winds drove us along we found ourselves suddenly in another and even harsher climate. This sudden change caused so many deaths in our vessels that we threw five or six sailors into the sea every day.

It was a plague that had infected our ships. Perhaps you will not be displeased if I give you an idea of it. You will see that I have become a great doctor on this voyage, and that I have not altogether forgotten the study I made of anatomy while I was taking my course in philosophy.

You must know, then, that the sudden change which takes place in the temperature, after leaving the mildest and most agreeable season of the year, brings about an entire revolution, all at once, in the human body, which contracts a disease peculiar to those regions, called the scurvy.

The extreme cold, and especially the tremendous quantity of nitre that exists in the straits, form fixed salts which arrest the circulation of the blood. These corrosive spirits give rise to acids, which, little by little, undermine the part where they occur; and the chyle, which becomes viscous, acid, salt and earthy, causes the thickening of the blood, which, being thus impeded in its circulation, gives rise at the same time to pains in the lower extremities, as in the legs, thighs and arms, which are the first parts to be attacked.

The parts affected become insensible, blackish, and, when one touches them, there remains a hollow such as one would make in a piece of dough.

It was most pitiful to see people completely paralyzed, so that they could not move themselves in their hammocks, and yet their minds were perfectly sane and clear.

The food that one is obliged to take at sea contributes not a little to the malady. Thus the quantity of acid in the salt beef and pork that they give the sailors causes a swelling in the gums and an obstruction in the salivary glands, which are intended to filter the lymph with the blood and carry it into the mouth by little ducts so as to serve as the first solvent in digestion. And, as all these little passages are blocked up by the excess of these penetrating salts, there is then spread through the mouth a thick, gluey and viscous humour. Then the blood, finding these ducts stopped, forms a mass of putrid matter which corrupts the gums, loosens the teeth and causes them all to drop out.

Some have a flux at the mouth, others have dysentery. The former drivel. The viscous matter which flows from the mouth causes gangrene in the glands and in the gums. They must then be given strong detergent gargles which can separate this thick matter. Lemon juice is very helpful.

Those who have dysentery are more liable to die. In these patients, there is formed in the region of the intestines an extremely corrosive humour. As soon as this juice is found to be corrupt, it follows of necessity that there are faintings and heart failures. For, as the heart can only exist by the circulation of a pure, clean and active blood, any other matter that forms in it cannot help hindering its ordinary course. And the gangrene, which forms in these patients, arrests the laws of the circulation of the blood.

The brain, being no longer bathed in its mild influences,

receives vapours which cause delirium, madness and then death. I have seen several who seemed to have a strong voice, a clear eye, and a clear tongue without any blackening or excoriation, and yet died while they were speaking.

One must use foods, therefore, which can dissolve the mass of the blood and by their sulphurous and volatile parts carry off the acids. These foods, by an insensible transpiration, dissipate the crudities of the mass, and are able to rally together the fibres of the blood. One should give the patients very little salt meat, but rice, peas, dried beans, detersivent injections and astringent opiates into which cordials enter; giving them plenty of fresh linen, which is a great relief in such cases.

This sickness only increases the appetite. The patients are as ravenous as dogs. I was not surprised, Sir, that this sudden change of climate on our return voyage should have caused to many deaths on our ship. There was a fermentation going on in the mass of the blood, which cause a gangrenous corruption. The heat wished to dilate what the cold had contracted; there was bound to be a combat. And nature, enfeebled by the dilation of the pores, caused an overflow which threw the whole machine out of gear.

Finally, after so many pains, labours, and misfortunes, we arrived at Belle Isle in Newfoundland on November 8. We proceeded to put our scurvied patients in the hospital of Port Louis, and we set out from there for Rochefort, where we discharged our ship.

23 The Bonaparte of the Cataracts

JOSEPH ACERBI

'It may possibly excite curiosity to know why a native of Italy, a country abounding in all the beauties of nature, and the finest productions of art, should voluntarily undergo the danger and fatigue of visiting the regions of the Arctic Circle.' Thus Acerbi in his 'Travels through Sweden, Finland and Lapland to the North Cape in the years 1789–91'. He goes on modestly to explain that 'men even of the most ordinary talents have often, by their humble efforts, given birth to exertion in others, which have been more happily directed and more successful'. In this extract we find him braving the cataracts of Muoniokoski: one wonders what he would have made of the rapids of the Ogowé that Mary Kingsley had to contend with.

At Kollare we had the good fortune to meet four of the most experienced boatmen we had seen in the whole course of our travels. There was one of them called Simon, whom we named by way of eminence, the *Bonaparte of the Cataracts*. It is impossible to give the reader an idea of his excellence of tactics, his courage, his address, the justness of his eye in judging from the surface of the water the nature of the bottom, and in ascertaining, with the most scrupulous precision, the depth of the river. Had it not been for the resolution and steadiness of this man, our expedition must have ended at Kollare; for the obstacles to be encountered between this place and Muonionisca are so seriously discouraging to common boatmen, that they would have refused to a man to conduct us any farther.

The passage from Kollare to Muonionisca is a distance of sixty-six miles, entirely upon the river Muonio, and constantly in opposition to cataracts and the current. The fortitude and perseverance with which those people bore this long and extraordinary labour, shew the astonishing power of habit. Where the river was too strong and violent for our boats, which owing to the weight they carried drew too much water, to make good their passage we were forced to disembark and haul our empty boats along the river.

The Finlanders who were employed in dragging the boat, kept on the bank, leaping from stone to stone, and sometimes they went up to the middle in water to disengage the rope from the rocks, where it had become entangled. Sometimes the boats themselves were obstructed in their passage by the rocks, in which case one of the men threw himself into the water, swam up to them, and set them afloat again. At last we came to a place where the extreme force of the cataract, the depth of the water, and the obstructions from the rocks, rendered it to appearance altogether impossible to continue our progress.

Our brave Simon was the only person who thought every thing possible. The rest seemed disposed to find fault with his daring projects, which they never lessened; but, on the contrary, magnified through their fears. But he was always the first to set an example of the most unwearied patience and activity; he constantly charged himself with the execution of the most arduous and laborious part of the undertaking, and never proposed a thing in which he did not reserve for himself the most difficult and hazardous offices it imposed: in short, no perils could daunt his spirit, no toils set bounds to his exertions. He hauled the boat, he disengaged it when it stuck fast; he was the first to leap into the water whenever occasion required, and seemed to do every thing himself alone.

While our Finlanders were displaying the most heroic perseverance on the river and on its banks, the utmost we could do was to keep up with them in the adjacent wood. It was not always possible to follow them close to the river, as we were not, like them, able to jump from one rock to another. The current too sometimes produced a giddiness in the head, and we were unwilling to wet our legs by wading through the water. Another species of fatigue still awaited us in the woods: we sunk here and there so deep in the moss that we thought we should be immersed in it up to our necks. We sometimes met with places so deep and boggy that it was highly dangerous to set a foot upon them.

The branches everywhere intercepted our passage, while the veils we wore on our faces to protect them from the stings of insects, caught hold of the branches, and were in danger of being torn in pieces by every twig. Tall fir and pine-trees, which the wind had levelled with the ground, and which time had almost converted into dust, lay scattered in the woods. We wished to escape the embarrassment of the moss, by stepping along the trees that lay in our way; but we found their substance generally so rotten and decayed that now and then they suddenly gave way under our feet, and we could with difficulty save ourselves from falling.

In this manner we had travelled about two English miles when notice was given us that the cataracts were becoming so formidable that there was no chance of carrying the boats farther up the river. To proceed without our boats was not to be thought of, it being impossible to get to Muonionisca but by crossing the river Muonio; and besides, there was another smaller river at the opposite side. The only expedient we had left was to haul the boats on shore, and to drag them about two miles through the woods, where we would come to a part of the river more quiet and practicable for sailing on.

Simon was the first to embrace this resolution; and without knowing that we had travelled on the sea drawn by horses,* he proposed that we should travel over the land through a thick wood in a boat. We were not inhuman enough, however, to take advantage of Simon's magnanimity, and to place ourselves in the boat, for its continual friction against the moss and trees rendered it so weighty that it required the whole force of our four boatmen to draw a single boat at once without any thing in it. At length we got to the end of two miles, and we were very glad to repose while our men returned for our baggage and the other boat. In the course of this journey, being invited by an uncommon noise of the river, we drew near to have a view of the famous cataract of Muonio-koski; and though we judged it impossible to descend with such a current, we were, nevertheless, bold enough to attempt and accomplish it on our return. As this cataract is the most dangerous that we passed in the whole course of our river navigation, I shall endeavour to give the reader a description, as near as I can, of the manner in which the passage is performed.

Let him imagine a place where the river is so hemmed in by narrow banks, and so compressed with rugged and shelving rocks, that the current is doubled in its rapidity; let him moreover represent to his mind the formidable inequalities in the bed of the river, occasioned by those rocks, which can only be passed by a sort of leap, and consequently make the water extremely turbulent; let him conceive that, for the space of an English mile, this river continues in the

* A joking reference to an incident earlier in the tour.

same state: and let him, after all this, consider the hazard to which a boat must be exposed that ventures itself on such a surface, where both the nature of the channel, and the amazing velocity of the current, seem to conspire to its destruction. You cannot perform this passage by simply following the stream; but the boat must go with an accelerated quickness, which should be at least double to that of the current.

Two boatmen, the most active and robust that can be found, must use their utmost exertions in rowing the whole time, in order that the boat may overcome the force of the stream, while one person is stationed at the helm to regulate its direction as circumstances may require. The rapidity of this descent is such that you accomplish an English mile in the space of three or four minutes. The man that manages the rudder can, with difficulty, see the rocks he must keep clear of: he turns the head of the boat directly in the line of the rock he means to pass, and when he is in the very instant of touching it, he suddenly makes a sharp angle and leaves it behind him.

The trembling passenger thinks that he shall see the boat dashed in a thousand pieces, and the moment after he is astonished at his own existence. Add to this, that the waves rush into the boat from all sides, and drench you to the skin; while, at other times, a billow will dash over the boat from side to side, and scarcely touch you. It is a situation which presents danger in such frightful shapes, that you could hardly open your eyes and refrain from trembling, though a person with the greatest certainty should assure you that you would not suffer any harm.

Several people, however, have perished in this place; and there were but two men in the village of Muonio who thought themselves qualified to conduct the descent: these were an old man of sixty-seven years of age, and his son of twenty-six. The old boatman had known this passage twenty years, and navigated it always with success, and in the course of that period he had taught his son his own dangerous calling. It is impossible to conceive any thing more striking and interesting than the collected and intrepid expression of the old man's countenance in the progress of the passage.

As our resolution to descend this cataract was not adopted rashly, but after a minute enquiry and cool reflection, we were prepared to observe the detail of our adventure in its most trifling circumstances. The old man never sat down, but stood upright, holding the rudder with both hands, which was tied on purpose for the occasion to the stern of the boat. In passing the smaller cataracts, they descend with the rudder untied, which they hold between their arms, and sit all the while.

When we were in the most critical moments of the passage, we had only to cast our eye on the old man's countenance, and our fears almost instantly vanished. In places of less difficulty he looked round to his son, to observe if he had proceeded with safety. It was plain his thoughts were more occupied about his son than himself; and indeed the young man grazed the rocks on two different occasions.

As soon as all danger was over, we drew in to the shore to repose and enjoy the triumph of our success. It was then we remarked that the son, who had piloted the second boat, looked extremely pale through terror; and my companion's servant, who had been in his boat, informed us that they had received two violent shocks, and that on both occasions he gave himself up for lost.